Student Study Guide

for use with

Essentials of
Psychology

Benjamin B. Lahey
University of Chicago

Prepared by
Steven Schneider
Pima Community College

Boston   Burr Ridge, IL   Dubuque, IA   Madison, WI   New York   San Francisco   St. Louis
Bangkok   Bogotá   Caracas   Kuala Lumpur   Lisbon   London   Madrid   Mexico City
Milan   Montreal   New Delhi   Santiago   Seoul   Singapore   Sydney   Taipei   Toronto

McGraw-Hill Higher Education

*A Division of The **McGraw-Hill** Companies*

Student Study Guide for use with
ESSENTIALS OF PSYCHOLOGY
BENJAMIN B. LAHEY

Published by McGraw-Hill Higher Education, an imprint of The McGraw-Hill Companies, Inc.,
1221 Avenue of the Americas, New York, NY 10020. Copyright © 2002 by The McGraw-Hill
Companies, Inc. All rights reserved.

This book is printed on acid-free paper.

2 3 4 5 6 7 8 9 0 BKM BKM 0 3

ISBN 0-07-243407-4

www.mhhe.com

Contents

Tips for Successful Studying

Some students take an introductory psychology course because they are considering psychology as a major; others take it because it is a required course for another major; still others take psychology out of a general interest and curiosity about their fellow human beings. Whatever the reason, whatever your major, you are certain to find some topics in this course to be most interesting. Biology/pre-med students will find the chapters dealing with biological psychology and sensation and perception to be particularly interesting. Education majors, parents, and future parents will find the developmental psychology chapter applicable and interesting. Are your interested in health, diet, and exercise? If so, you will find the health psychology chapter to be intriguing. You don't have to be a social scientist to wonder whether intelligence tests are valid, how the human memory system works, what causes mental disorders, or what attracts people to each other. These issues and many others will be explored in your introductory psychology course.

I have taught thousands of introductory psychology students over the past 20 years, and I would like to share some observations about students who succeed in the course and those who fail to live up to their (and my) expectations in the course.

1. Successful students are well organized. Some of my most successful students have been some of my busiest students—those with part-time or full-time jobs, parents with many familial obligations, and students carrying an incredible course load. Their ability to organize their lives and manage their time, however, allowed them to accomplish their tasks efficiently and effectively. To be well organized, you should use a semester calendar that clearly indicates deadlines for papers, exam dates, and other important dates. Keep your course outlines in a safe place so that you can refer to them during the semester. Be certain that you know the office hours and office phone numbers of your instructors. Make and adhere to a weekly schedule for yourself that builds in all the important activities, including class time, work time, study time, *and* relaxation time.

2. Successful students come to class. As you begin college, one difference you may note from your previous educational experiences is that your instructor may not take attendance. That doesn't signify a lack of concern on the part of your instructor—after all, it's *your* tuition and textbook money. What it does mean is that you are responsible for the decision to come to class or not. Both casual observation and the results of research studies show that students who attend class do better than those who don't attend.

3. Read the material before going to class. My most successful students over the years generally read the text before coming to class. They had a pretty good idea what the lecture was going to be about. This also helped them organize their note taking while in class.

4. Take good notes and review them. In your efforts to be a good learner, it is usually a mistake to try to take down everything that is said in class. Instead, try to outline the lecture, using Roman numerals and letters for the major and minor points. This technique can be particularly effective if the instructor lectures from an outline. Review your notes as soon after class as possible. It is somewhat dismaying while studying for an exam to see notes in your handwriting that you don't even remember writing.

5. Focus on key terms and concepts. A large and important part of most introductory courses consists of learning the language of the field you are studying. This is necessary in order to communicate with and to think like the professionals in the field. The implication is that, when you study, you need to learn the language of psychology. You are likely to be tested on the terminology and, even if you are not tested directly on the terms, you will almost certainly be expected to know and understand them.

6. Consider using the SQ3R method for studying. The SQ3R method of studying is a tried and tested technique. Research conducted with students who use this technique indicates significantly greater comprehension of text material. This is how it works:

Survey: Although the temptation when you begin studying is to open the text and begin reading, this technique suggests that you should first get an overview of the material. Read the chapter outline (found in the text) and the chapter overview (found in this study guide). Skim through the text, noting the major headings as well as the charts and pictures. This activity will allow you to get a feel for the chapter, as well as to see how the chapter is organized.

Question: As you survey the chapter, begin noting questions about the material. You may use the Learning Objectives section in this study guide to help you formulate questions about the text. The questions that you formulate will help you pick out the most important parts of the text as you read.

Read: When you have formulated questions, reading the text now becomes purposeful; that is, you are reading in order to answer the questions. As you find the material that answers your questions, consider highlighting it or marking an *X* in the margin. Consider taking notes of the major points as you read the text.

Recite: After you have finished a section of the text, stop and state the answers to the questions in your own words (not the author's). This will help give you practice pronouncing some difficult terminology and will test whether the material you have just learned makes sense to you. Recitation is also a very efficient system; material that has been recited is remembered much longer than material not recited. Recitation is particularly effective when studying for essay exams, since it may stimulate the questions you will receive on the exam.

Review: Virtually everybody who sees a movie for the second time comments that the experience was much different from the first viewing. People often say they "got something completely different" from seeing the movie a second time. A similar situation exists when reading a chapter of your text. Review the material soon after reading it. You may test yourself by working through the guided review for each chapter that is included in this study guide. Try to answer the multiple-choice questions in the study guide. These are keyed to the learning objectives found at the beginning of each study guide chapter.

7. *Prepare for exams.* The most widespread method used by instructors to asses what you have learned is to give you an exam. Whereas some students welcome the challenge, for many it provides an exercise in terror. Test anxiety is widely recognized to be a major problem for many students. Some hints for preparing for and taking exams can help. Find out as much as you can about the exam beforehand (remaining, of course, within the bounds of conventional morality and the law!). What material will be covered? Will it be multiple-choice, essay, fill-in, or matching? How much time will be allotted? How much weight will be given to various topics? The answers to these questions should help guide your preparation for the exam. Try to study always in the same place and on a regular basis. It should be a quiet, well-lit area and should contain minimal distractions. Use your study area only for studying. Generally speaking, you study most efficiently when you study alone. Take breaks when you study. Studying is a fatiguing activity, and most students can benefit from a short break every 20 minutes or so. It is certainly time to take a break when you reach the end of a page and then realize you haven't retained a word on the page. Take a break instead of fighting it. The type of test for which you are preparing should dictate how you prepare—for example, study for an essay exam by asking yourself essay questions and writing out good answers. Prepare for a multiple-choice exam by answering multiple-choice questions (be sure to review those in the study guide). Solid preparation, a good night's sleep the night before an exam, and relaxing instead of cramming just prior to the exam should help minimize test anxiety. If your anxiety is severe, seek the advice of a counselor. Many colleges offer courses designed to help deal with test anxiety.

I hope you enjoy and benefit from your psychology course. I also hope that you find this *Student Study Guide* to be a helpful resource. I welcome your comments, opinions, and suggestions for improvements. My address is Steve Schneider, c/o Psychology Department, Pima Community College, 2202 W. Anklam Rd., Tucson AZ 85709. My e-mail address is: SSCHNEIDER@pimacc.pima.edu.

To the Student: Before You Begin

This *Student Study Guide* has been written to assist you as you read *Essentials of Psychology* by Benjamin B. Lahey. This guide will help you to learn the essential concepts, facts, and theories that are covered in the text; please remember, however, that it is not intended to be used as a substitute for the textbook. This study guide should be used to help you identify essential information, to help you review, to indicate the gaps in your learning, to stimulate your thinking about the ideas in the text, and to test what you have learned. Each chapter of the *Student Study Guide* is divided into the following sections:

Learning Objectives

You can use the learning objectives in two different ways. First, examine the objectives *before* you read the chapter to get an overview of the major topics that will be covered in the text. Pay attention to the terms, concepts, and names mentioned in the objectives. Second, after you have completed reading the chapter, return to the objectives; you should now be able to perform the activities listed in the objectives. You may write your responses to the objectives in the space provided. If you find an objective that seems unclear to you, return to the text and reread that section. The page numbers following each objective refer to the location of the material in the text.

Chapter Overview

The chapter overview is a relatively brief survey of the material in the chapter. It should be read before and after you read the text. The first reading will help to prepare (and intrigue) you for the topics covered in the textbook. The second reading will help you to see how the information you have just read in the chapter fits together.

Key Terms Exercise and Who Am I?

The key terms exercise is intended to test your understanding of the key terms that are listed at the beginning of each chapter in the textbook. These matching exercises are grouped according to topic; therefore, some exercises contain only a few terms while others contain more. For your convenience, the key terms are page-referenced to the textbook, and the correct answers immediately follow each exercise. To get the maximum benefit from this activity, keep the answers covered until you have completed all the answers.

Some chapters contain the names of a large number of psychologists. The "Who Am I?" exercise will test your ability to match the names of the psychologists with their contributions to the field. As with the key terms exercise, page references to the text follow the names of the psychologists, and the correct answers immediately follow each exercise (remember to keep the answers covered while you do the exercise).

Guided Review

The guided review is deigned to be a challenging and comprehensive fill-in-the-blanks exercise. The answers are found in the Answer Section that appears later in the chapter. This exercise will help point out the terms or sections of the text you need to review. When all of the blanks have been correctly filled in, you will have a thorough summary of the chapter for future reference and review.

Concept Checks

These fill-in exercises are designed to allow you to check your understanding of several important concepts from each chapter.

Extending the Chapter

This section contains questions from the "Application of Psychology" section of the text and other questions that relate the text material to personal issues, societal issues, and so on. Please note that many of these questions are asking for your opinion about issues, hence there are no right or wrong answers.

Practice Quiz

The practice quiz consists of three sections:

1) *Short answer questions*, with sample answers provided in the Answer section.

2) *Multiple choice questions*, with expanded answers provided in the Answer section. One important note: The multiple-choice questions correspond to the learning objectives found at the beginning of every Study Guide chapter. If you miss a multiple-choice question, you might want to review the corresponding learning objective.

3) *True-False questions*, with answers provided at the end of the Answer section.

Chapter 1   What Is Psychology?

Learning Objectives

1. Describe Aristotle's role in the history of psychology and understand the definition of psychology. (p. 4)

2. Identify and define the four goals of psychology. (p. 5)

3. Identify and compare early views of psychology that focused on the elements of conscious experience, including Wundt, Titchener, the structuralists, Alston, and the Gestalt psychologists. (p. 7)

4. Identify and compare views in psychology that focused on the functions of the conscious mind, and the functionalists. Also, explain functionalism's influence on contemporary psychology. (p. 8)

5. Describe the origins of behaviorism and social learning theory. (p. 9)

6. Identify the early views of psychology that focused on the nature of the unconscious mind. (p. 11)

7. Describe both the neuroscience and sociocultural perspectives and explain their influence on contemporary psychology. (p. 13)

8. Identify and define the terms associated with the sociocultural perspective. (p. 13)

9. Describe the differences between basic and applied areas of psychology; list and describe examples of both areas. (p. 14)

10. Identify three descriptive methods used in psychology and discuss how they are used. (p. 19)

11. Describe the correlational method. (p. 20)

12. Explain the statement: "Correlation does not necessarily mean causation." (p. 21)

13. Understand how and when formal experiments are used. (p. 22)

14. Distinguish between a dependent and an independent variable; distinguish between a control group and an experimental group. (p. 23)

15. List and define the five major ethical principles of research with human participants. (p. 23)

16. Understand why psychologists use animals in research and describe the ethical principles associated with animal studies. (p. 24)

Chapter Overview

Psychology is defined as the science of behavior and mental processes. Psychology is considered to be a science because psychologists acquire knowledge through systematic observation. The four main goals of psychology are to describe, predict, understand, and influence behavior and mental processes.

The influential early psychologists and their areas of interest include Wilhelm Wundt, Edward Titchener and J. Henry Alston (structuralism), Max Wertheimer (Gestalt psychology), William James (functionalism), Hermann Ebbinghaus and Mary Whiton Calkins (human memory), Alfred Binet (measurement of intelligence), Ivan Pavlov, John B. Watson and Margaret Floy Washburn (behaviorism), and Sigmund Freud (psychoanalysis). Humanistic psychologists believe that humans determine their own fates through the decisions they make.

Although some contemporary behaviorists continue to rule out the study of mental processes, other behaviorists, like Bandura, stress the importance of cognition. Contemporary psychoanalysts continue to emphasize unconscious conflicts, but suggest that motives other than sex and aggression are important.

A contemporary approach, the neuroscience perspective, studies the relationship between the nervous system, heredity, hormones, and behavior. A contemporary perspective that emphasizes culture, gender, and ethnic factors is the sociocultural perspective.

Modern psychologists work in basic or applied fields. Psychologists who work in basic areas conduct basic research, whereas applied psychologists put psychological knowledge to work helping people in a variety of settings.

Psychologists use three major scientific methods: 1) descriptive methods, which help to describe behavior and which include the use of surveys, naturalistic observation, and clinical methods; 2) correlational studies, which help to predict behavior by studying the relationship between variables; and 3) formal experiments, which study the cause-and-effect relationships between variables, and help psychologists to understand and influence behavior.

Formal experiments usually involve an experimental group, which receives the independent variable, and a control group. Differences in the dependent variable between the groups are believed to be caused by the independent variable.

Psychologists adhere to ethical principles of research, which protects the rights of human participants by avoiding coercion, uninformed participation, and unnecessary deception, by offering subjects the results of the studies in which they participate, and by ensuring confidentiality. In conducting research with animals, psychologists are guided by the principles of necessity, health, and humane treatment.

Key Terms Exercise

For each of the following exercises, match the key terms on the left with the correct definitions on the right. Page references to the text follow the terms so that you may refer to the text for any items you answer incorrectly or do not understand completely. You may check your responses immediately by referring to the answers that follow each exercise.

Psyche and Science=Psychology

_e_ 1. psychology (p. 4)
_c_ 2. behavior (p. 5)
_a_ 3. mental processes (p. 5)
_d_ 4. theory (p. 5)
_b_ 5. introspection (p. 7)

a.   private thoughts, emotions, feelings, and motives that others cannot directly observe
b.   looking inward at one's own consciousness
c.   observable and measurable human action
d.   a tentative explanation of facts and relationships in science
e.   the science of behavior and mental processes

ANSWERS

1. e	4. d
2. c	5. b
3. a	

The Many Viewpoints in Psychology and Their Origins

_____ 1. structuralism (p. 7)
_____ 2. Gestalt psychology (p. 8)
_____ 3. functionalism (p. 9)
_____ 4. cognition (p. 9)
_____ 5. cognitive psychology (p. 9)
_____ 6. behaviorism (p. 10)
_____ 7. social learning theory (p. 10)
_____ 8. psychoanalysis (p. 11)
_____ 9 .humanistic psychology (p. 11)

a.   the approach that believes that people control their own fates
b.   the school of psychology that emphasized the functions of consciousness
c.   an approach that emphasizes learning and the measurement of behavior
d.   an approach that studies the mind in terms of large, meaningful units
e.   techniques based on Sigmund Freud's theory of the unconscious
f.   the school of psychology that used introspection to determine the structure of the mind
g.   intellectual processes of perceiving, believing, thinking, and so on
h.   states that most of our behaviors are learned from others in society
i.   viewpoint that emphasizes such cognitive processes as perception, memory, and thinking

ANSWERS

1. f	6. c
2. d	7. h
3. b	8. e
4. g	9. a
5. i	

Contemporary Perspectives

_____ 1. neuroscience perspective (p. 13)
_____ 2. sociocultural perspective (p. 13)
_____ 3. culture (p. 13)
_____ 4. ethnic group (p. 13)
_____ 5. ethnic identity (p. 13)
_____ 6. gender identity (p. 14)
_____ 7. cultural relativity (p. 14)
_____ 8. applied psychologist (p. 15)

a. a group of persons who are descendants from a common group of ancestors
b. an approach that emphasizes one's culture, ethnic identity, and gender identity
c. thinking about other cultures in relative rather than in judgmental terms
d. patterns of behavior, beliefs and values shared by a group of people
e. a person's sense of belonging to a particular ethnic group
f. one's view of oneself as male or female
g. a psychologist who uses psychological knowledge to prevent and to solve human problems
h. the viewpoint that emphasizes the nervous system in explaining behavior and mental disorders

ANSWERS

1. h	5. e
2. b	6. f
3. d	7. c
4. a	8. g

Scientific Methods

_____ 1. scientific methods (p. 19)
_____ 2. survey method (p. 20)
_____ 3. naturalistic observation (p. 20)
_____ 4. clinical method (p. 20)
_____ 5. correlational method (p. 21)
_____ 6. formal experiment (p. 22)
_____ 7. independent variable (p. 23)
_____ 8. dependent variable (p. 23)

a. the method of observing people while they receive psychological help
b. a research method that measures the strength of relationship between two variables
c. the variable whose value depends on the independent variable
d. a research method that records behavior in natural life settings
e. methods of gathering information based on observation
f. the variable whose value can be controlled by the experimenter
g. a research method using interviews and questionnaires
h. a method that allows the researcher to manipulate the independent variable in order to study its effect on the independent variable

ANSWERS

1. e	5. b
2. g	6. h
3. d	7. f
4. a	8. c

Who Am I?

Match the psychologists on the left with their contributions to the field of psychology on the right. Page references to the text follow the names of the psychologists so that you may refer to the text for further review of these psychologists and their contributions. You may check your responses immediately by referring to the answers that follow each exercise.

Part I

_b_ 1. Aristotle (p. 4)
_f_ 2. J. Henry Alston (p. 7)
_a_ 3. William James (p. 7)
_d_ 4. Ivan Pavlov (p. 10)
_e_ 5. John B. Watson (p. 10)
_c_ 6. Albert Bandura (p. 10)

a. I taught the first course on psychology and founded the functionalist approach to psychology.

b. I was a philosopher who believed in the importance of observation.

c. I am a cognitive behaviorist who believes mental processes can't be ignored.

d. I identified a simple form of learning called conditioning.

e. I believed that only outward behavior can be studied, and I founded the behaviorist approach to psychology.

f. I am best known for my research on warmth and cold sensations and for being the first African-American to publish research in an APA journal.

ANSWERS

1. b	4. d
2. f	5. e
3. a	6. c

Part II

_c_ 1. Wilhelm Wundt (p. 7)
_a_ 2. Max Wertheimer (p. 8)
_e_ 3. Sigmund Freud (p. 11)
_d_ 4. Margaret Floy Washburn (p. 10)
_b_ 5. B. F. Skinner (p. 10)

a. I studied perception and helped found the Gestalt approach to psychology.

b. As a behaviorist, I believed that learning shapes our behavior.

c. I opened the Laboratory for Psychology in Leipzig, Germany, in 1879 and used a technique called introspection.

d. I was the first woman to receive a Ph.D. in psychology, and I taught for many years at Vassar College.

e. My techniques of psychoanalysis helped patients to explore their unconscious minds.

ANSWERS

1. c	4. d
2. a	5. b
3. e	

Review At A Glance
(Answers to this section may be found on page 17)

Psyche and Science=Psychology: Definition of Psychology

The ancient Greek philosopher, Aristotle, used the term ___(1)___ to refer to the essence of life. Aristotle believed that psyche escaped as a person took his last dying ___(2)___.

Psychology is defined as the science of ___(3)___ and ___(4)___ processes. Modern psychology uses careful, controlled observation and therefore is considered to be a ___(5)___. Psychologists study the overt actions of people that can be directly observed; these actions are referred to as ___(6)___. Psychologists also study thoughts, feelings, and motives that cannot be directly observed; these are referred to as mental ___(7)___.

Goals of Psychology

The goals of psychology are to ___(8)___, ___(9)___, ___(10)___, and ___(11)___ behavior and mental processes. Although psychology is a science, current explanations are always subject to revision. These tentative explanations of facts and relationships are known as ___(12)___.

The Many Viewpoints in Psychology and Their Origins

Psychology, like other sciences, emerged from the general field of ___(13)___. In 1879, Wilhelm ___(14)___ founded a psychological laboratory in Leipzig, Germany. Wundt and his student, Edward ___(15)___ studied consciousness using a method of looking inward at one's own experiences; this technique is called ___(16)___. Wundt and his followers were interested in the elements and structures of the mind; they were thus called ___(17)___. An early structuralist named J. Henry Alston studied the sensations of ___(18)___ and ___(19)___. Alston is the first African-American researcher to ___(20)___ an article in a journal of the APA.

In Germany, Max Wertheimer and his associates popularized a different approach to the study of consciousness, called ___(21)___ psychology. They believed that the mind could not be broken down into raw elements because "the ___(22)___ is different than the sum of its parts." Gestalt psychologists demonstrated their approach with examples of apparent movement, called the ___(23)___ phenomenon.

The first course on psychology was taught in 1875 by William ___(24)___. He believed that the process of consciousness helps the human species to ___(25)___. His approach, which emphasized the purposes or functions of consciousness, is called ___(26)___. The influence of functionalism is seen today in the study of ___(27)___ psychology.

In the 1890s, Russian physiologist Ivan Pavlov identified a simple form of learning called ___(28)___. Pavlov's ideas were popularized in the U.S. by John B. Watson, who believed that only ___(29)___ behavior could be scientifically understood. The school of psychology based on the ideas of Pavlov and Watson is called ___(30)___. Another influential early behaviorist, and the first woman to receive a Ph.D. in psychology, was Margaret Floy ___(31)___. Most contemporary behavioral psychologists integrate the study of behavior with the study of ___(32)___. Albert Bandura is associated with this viewpoint, also called ___(33)___ _____ theory.

Sigmund Freud was an influential founder of psychology who believed that conscious experiences were not as important as the ___(34)___ mind. He believed the roots of psychological problems involved ___(35)___ and ___(36)___ motives. The process Freud formulated to help people with psychological problems is called ___(37)___. Modern psychoanalysts still believe that unconscious ___(38)___ are the chief source of psychological problems, however, many psychoanalysts also stress the importance of other motives as well.

Abraham Maslow and Carl Rogers have popularized the ___(39)___ approach, which holds that humans determine their own fates through the decisions they make.

Contemporary Perspectives in Psychology

Psychologists who are interested in the role played by the brain in such areas as emotion, reasoning, and speaking are approaching psychology from the ___(40)___ perspective. A contemporary perspective that emphasizes cultural, gender, and ethnic factors is called the ___(41)___ perspective. The patterns of behavior, beliefs, and values shared by a group of people is referred to as ___(42)___. A group of people who descended from a common group of ancestors is called an ___(43)___ group. A person's sense of belonging to a particular ethnic group is referred to as ethnic ___(44)___. A person's view of himself or herself as male or female is called ___(45)___. The sociocultural perspective encourages the view of other cultures as being different rather than inferior; this view is called cultural ___(46)___. The sociocultural perspective also emphasizes ___(47)___ differences among members of different ethnic groups, cultures, and genders.

For many years the field of psychology was dominated by ___(48)___ _____. Until recently, the contributions of women and ___(49)___ _____ were ignored in most textbooks. Although the number of women and ethnic minorities in psychology has grown in recent years, ___(50)___ continues to play a negative role in psychology.

Specialty Areas of Modern Psychology

Psychologists who work in ___(51)___ areas conduct research. Psychologists who use basic knowledge to solve and prevent human problems are called ___(52)___ psychologists. The largest specialties within experimental psychology are 1) ___(53)___ psychology, which studies the nervous system and its relationship to behavior; 2) ___(54)___ and ___(55)___ which studies how the sense organs operate and how we interpret information; 3) ___(56)___ and ___(57)___, which focuses on the ways in which we acquire and remember information; 4) ___(58)___, which studies intelligent action; 5) ___(59)___ psychology, which focuses on changes during the lifespan; 6) ___(60)___

__ and ___(61)___, which studies needs and states that activate behavior, as well as feelings and moods; 7) (62)___, the field that focuses on our consistent ways of behaving; 8) ___(63)___ psychology, the area that studies the influence of others on our behavior, and 9) the area that focuses on ethnic, cultural, and gender issues, ___(64)__ psychology.

The majority of psychologists are ___(65)___ psychologists. The major specialties within applied psychology are 1) ___(66)___ psychology, the field concerned with personal problems and abnormal behavior; 2) ___(67)___ psychology, which focuses on personal or school problems and career choices; 3) ___(68)___ - psychology, which deals with work-related psychological issues; 4) ___(69)___ and school psychology, which focuses on learning and other school-related issues; and 5) ___(70)___ psychology, which studies the relationship between psychology and health.

Scientific Methods: How We Learn About Behavior and Mental Processes

The simplest of the scientific methods involves ___(71)___. An example of this method involves asking people questions directly; this is the ___(72)___ method. Another descriptive approach, called ___(73)___ observation, involves observing and recording behavior in real-life settings. A third technique, observing people who are receiving help from a psychologist, is the ___(74)___ method.

To understand the relationship between variables, psychologists use a technique called the ___(75)___ method. When psychologists observe factors whose numerical values can vary, they are studying ___(76)___. The main difference between naturalistic observation and correlational studies is that correlational studies use ___(77)___ _____. It's important to remember that, when two variables correlate, it does not necessarily mean that one variable ___(78)___ the other.

The most useful method of observation is the ___(79)___ experiment. This approach allows the researcher to draw conclusions about ___(80)___ - and- _____ relationships. Formal experiments compare quantitative measures of behavior under ___(81)___ _____. In formal experiments, the factor that is controlled by the researcher is called the ___(82)___ variable. The factor that depends on the effects of the independent variable is the ___(83)___ variable. In a study designed to test the effects of caffeine on job performance, caffeine is considered the ___(84)___ variable, while job performance is the ___(85)___ variable. For simple experiments, two groups of participants are used. The group that receives the independent variable is called the ___(86)___ group, whereas the group that does not is called the ___(87)___. Two drawbacks regarding experiments are that they are somewhat (88)___ not all results are necessarily ___(89)___.

Ethical Principles of Research

The following issues are important ethical principles for psychological research with human participants. Individuals should not be pressured into participating in research; that is, there should be freedom from ___(90)___. When a full description of the experiment is made available to potential participants, the principle being followed is ___(91)___. Except under certain circumstances, it is not considered ethical to misrepresent the true purpose of a study. Such misrepresentation is called limited ___(92)___. When participants are provided with the results of the study, this is termed ___(93)___. Participants must be assured of their anonymity; that is, their ___(94)___ must be protected. Psychologists conduct research with animals for several reasons. In many cases, for example with brain research, it would be unethical to do the research with ___(95)___. Also, using animals allows psychologists to conduct experiments that are more precisely ___(96)___. Psychologists have also learned much by comparing the behavior of animals of different ___(97)___. Finally, psychologists are interested in learning about other animal species. Animal research is considered ethical only when all of the following conditions are met: ___(98)___, health, and ___(99)___ treatment.

Concept Checks

Fill in the missing components of the following concept boxes. The correct answers are located in the "Answers" section at the end of the chapter.

Early Approaches to Psychology

Approach	Focus	Key names
structuralists		Wundt, Titchener, Alston
	human consciousness cannot be broken down into its elements; the phi phenomenon illustrates the "whole is different than the sum of its parts"	
functionalists		William James
behaviorism		Pavlov, Watson, Washburn

Contemporary Perspectives

Perspective	Focus
	Behavior is learned from others in society
Sociocultural perspective	
Humanistic perspective	
	Emphasizes the relationship between the nervous system, hormonal and genetic factors, and behavior
Psychoanalysis	

Research Methods

Method	Explanation	Advantage/disadvantage
survey method	a descriptive approach that uses interviews and questionnaires	
	a descriptive approach in which behavior is recorded in natural settings	**adv**: allows observation of behavior in its natural context; **disadv**: observers may influence "natural" settings
clinical method		**adv**: in-depth study of a person's behaviors, thoughts and so on; **disadv**: very small sample size
correlational studies		**adv**: allows researchers to understand strength of relationship between variables; **disadv**: correlation does not prove causation
formal experiment	researchers study the effect of the independent variable on the dependent variable	

Extending the Chapter: Psychology, Societal Issues, and Human Diversity

These questions may be assigned to you. Whether or not they are assigned, they are designed to be challenging questions to encourage you to think independently about the material in the chapter. Many of the questions have no right or wrong answers.

1. Which contemporary approach to psychology makes the most sense to you? Why?

2. A high school freshman takes her first puff on a cigarette. How might the following perspectives view this behavior: social learning theory, humanistic theory, the neuroscience perspective, and the sociocultural perspective?

3. Describe the advantages and disadvantages of being a member of an individualistic culture (You may substitute collectivist culture, if you are more familiar with a collectivist culture).

4. How do the various perspectives view the issue of responsibility for one's own behavior?

5. Most Western research psychologists would agree that the scientific method is the only certain way to acquire valid information about psychology. What other approaches do different cultures use to acquire credible information about behavior and mental processes? (Hint: palm reading, astrology, reading tea leaves, and others)

6. Explain the arguments both favoring and opposing the use of animals in research. What is your opinion? Why?

7. Are psychologists able to study behavior and mental processes with the same degree of objectivity with which other scientists (for example, geologists) approach their disciplines? Defend your answer.

Practice Quiz

The practice quiz consists of three sections: 1) Short answer questions, 2) Multiple choice questions, and 3) True-False questions. At the end of the chapter you will find suggested answers to the short answer questions, answers and explanation for the multiple choice questions, and answers to the true-false questions.

Short Answer Questions

1. List and describe the goals of psychology.

_____

_____

2. Explain the concept of cultural relativity.

_____

_____

3. List and describe ethical issues involved in conducting research with humans.

_____

_____

Multiple Choice Question

1. The author defines psychology as the science of behavior and
   a. mental processes.
   b. overt actions.
   c. phenomena.
   d. Observation.
   LO 1

2. Psychology is considered to be a science because psychologists
   a. use logic to develop their theories.
   b. use careful and controlled observation.
   c. can be completely objective in their study of human behavior.
   d. have developed techniques to let them understand private thoughts and emotions.
   LO 1

3. Which of the four goals of psychology is achieved when we can explain behavior?
   a. describe
   b. predict
   c. understand
   d. influence
   LO 2

4. Surveys are conducted in order to achieve which of the following goals of psychology?
   a. describe
   b. predict
   c. understand
   d. explain
   LO 2

5. If a man wearing a fake beard and a black academic robe asks you to describe the sensations of biting into an apple,
   a. leave the area immediately.
   b. he's probably a behaviorist trying to condition you.
   c. he's probably a psychoanalyst looking into your unconscious mind.
   d. he's probably a structuralist asking you to do introspection.
   LO 3

6. What was the focus of structuralism?
   a. mental processes
   b. observable events
   c. unconscious thought
   d. mental elements
   LO 3

7. According to William James, psychology should emphasize
   a. what the mind can do.
   b. the basic structure of the mind.
   c. the factors that have aided our evolution.
   d. a and c above.
   LO 4

8. When Pavlov discovered that his dogs associated the sound of the bell with food, he called this
   a. functionalism.
   b. conditioning.
   c. introspection.
   d. the phi phenomenon.
   LO 5

9. Social learning theory has attempted to integrate the ideas of behaviorism with the study of
   a. the unconscious.
   b. Gestalt psychology.
   c. humanistic psychology.
   d. cognition.
   LO 5

10. Which of the following ideas is most likely to be associated with humanistic psychology?
    a. self-concept
    b. cultural relativism
    c. the phi phenomenon
    d. introspection
    LO 6

11. According to Freud, innate motives that are at the root of psychological problems are sex and
    a. social needs.
    b. physical need.s
    c. guilt.
    d. aggression.
    LO 6

12. In the early 1900s, Ramon y Cajal identified
    a. the structure of the unconscious.
    b. neurons.
    c. hormones.
    d. the basic principles of heredity.
    LO 7

13. In order to fully understand people, it is necessary to understand the beliefs and values of their culture, according to
    a functionalism.
    b. structuralism.
    c. the sociocultural perspective.
    d. the neuroscience perspective.
    LO 7

14. According to the sociocultural perspective, which of the following refers to a person's sense of belonging to a particular ethnic group?
    a. cultural relativity
    b. ethnic identity
    c. gender identity
    d. racial identity
    LO 8

15. Cultural relativity promotes the idea that
    a. some cultures are more advanced than others.
    b. some cultures operate on a higher moral plane than others.
    c. it is useful to think about different cultures in judgmental terms.
    d. cultures should be thought of as being different rather than superior or inferior.
    LO 8

16. Which of the following is *not* considered a "basic" area of psychology?
    a. sensation and perception
    b. cognition
    c. counseling psychology
    e. personality
    LO 9

17. A "basic" area of psychology that studies ways in which our behavior is influenced by other people is called
    a. personality.
    b. motivation and emotion.
    c. social psychology.
    d. developmental psychology.
    LO 9

18. Of the research methods described in the text, which are described as the simplest methods?
    a. correlational
    b. descriptive
    c. quantitative
    d. experimental
    LO 10

19. A psychology student wishes to find out more about test anxiety. She constructs a "Test Anxiety Questionnaire" and gives it to other students. Which technique is she using?
    a. survey method
    b. correlational method
    c. clinical method
    d. formal experiment
    LO 10

20. If you were interested in describing "Happy Hour" behavior among college students, which technique would be most likely to yield accurate data?
    a. survey method
    b. formal experiment
    c. naturalistic observation
    d. clinical method
    LO 10

21. In a research study, participants recorded the number of cigarettes smoked per day. "Number of cigarettes smoked per day" is referred to as a(n)
    a. sample.
    b. variable.
    c. coefficient.
    d. hypothesis.
    LO 11

22. Psychologists seeking to establish a relationship between family income and years of formal education would use which research method?
    a. the clinical method
    b. naturalistic observation
    c. formal experiments
    d. correlational methods
    LO 11

23. If criminal activity were found to increase as temperatures increase, researchers could conclude that
    a. warm weather causes crime.
    b. crime causes warm weather.
    c. crime and temperature are positively correlated.
    d. crime and temperature have a correlation coefficient of zero.
    LO 12

24. The goal of correlational research is to
    a. prove cause-and-effect relationships.
    b. show the degree of relationship between two variables.
    c. manipulate the independent variable.
    d. observe behavior in its natural environment.
    LO 12

25. Which of the following is an advantage of using formal experimental methods?
    a. Only these methods can establish whether there is any relationship between two variables.
    b. Only these methods allow behavior to be observed as it naturally occurs.
    c. Only these methods allow researchers to determine people's opinions about various issues.
    d. Only these methods allow scientists to determine cause-and-effect relationships.
    LO 13

26. If a researcher wished to determine whether one variable was the cause of another variable, which research method would she use?
    a. correlational study
    b. formal experiment
    c. survey
    d. naturalistic observation
    LO 13

27. A psychologist studied the effect of blood alcohol on driving behavior. In this study the driving behavior was the _____ variable.
    a. control
    b. independent
    c. dependent
    d. manipulated
    LO 14

28. The purpose of the control group is to
    a. control the outcome of the study.
    b. control the behavior of the participants.
    c. have a group that receives none of the independent variable.
    d. have a group that receives none of the dependent variable.
    LO 14

29. Sandra participates in a research study. When she is finished with her participation, she receives a copy of the complete results of the study. The researchers are practicing the principle of
   a. informed consent.
   b. adequate debriefing.
   c. confidentiality.
   d. freedom from coercion.
      LO 15

30. If a student is *required* to participate in a research study in order to pass a course, this is a violation of the ethical principle of
   a. confidentiality.
   b. freedom from coercion.
   c. informed consent.
   d. Debriefing.
      LO 15

31. To be considered ethical, which of the conditions must researchers using animals meet?
   a. necessity
   b. health
   c. humane treatment
   d. all of the above
      LO 16

32. Which of the following represents an advantage of using nonhuman animals in research?
   a. more precisely controlled research
   b. unethical to do research with humans
   c. learn about other species
   d. all of the above
      LO 16

True False Questions

_____1. Psychology is defined as the science of behavior and mental processes.

_____2. According to the text, one of the goals of psychology is to control behavior.

_____3. William James was an influential early structuralist.

_____4. Cognitive psychology is a modern version of functionalism.

_____5. Watson's approach to behaviorism emphasized the importance of cognition.

_____6. Humanistic psychologists believe each person can control her own destiny.

_____7. The sociocultural perspective is not as influential as it once was.

_____8. Surveys can yield information about the cause and effect of behavior.

_____9. In formal research, the group that receives the independent variable is called the experimental group.

_____10. Requiring students to participate in research violates the ethical principle of freedom from coercion.

ANSWER SECTION

Concept Checks

Early Approaches to Psychology

Approach	Focus	Key names
structuralists	sought to determine the structure of the mind through introspection	Wundt, Titchener, Alston
Gestalt psychology	human consciousness cannot be broken down into its elements; the phi phenomenon illustrates the "whole is different than the sum of its parts."	Wertheimer
functionalists	emphasized the *functions* of consciousness, rather than the structure	William James
behaviorism	psychology should study only overt, measurable behavior	Pavlov, Watson, Washburn

Contemporary Perspectives

Perspective	Focus
Social learning theory	behavior is learned from others in society
Sociocultural perspective	emphasizes the importance of culture, ethnic identity, and gender identity
Humanistic perspective	humans determine their own fates through the decisions they make
Neuroscience perspective	emphasizes the relationship between the nervous system, hormonal and genetic factors, and behavior
Psychoanalysis	conflicts in the unconscious mind are the main source of psychological problems
Cognitive perspective	this perspective emphasizes the processes involving perceiving, believing, thinking, knowing, and so on

Research Methods

Method	Explanation	Advantage/disadvantage
survey method	a descriptive approach that uses interviews and questionnaires	**adv**: can collect a great deal of information in a short amount of time; **disadv**: accuracy of information is questionable
naturalistic observation	a descriptive approach in which behavior is recorded in natural settings	**adv**: allows observation of behavior in its natural context; **disadv**: observers may influence "natural" settings
clinical method	a descriptive approach that studies people while they receive help from a psychologist	**adv**: in-depth study of a person's behaviors, thoughts and so on; **disadv**: very small sample size
correlational studies	measures the strength of relationship between 2 variables	**adv**: allows researchers to understand strength of relationship between variables; **disadv**: correlation does not prove causation
formal experiment	researchers study the effect of the independent variable on the dependent variable	**adv**: allows researchers to understand cause-and-effect relationship; **disadv**: may require "artificial" setting, for example, a laboratory

Answers to Review At A Glance

1. psyche
2. breath
3. behavior
4. mental
5. science
6. behavior
7. processes
8. describe
9. predict
10. understand
11. influence
12. theories
13. philosophy
14. Wundt
15. Titchener
16. introspection
17. structuralists
18. heat
19. cold
20. publish
21. Gestalt
22. whole
23. phi
24. James
25. survive
26. functionalism

27. cognitive
28. conditioning
29. outward
30. behaviorism
31. Washburn
32. cognition
33. social learning
34. unconscious
35. sexual
36. aggressive
37. psychoanalysis
38. conflicts
39. humanistic
40. biological
41. sociocultural
42. culture
43. ethnic
44. identity
45. gender identity
46. relativity
47. individual
48. white males
49. ethnic minorities
50. prejudice
51. basic
52. applied

53. biological
54. sensation
55. perception
56. learning
57. memory
58. cognition
59. developmental
60. motivation
61. emotion
62. personality
63. social
64. sociocultural
65. applied
66. clinical
67. counseling
68. industrial-organizational
69. educational
70. health
71. description
72. survey
73. naturalistic
74. clinical
75. correlation
76. variables
77. quantifiable data
78. perfect

79. negative	86. independent	93. debriefing
80. causes	87. dependent	94. confidentiality
81. formal	88. experimental	95. humans
82. cause-and-effect	89. control	96. controlled
83. different conditions	90. coercion	97. species
84. independent	91. informed consent	98. necessity
85. dependent	92. deception	99. humane

Sample Answers for Short Answer Questions

1. **List and describe the goals of psychology.**

   The goals of psychology are: 1) to describe psychological phenomena more accurately and completely; 2) to predict future behavior; 3) to understand behavior and mental processes well enough to explain them; and 4) to influence behavior in beneficial ways.

2. **Explain the concept of cultural relativity.**

   The sociocultural perspective emphasizes the concept of cultural relativity. This notion encourages thinking about cultures in relative rather than in judgmental terms. It suggests that different cultures, ethnic groups and genders are different, rather than to superior or inferior when compared with another.

3. **List and describe ethical issues involved in conducting research with humans.**

   The text lists five ethical issues: 1) freedom from coercion, which means individuals should not be pressured into participating in research; 2) informed consent, which generally obligates a researcher to fully describe the purpose of the study before they are asked to participate; 3) limited deception, which spells out the conditions under which participants might be deceived about their participation; 4) adequate debriefing, which gives participants the right to know the results of the study; and 5) confidentiality, which obligates researchers to keep confidential everything they learn about a participant.

Multiple Choice Answers

1. The answer is *a*. Overt actions are of special interest to behavioral psychologists, and all scientists are interested in the observation of phenomena.
2. The answer is *b*. Logic alone doesn't comprise science. Choices c and d are debatable.
3. The answer is *c*. We understand behavior when we can *explain* our knowledge of facts and relationships in psychology, in addition to describing and predicting.
4. The answer is *a*. Surveys don't try to influence behavior; they try to take a sort of snapshot of behavior, that is, they try to describe behavior.
5. The answer is *d*. The beard and robe are meant to conjure up the image of Edward Titchener, an influential structuralist. Introspection was the technique that structuralists used to look inward in an effort to isolate the basic elements of the mind.
6. The answer is *d*. Structuralists like Wundt and Titchener used introspection in an effort to understand the elements of the mind. Unconscious thought was a topic of great import to the psychoanalysts, and observable events were important to the behaviorists.

7. The answer is *d* (*a* and *c*). James was interested in studying the functions of the mind, rather than the individual structures of the mind. He was also interested in topics he considered to be evolutionarily important.

8. The answer is *b*. Functionalism was a school of thought popularized by William James; the phi phenomenon is a Gestalt psychology term dealing with the perception of movement.

9. The answer is *d*. Social learning theory has its roots in behaviorism, but has attempted to broaden the perspective by also emphasizing the importance of cognition.

10. The answer is *a*. Humanistic psychologists have emphasized that humans determine their fates through the decisions they make. According to their view, society often makes it difficult to have an accurate self-concept.

11. The answer is *d*. Although Freud emphasized these two motives, later psychoanalysts emphasized other motives, such as the need to feel adequate in social relationships.

12. The answer is *b*. This research was instrumental in the development of the neuroscience perspective.

13. The answer is *c*. As the world continues to shrink in the 21st century, this perspective is likely to increase in importance.

14. The answer is *b*. Cultural relativity is the idea that cultures are best thought of in relative rather than judgmental terms. Gender and racial identity refer to one's sense of belonging to a gender or racial group.

15. The answer is *d*. This notion emphasizes viewing other cultures in *relative* rather than in judgmental terms.

16. The answer is *c*. Basic areas of psychology emphasize research and adding to the knowledge base of psychology. Counseling psychology is considered to be an applied field of psychology.

17. The answer is *c*. All of the other choices are also areas of basic or experimental psychology.

18. The answer is *b*. Descriptive methods seek only to describe what exists. These methods are not looking for relationships between variables or seeking to explain the causes of behavior.

19. The answer is *a*. The correlational method is used to discover the relationship between variables. The clinical method involves observing people who are receiving help for psychological problems. Formal experiments involve manipulation of the independent variable to study its effect on the dependent variable.

20. The answer is *c*. Naturalistic observation allows the researcher to observe behavior as it naturally occurs. Presumably, this approach would allow a researcher more accurate information than merely surveying college students. Formal experiments are not intended to be descriptive, and the clinical method involves observing people while they receive help for psychological problems.

21. The answer is *b*. Since the number of cigarettes smoked per day varies from person to person, and from day to day for the same person, it is a variable. A hypothesis would seek to relate this variable to another variable.

22. The answer is *d*. Correlational methods are used to discover the degree of relationship between variables, such as income and education.

23. The answer is *c*. This is a reminder that the fact that two variables have a positive correlation doesn't prove that one variable causes the other.

24. The answer is *b*. Answers a and c refer to formal research, whereas answer d refers to naturalistic observation.

25. The answer is *d*. Correlational techniques can only suggest that a relationship between variables exists; formal experimental methods can determine whether one variable is the cause of the other. Answer b refers to naturalistic observation, whereas answer c refers to survey methods.

26. The answer is *b*. Formal experiments are the only type of research that allow researchers to make conclusions about cause and effect.

27. The answer is *c*. Since driving behavior depends upon the blood alcohol level of the driver, it is considered the dependent variable. In this experiment, blood alcohol level is the independent variable.

28. The answer is *c*. None of the other answers make any sense.

29. The answer is *b*. Each of the other choices also refers to ethical principles of research.

30. The answer is *b*. Forcing anybody to participate in research is unethical.

31. The answer is *d*. "Necessity" implies that the study must be necessary to significantly advance psychology, "health" refers to the requirement that all animals must be well-cared for, and "humane treatment" means efforts must be made to minimize discomfort to animals.

32. The answer is *d*. Other advantages include learning how to protect endangered species.

Answers to True-False Questions

1. T   6. T

2. F   7. F

3. F   8. F

4. T   9. T

5. F   10. T

Chapter 2   **Biological Foundations of Behavior**

Learning Objectives

1. Understand the importance of the neuron and differentiate among the neuron's cell body, dendrite, and axon. (p. 32)

2. Summarize the processes of neural transmission and synaptic transmission. (p. 33)

3. Distinguish between the central nervous system and the peripheral nervous system and explain the differences among afferent neurons, efferent neurons, and interneurons. (p. 38)

4. List the functions of the somatic and autonomic nervous systems and describe the roles of the sympathetic and parasympathetic divisions of the autonomic nervous system. (p. 39)

5. Describe the techniques that provide images of the brain and brain functions. (p. 43)

6. List the three major divisions of the brain and know their principal components. (p. 44)

7. Explain the basic functions of the hindbrain and midbrain. (p. 44)

8. Summarize the functions of the regions of the forebrain, specifically the thalamus, hypothalamus, limbic system, and cerebral cortex. (p. 44)

9. Identify the location and functions of the four cortical lobes and the association areas of the cerebral cortex. (p. 46)

10. Explain how the two cerebral hemispheres communicate and describe the changes that occur if the corpus callosum is severed. (p. 49)

11. Discuss the role of the cerebral cortex in processing intellectual and emotional information. (p. 50)

12. Identify the endocrine glands and understand how the endocrine system communicates and how it regulates body processes. (p. 54)

13. Identify the hormones related to each endocrine gland and understand their functions. (p. 55)

14. Describe the relationship between genes and chromosomes and understand how dominant and recessive genes affect physical and behavioral traits. (p. 58)

15. Summarize the role of twin studies and adoption studies in genetic research. (p .60)

16. Understand inheritance in terms of its influence on personality development and abnormal behavior. (p. 61)

17. (From the *Application of Psychology* section) Describe the relationship between the brain and schizophrenia. (p. 63)

Chapter Overview

The human nervous system is a complex network of neural cells that carry messages and regulate bodily functions and personal behavior. The individual cells of the nervous system are called neurons. The parts of a neuron include the cell body, dendrites and axons. Neurons are separated from each other by a tiny synaptic gap. Chemical substances called neurotransmitters transmit electrical messages across the synapse.

The central nervous system is composed of the brain and the spinal cord. The peripheral nervous system carries messages to and from the rest of the body. It is composed of both the somatic and autonomic nervous system. The autonomic nervous system consists of the sympathetic division, which activates internal organs, and the parasympathetic division, which calms internal organs.

Scientists have developed brain-imaging techniques that can create images of the activities of the living brain. These techniques include the EEG, the PET scan, and the MRI.

The brain has three major parts. The first of these, the hindbrain, contains a) the medulla, which controls breathing and a variety of reflexes; b) the pons, which is concerned with balance, hearing, and some parasympathetic functions; and c) the cerebellum, which is chiefly responsible for maintaining muscle tone and coordinating muscular movements. A second part of the brain, the midbrain, is a center for reflexes related to vision and hearing.

The forebrain, the third major part of the brain, includes two distinct areas. The first area contains the thalamus, a switching station that routes sensory information to the appropriate areas of the brain, the hypothalamus, which is involved with our motives and emotions, and most of the limbic system. The second area contains the cerebral cortex, which controls conscious experience, intellectual activities, the senses, and voluntary actions. The cortex contains two cerebral hemispheres connected by the corpus callosum. Each hemisphere of the cortex contains four lobes: the frontal lobe is involved with speaking and voluntary movement; the parietal lobe is involved with the sense of touch; the temporal lobe is involved with hearing and understanding language; and the occipital lobe is involved with vision. The cerebral cortex is also important in processing emotions.

The endocrine system contains glands that secrete hormones. This system influences emotional arousal, metabolism, sexual functioning, and other bodily processes. The pituitary gland is referred to as the master gland, since its hormones help to regulate the activity of the other glands. The adrenal glands secrete epinephrine and norepinephrine, which are involved in emotional arousal and which affect the metabolic rate and sexual arousal. The islets of Langerhans secrete glucagon and insulin, which control blood sugar and energy levels. The gonads produce sex cells for human reproduction and also estrogen and testosterone, which are important to sexual functioning and the development of secondary sex characteristics. The thyroid gland secretes thyroxin, which helps control the metabolic rate. The parathyroid glands secrete parathormone, which controls the level of nervous activity. The pineal gland, attached to the top of the thalamus, secretes melatonin.

Human characteristics and behaviors are influenced by genetic inheritance. Characteristics that are inherited are passed on through genes containing DNA. Genes are found in the cell nucleus on strips called chromosomes. Most normal human cells contain 46 chromosomes arranged in 23 pairs. The sex cells, however, each contain only 23 chromosomes and are capable of combining into a new zygote with a unique set of chromosomes.

Researchers interested in hereditary influences on behavior have used twin studies and adoption studies. Although inheritance plays a significant role in influencing human behavior, environmental and other personal factors also play important roles.

Research into schizophrenia underscores the influence of the brain in both normal and disturbed behavior.

Key Terms Exercise

For each of the following exercises, match the key terms on the left with the correct definitions on the right. Page references to the text follow the terms so that you may refer to the text for any items you answer incorrectly or do not understand completely. You may check your responses immediately by referring to the answers that follow each exercise.

The Nervous System (I)

_____ 1. brain (p. 32)
_____ 2. spinal cord (p. 32)
_____ 3. neuron (p. 32)
_____ 4. cell body (p. 32)
_____ 5. dendrites (p. 32)
_____ 6. axons (p. 32)
_____ 7. nerve (p. 33)

a. a thick bundle of long neurons outside the spine
b. the mass of neural cells and related cells encased in the skull
c. the nerve fibers in the spinal column
d. neuron endings that transmit messages to other neurons
e. extensions of the cell body that receive messages from other neurons
f. an individual cell of the nervous system
g. the central part of the nerve cell, containing the nucleus

ANSWERS
1. b   5. e
2. c   6. d
3. f   7. a
4. g

The Nervous System (II)

_____ 1. ions (p. 33)
_____ 2. myelin sheath (p. 35)
_____ 3. synapse (p. 35)
_____ 4. neurotransmitters (p. 35)
_____ 5. central nervous system (p. 38)
_____ 6. peripheral nervous system (p. 38)

a. the junction between neurons
b. the brain and nerve fibers of the spinal cord
c. electrically charged particles
d. chemical substances that help carry messages across synapses
e. nerves that branch off from the brain and spinal cord to all parts of the body
f. a fatty coating that encases and insulates many axons

ANSWERS

1. c   4. d
2. f   5. b
3. a   6. e

The Nervous System (III)

_____ 1. afferent neurons (p. 38)
_____ 2. efferent neurons (p. 38)
_____ 3. interneurons (p. 39)
_____ 4. somatic nervous system (p. 39)
_____ 5. autonomic nervous system (p. 40)
_____ 6. sympathetic division (p. 40)
_____ 7. parasympathetic division (p. 40)

a. carries messages from the body to the central nervous system
b. helps process simple reflexes in the brain and spinal cord
c. activates the visceral organs during emotional arousal
d. generally calms the visceral organs after arousal
e. the system that controls involuntary action and regulates emotion
f. the system that receives messages from the sense organs, muscles, joints and skin and carries messages from the central nervous system to the skeletal muscles
g. carries messages from the central nervous system to the organs and muscles

ANSWERS

1. a   5. e
2. g   6. c
3. b   7. d
4. f

Structures and Functions of the Brain (I)

_____ 1. hindbrain (p. 44)
_____ 2. medulla (p. 44)
_____ 3. pons (p. 44)
_____ 4. cerebellum (p. 44)
_____ 5. midbrain (p. 44)
_____ 6. forebrain (p. 44)
_____ 7. thalamus (p. 45)

a. routes messages to appropriate parts of the brain involved in balance, hearing, and some parasympathetic functions

b. involved in balance, hearing, and some parasympathetic functions

c. two structures that are responsible for maintaining muscle tone and muscular conditioning

d. the swelling at the top of the spinal cord, responsible for breathing and a variety of reflexes

e. a small area at the top of the hindbrain that mainly serves as a reflex center for orienting the eyes and ears

f. lowest part of the brain, primarily responsible for "housekeeping" functions

g. part of the brain that contains the thalamus, hypothalamus, most of the limbic system and the cerebral cortex

ANSWERS

1. f   5. e
2. d   6. g
3. b   7. a
4. c

Structures and Functions of the Brain (II)

_____ 1. hypothalamus (p. 45)
_____ 2. limbic system (p. 45)
_____ 3. cerebral cortex (p. 46)
_____ 4. frontal lobes (p. 46)
_____ 5. parietal lobes (p. 48)
_____ 6. temporal lobes (p.48)
_____ 7. occipital lobes (p. 48)

a. the largest structure of the forebrain, controlling conscious experience and intelligence

b. involved in motivation, emotion, and the functions of the autonomic nervous system

c. a neural system composed of the amygdala, the hippocampus, the septal area, and the cingulate cortex

d. contains the somatosensory area

e. contains the visual area

f. contains both Broca's area and the motor area

g. contains the auditory areas

ANSWERS

1. b   5. d
2. c   6. g
3. a   7. e
4. f

Endocrine System and Genetic Influences (I)

_____ 1. endocrine system (p. 54)
_____ 2. hormones (p. 54)
_____ 3. pituitary gland (p. 54)
_____ 4. adrenal glands (p. 55)
_____ 5. islets of Langerhans (p. 56)
_____ 6. gonads (p. 56)

a. chemical substances that control internal organs
b. the system of glands that produces hormones
c. play an important role in emotional arousal
d. embedded in the pancreas and helps regulate blood sugar levels
e. produce the sex cells and secrete hormones
f. the body's "master gland"

ANSWERS
1. b   4. c
2. a   5. d
3. f   6. e

Endocrine System and Genetic Influences (II)

_____ 1. thyroid gland (p. 56)
_____ 2. parathyroid glands (p. 56)
_____ 3. pineal gland (p. 56)
_____ 4. gene (p. 58)
_____ 5. chromosomes (p. 58)

a. secrete parathormone, which is important in nervous system functioning
b. provide instructions to the organism through DNA
c. strips in the cell nucleus that contain genes
d. secretes thyroxin, which helps regulate metabolism
e. secretes melatonin, important in the regulation of biological rhythms.

ANSWERS
1. d   4. b
2. a   5. c
3. e

Review At A Glance

(The answers to this section begin on page 40)

Nervous System: The Biological Control Center

The complex mass of nerve cells encased in the skull is the ___(1)___. The brain is connected to a bundle of long nerves running through the spine, called the ___(2)___ ___(3)___. The most important unit of the nervous system is the individual nerve cell, or ___(4)___. The central part of the neuron is called the ___(5)___ ___; it contains the cell's control center, or ___(6)___. The small branches extending out from the cell body receive messages from other neurons and are called ___(7)___. The small branches at the other end of the nerve cell transmit messages to other neurons; these are ___(8)___. The nervous system contains about ___(9)___ ___ neurons. Each neuron can receive messages from, or transmit messages to ___(10)___ to ___(11)___ other neural cells. A bundle of long neurons outside the brain and spinal cord is a ___(12)___.

Neurons, the "wires" of the nervous system, also contain built-in supplies of ___(13)___ power. The fluids inside and outside the neuron contain electrically charged ___(14)___. The overall ion charge within the cell membrane is ___(15)___, while the fluid outside the cell membrane, which contains sodium ions, is ___(16)___. The cell membrane allows some chemicals to pass through, but not others; it is ___(17)___.

In its normal resting state, with mostly negative ions inside and mostly positive ions outside, the neuron is electrically ___(18)___. When the membrane is stimulated and positively charged sodium ions enter the neuron, the process is termed ___(19)___. Neural transmission operates according to the ___(20)___ principle. If sufficient depolarization occurs, the axon conducts a neural impulse, known as an ___(21)___ ___. The action potential travels the length of the ___(22)___. A drug that interrupts the flow of depolarization is ___(23)___. Axons are insulated by a fatty covering called a ___(24)___ ___. The myelin sheath improves the capacity of the neuron to conduct ___(25)___ impulses. The myelin sheath grows thicker in late ___(26)___. A disease that destroys the myelin sheath of many neurons is ___(27) -___ ___.

Although neurons are linked together, there is a small gap between them called the ___(28)___. Neural messages can be transmitted across the synaptic gap if the axon produces ___(29)___. Neurotransmitters are stored in synaptic vessicles located in the synaptic ___(30)___. Neurotransmitters float across the gap and fit into receptor sites on the adjacent ___(31)___; this causes an ___(32)___ ___ that allows the neural message to continue. The chemical structure of some drugs is similar enough to a neurotransmitter to fit the receptor sites of the ___(33)___. Other drugs block receptor sites; drugs such as Prozac reduce the reabsorption of a ___(34)___.

Divisions of the Nervous System

The nervous system consists of two major divisions: 1) the brain and spinal cord, collectively called the ___(35)___ ___ ___, and 2) the nerves that branch off the brain and spinal cord to the rest of the body, called the ___(36)___ ___ ___. Messages that come from the body into the central nervous system are carried by ___(37)___ neurons. Messages going out from the central nervous system are carried by ___(38)___ neurons. Simple reflexes are processed in the brain and spinal cord by ___(39)___.

The peripheral nervous system consists of two divisions. The first is called the ___(40)___ nervous system; it carries messages from the central nervous system to the skeletal muscles and receives messages from the sense organs, muscles, joints, and skin. The second, the ___(41)___ nervous system, carries messages to and from the glands and visceral organs; it automatically controls many essential functions of the body, regulates emotion, and helps to control our ___(42)___. The autonomic nervous system itself contains two further divisions: 1) a division that tends to activate the internal organs, called the ___(43)___ division, and 2) a division that generally "calms" the internal organs, called the ___(44)___ division. The clusters of neural cell bodies, called ___(45)___, are organized differently for the sympathetic and parasympathetic divisions. This organization allows the parasympathetic division to operate more ___(46)___.

Structures and Functions of the Brain

One brain-image technique that records the brain's electrical activity is called the ___(47)___, or ___(48)___. A second technique uses a computer interpretation of an X-ray-like image; this technique is called ___(49)___ _____, or ___(50)___ _____. A third technique detects and interprets activity from the nuclei of atoms in living cells; this approach is called ___(51)___ _____ _____, or ___(52)___. A type of MRI that measures brain activity by measuring the oxygen use of groups of neurons is called a ___(53)___ MRI.

The lowest part of the brain, responsible for routine functions, is the ___(54)___. The hindbrain has three main structures: 1) a part responsible for controlling breathing and a variety of reflexes, called the ___(55)___; 2) a structure involved in balance, hearing, and some parasympathetic functions, called the ___(56)___; and 3) a part that is mainly responsible for maintaining muscle tone and muscular coordination, called the ___(57)___.

The small area at the top of the hindbrain that serves primarily as a reflex center for orienting the eyes and ears is the ___(58)___. The forebrain consists of two main parts. The first contains a structure that primarily routes messages to the appropriate parts of the brain called the ___(59)___ and the ___(60)___, a tiny structure involved with motives, emotions, and the functions of the autonomic nervous system.

The hypothalamus influences emotional arousal by working with a complex brain system called the ___(61)___ system. A part of the limbic system that is involved in the emotions of fear and rage is the ___(62)___. A limbic structure that is believed to tie together memories stored in different parts of the cerebral cortex is the ___(63)___. Other limbic structures that process cognitive information in emotions are the ___(64)___ area and the (65) cortex.

Cerebral Cortex: Sensory, Cognitive, and Motor Functions

The largest structure in the forebrain, called the cerebral cortex, is involved in ___(66)___ experience, language, and ___(67)___. The cortex is frequently called the "___(68)___" matter of the brain, while the cerebrum is the ___(69)___ matter.

Each hemisphere contains four lobes, and each lobe performs different cognitive functions. The ___(70)___ lobes play an important role in organizing behavior and in predicting the consequence of behavior. The left hemisphere contains ___(71)___ area, which is involved in our ability to speak language. Broca's research on stroke victims who were left ___(72)___ found that the strokes had occurred in this area of the brain. Another area of the frontal lobe, which is involved in the control of voluntary motor movement, is called the ___(73)___ area. The unfortunate case of Phineas Gage demonstrated the role of the ___(74)___ lobes in the inhibition of socially inappropriate behavior. A more recent case, that of "J.Z.," further demonstrated the role of the frontal lobes in controlling ___(75)___ aspects of our behavior. The ___(76)___ lobes contain the somatosensory area, which is involved in the sense of ___(77)___ and other body senses. The temporal lobes, extending backward from the temples, are involved with the sense of ___(78)___. In the left temporal lobe, ___(79)___ area plays an important role in understanding spoken language. Damage to this area, called Wernicke's ___(80)___, leaves victims unable to understand language spoken to them by others, although they can speak normally. The ___(81)___ lobes contain the visual area and play an essential role in processing sensory information from the eyes. Association areas are sometimes called the ___(82)_____ of the cortex.

The cerebral cortex consists of two cerebral hemispheres joined by the ___(83)_____. The corpus callosum allows ___(84)___ between the two hemispheres. The left hemisphere tends to handle ___(85)___ information and the right side tends to handle visual and ___(86)___ information.

Patients who have had the corpus callosum surgically severed are referred to as ___(87)___-_____ patients. Research with these patients has revealed the localization of language expression abilities in the ___(88)_____.

The results of a variety of studies, starting with Broca's research in 1861 and continuing through studies conducted in the 1990s, suggest that the two cerebral hemispheres process different aspects of ___(89)___. The right hemisphere plays an important role in expressing emotions and in ___(90)___ the emotions expressed by others. Research suggests that positive emotions are processed more in the ___(91)___ hemisphere and negative emotions are processed more in the ___(92)___ hemisphere.

Endocrine System: Chemical Messengers of the Body

Another system that plays a role in communication and regulation of bodily processes is the ____(93)____ system. This system consists of ____(94)____ that secrete neuropeptides and hormones into the bloodstream. The hormones are regulated by the brain, particularly by the ____(95)____. Some hormones are chemically identical to some of the ____(96)____. Hormones aid the ability of the ____(97)____ to control the body. The following glands are the most important from a psychological standpoint:

1. Located near the bottom of the brain and largely controlled by the hypothalamus is the ____(98)____ gland. This gland secretes hormones that help regulate the other glands and is frequently referred to as the ____(99)____. _____. The pituitary regulates the body's reactions to ____(100)____ and resistance to ____(101)____.

2. The glands that sit atop the kidneys and play an important role in emotional arousal are the ____(102)____ glands. These glands secrete two hormones that help the body prepare for stress, ____(103)____ and ____(104)____.

3. The glands that are embedded in the pancreas and regulate the blood sugar level are the ____(105)____ _____. These glands secrete ____(106)____ and ____(107)____.

4. The glands responsible for sex cell production are the ____(108)____. In females, the glands are the ____(109)____, whereas in males they are the ____(110)____. The most important sex hormones are ____(112)____ in females and ____(112)____ in males.

5. The gland that helps regulate metabolism is the ____(113)____ gland. This gland secretes the hormone ____(114)____, which is necessary for mental development in children and for control of weight and level of activity in adults. A deficiency of thyroxin can cause a type of mental retardation called ____(115)____.

6. Embedded in the thyroid are four glands called the ____(116)____ glands. These secrete a hormone called ____(117)____, which is important in the functioning of the nervous system.

7. Attached to the top of thalamus is the ____(118)____ gland which secretes ____(119)____.

Genetic Influences on Behavior: Biological Blueprints?

The problem of distinguishing the influence of heredity from that of the environment is referred to as separating ____(120)____ from ____(121)____. In a seabird called the tern, knowing how to build a nest is part of the bird's ____(122)____ inheritance. Among human beings, inheritance seems to ____(123)____ much of our behavior, although we do not inherit specific patterns of behavior.

Inherited characteristics are passed on through genetic material called ____(124)____, which are found in the nuclei of all human cells. Genes provide their instructions through a complex substance called ____(125)____, which stands for ____(126)____ _____. Genes are arrayed in the cells on strips called ____(127)____. All human cells except sex cells have ___(128)___ chromosomes, arranged in 23 pairs, and each chromosome carries ___(129)___ of genes. Sex cells are called ___(130)___ and contain ___(131)___ unpaired chromosomes. A sperm unites with an ovum through the process of ___(132)___; in this process, a new cell, called a ___(133)___, is formed. Zygotes contain 23 ___(134)___ of chromosomes, with the mother and father each contributing half. On the average, brothers and sisters will have about ___(135)___ percent of their genes in common; the exception is ___(136)___ twins, who are formed from a single zygote and share all their genes.

When the gene contributed by one parent conflicts with the gene contributed by the other parent for the same characteristic, the ___(137)___ gene will normally reveal its trait. Some traits are revealed only when the same gene has been contributed by both parents; these are ___(138)___ genes.

The presence of an additional 21st chromosome can result in ___(139)___ syndrome.

Although researchers have studied genetic influences on animals, selective breeding experiments is not conducted with humans for ___(140)___ reasons. Instead, researchers have used two descriptive research methods. The first method involves comparing the characteristics of identical or ___(141)___ twins with dizygotic twins, formed from the fertilization of two ova by two sperm cells. The second method compares the characteristics of ___(142)___ children with those of both their biological parents and their adoptive parents. Research strongly suggests that much of our behavior, both normal and abnormal, is influenced by ___(143)___ factors. The research also implies that ___(144)___ factors play powerful roles in shaping our personalities.

Applications of Psychology: Madness and the Brain

The central feature of schizophrenia is a marked abnormality of ___(145)___ _____. Brain-imaging techniques reveal a shrunken cerebral cortex and enlarged ___(146)___ in persons with schizophrenia. Recent findings indicate that the ___(147)___ may not function normally in individuals with schizophrenia. Evidence also exists that ___(148)___ can cause persons who are genetically predisposed to have episodes of schizophrenia. According to Mednick's "double strike" theory, schizophrenia is most likely to occur in those who 1) have a ___(149)___ _____ and 2) who suffered some health complication during ___(150)___ or ___(151)___.

Concept Check

Fill in the missing components of the following concept boxes. The correct answers are located in the "Answers" section at the end of the chapter.

Structure of a Neuron/Neural Transmission

Structure	Function
cell body	
	receives neural messages from other neurons
axons	
polarized state	
	process during which positively charged ions flow into the neuron
action potential	
	a protective fatty coating that covers and protects many axons

Structures and Functions of the Brain

Structure	Function
hindbrain	
hypothalamus	
	This is a neural system composed of the amygdala, hippocampus, septal area, and cingulate cortex. It is also involved in emotional behavior (both arousal and cognitive aspects).
cerebral cortex	
lobes of the cerebral cortex	
	This is a neural system involved in helping to arouse the cerebral cortex.

Endocrine Glands and Functions

Name of gland	Function
pituitary gland	
	involved in physical and emotional arousal
	help to regulate the level of sugar in the blood
gonads	
	helps to regulate metabolism
parathyroid glands	
	largely responsible for regulating biological rhythms such as sleep and wakefulness and menstrual cycles in females

Extending the Chapter: Psychology, Societal Issues, and Human Diversity

These questions may be assigned to you. Whether or not they are assigned, they are designed to be challenging questions to encourage you to think independently about the material in the chapter. Many of the questions have no right or wrong answers.

I. From the *Applications of Psychology* section

1. Discuss the results of brain imaging research on persons with schizophrenia.

2. Summarize the research on the causes of schizophrenia.

II. Psychology, Societal Issues, and Human Diversity

1. As researchers unlock the genetic factors that influence behavior, how might this affect the way society views individual responsibility for behavior?

2. Research topic: Researchers are beginning to appreciate how a child's early environment can influence the physical development of the brain.

Practice Quiz

The practice quiz consists of three sections: 1) Short answer questions, 2) Multiple choice questions, and 3) True-False questions. At the end of the chapter you will find suggested answers to the short answer questions, answers and explanation for the multiple choice questions, and answers to the true-false questions.

Short Answer questions

1. Explain the relationship between inheritance, genes, DNA, and chromosomes.

_____

_____

_____

2. Distinguish between dominant and recessive traits.

_____

_____

_____

3. Describe the research methods used to help sort out the influences of nature and nurture in humans.

_____

_____

_____

Multiple Choice Questions

1. The part of the neuron that receives messages from other neurons is called the
   a. dendrite.
   b. axon.
   c. cell body.
   d. synapse.
   LO 1

2. The part of the axon responsible for transmitting messages to the next neuron is the
   a. dendrite.
   b. myelin sheath.
   c. cell body.
   d. axon.
   LO 1

3. When positively charged ions enter the neuron, the process is called
   a. polarization.
   b. depolarization.
   c. semipermeability.
   d. synaptical transmission.
   LO 2

4. A "flowing storm of ions" characterizes
   a. synaptic transmission.
   b. neural transmission.
   c. neurotransmitters.
   d. none of the above.
   LO 2

5. Which of the following chemical substances makes it difficult for messages to be transmitted across synapses?
   a. excitatory neurotransmitters
   b. inhibitory neurotransmitters
   c. regulatory neurotransmitters
   d. all of the above
   LO 2

6. Which of the following transmit messages from the body into the nervous system?
   a. afferent neurons
   b. efferent neurons
   c. association neurons
   d. transmittal neurons
   LO 3

7. The central nervous system is the primary location of
   a. efferent neurons.
   b. afferent neurons.
   c. interneurons.
   d. nerves.
   LO 3

8. Which division of the nervous system is composed of all the nerves that branch from the brain and spinal cord?
   a. peripheral nervous system
   b. afferent nervous system
   c. central nervous system
   d. somatic nervous system
   LO 3

9. All of the following are functions of the autonomic nervous system *except*
   a. breathing.
   b. voluntary movements.
   c. sweating.
   d. sexual arousal.
   LO 4

10. Activation of the internal organs is carried out by the
    a. sympathetic nervous system.
    b. parasympathetic nervous system.
    c. somatic nervous system.
    d. all of the above.
    LO 4

11. For what purpose are PET scans and MRI used?
    a. observing the process of depolarization
    b. observing images of the brain
    c. measuring the responsiveness of the autonomic nervous system
    d. measuring the sensitivity of the skin's pain receptors
    LO 5

12. The hindbrain structure responsible for maintaining muscle tone and coordination of muscle movements is the
    a. medulla.
    b. pons.
    c. cerebellum.
    d. thalamus.
    LO 6

13. The hypothalamus is located within the
    a. midbrain.
    b. thalamus.
    c. medulla.
    d. forebrain.
    LO 6

14. A small area at the top of the hindbrain that helps regulate sensory reflexes is called the
    a. medulla.
    b. pons.
    c. forebrain.
    d. midbrain.
    LO 7

15. If a person's cerebellum was damaged in an accident, you would expect the person to have a problem with
    a. breathing and heart rate.
    b. seeing and hearing.
    c. talking and understanding.
    d. balance and muscle coordination.
    LO 7

16. The hypothalamus plays a role in each of the following *except*
    a. motives and emotions.
    b. regulating body temperature.
    c. aggression.
    d. routing incoming stimuli.
    LO 8

17. According to the text, the most dramatic function of the limbic system is carried out by the
    a. hippocampus.
    b. cingulate cortex.
    c. amygdala.
    d. septal area.
    LO 8

18. People who experience Wernicke's aphasia have had damage to the
    a. frontal lobe.
    b. somatosensory area.
    c. temporal lobe.
    d. occipital lobe.
    LO 9

19. The processing of sensory information from the eyes is carried out in which lobe of the cerebral cortex?
   a. frontal
   b. parietal
   c. temporal
   d. occipital
   LO 9

20. The structure that allows communication between the two cerebral hemispheres is called the
   a. corpus callosum.
   b. cingulate cortex.
   c. reticular formation.
   d. association area.
   LO 10

21. Research with split-brain patients has revealed the localization of what types of abilities in the left hemisphere?
   a. emotional expression
   b. recognition of stimuli
   c. abstract thinking
   d. language expression
   LO 10

22. Research suggests that positive emotions are more likely to be processed in the
   a. corpus callosum.
   b. left hemisphere.
   c. right hemisphere.
   d. amygdala.
   LO 11

23. The gland that is often considered to be the master gland is the
   a. adrenal.
   b. pituitary.
   c. gonads.
   d. thyroid.
   LO 12

24. How are hormones different from neurotransmitters?
   a. hormones are chemical messengers
   b. hormones are carried in the bloodstream
   c. hormones are not regulated by the brain
   d. hormones are by-products of neurotransmitters
   LO 12

25. The gland(s) that produce(s) male and female sex hormones is (are) the
   a. pituitary gland.
   b. thyroid gland.
   c. adrenal glands.
   d. gonads.
   LO 13

26. Which of the following is *not* correct?
   a. Chromosomes contain genes, which are made of DNA.
   b. A normal human cell contains 46 chromosomes.
   c. A normal gamete contains 23 chromosomes.
   d. DNA is made of genes, which contain chromosomes.
   LO 14

27. How is it possible for two brown-eyed parents to have a blue-eyed child?
   a. if both parents contribute a recessive gene
   b. if both parents contribute a dominant gene
   c. if one parent contributes a recessive gene and one parent contributes a dominant gene
   d. It's impossible for two brown-eyed parents to have a blue-eyed child unless they adopt.
   LO 14

28. Down syndrome
   a. is caused by the presence of an additional 21st chromosome.
   b. can cause mental retardation.
   c. causes obvious physical irregularities.
   d. all of the above.
   LO 14

29. Which of the following characterizes dizygotic twins?
   a. They are formed when two different eggs are fertilized by different sperm cells.
   b. They are formed by a single fertilized egg
   c. They are identical in appearance.
   d. They are identical in genetic structure.
   LO 15

30. To determine the influence of inheritance on behavior, psychologists have used what type of research?
   a. adoption studies
   b. twin studies
   c. formal experiments
   d. *a* and *b* above
   LO 15

31. Which of the following is characteristic of monozygotic twins?
    a. They are referred to as identical twins.
    b. They are formed from a single ovum.
    c. They are virtually identical in genetic structure.
    d. All of the above.
    LO 16

32. Research on the role of inheritance in personality and abnormal behavior suggests that
    a. personality is inherited.
    b. abnormal behavior is inherited.
    c. personality and abnormal behavior may be influenced in part by inheritance.
    d. none of the above.
    LO 16

33. Each of the following has been demonstrated in the brains of schizophrenics *except*
    a. greatly enlarged ventricles.
    b. a smaller hippocampus.
    c. a larger cerebral cortex.
    d. low levels of frontal lobe activity.
    LO 17

34. According to Mednick, schizophrenia is likely in persons who
    a. have a genetic predisposition.
    b. suffer a health complication during pregnancy or birth.
    c. live with a schizophrenic parent.
    d. a and b above.
    LO 17

True-False Questions

_____1. In the neuron, the axon transmits messages to other neurons.

_____2. Messages are carried across the synapse by neurotransmitters.

_____3. The sympathetic nervous system generally "calms" internal organs.

_____4. The midbrain contains three essential structures: the medulla, the pons and the cerebellum.

_____5. The occipital lobes process sensory information from the eyes.

_____6. Generally, the left hemisphere plays a greater role in the expression of emotions.

_____7. Some hormones are chemically identical to neurotransmitters.

_____8. The thyroid gland is referred to as the "master" gland.

_____9. Monozygotic twins are referred to as identical twins.

_____10. The IQs of adopted children are more similar to their adoptive parents than to their biological parents.

ANSWER SECTION

Concept Check

Structure of a Neuron/Neural Transmission

Structure	Function
cell body	contains the nucleus
dendrite	receives neural messages from other neurons
axons	transmits messages to other neurons
polarized state	the resting state of a neuron, in which ions are generally inside the cell membrane and positive ions are generally outside
depolarization	process during which positively charged ions flow into the neuron
action potential	triggered by depolarization, a neural message travels the length of the axon
myelin sheath	a protective fatty coating that covers and protects many axons

Structures and Functions of the Brain

Structure	Function
hindbrain	Its main responsibility is in general "housekeeping functions; the medulla controls breathing and other reflexes; the pons helps control balance and hearing; the cerebellum helps maintain muscle tone and coordinates muscular movements.
hypothalamus	This is the part of the forebrain involved in motivation and emotion, such as eating, drinking, sexuality, pleasure, anger, and fear. It also helps regulate body temperature, endocrine activity, immune system functioning, aggression and even pleasure.
limbic system	This is a neural system composed of the amygdala, hippocampus, septal area, and cingulate cortex. It is also involved in emotional behavior (both arousal and cognitive aspects).
cerebral cortex	The largest forebrain structure and is involved in conscious experience, voluntary action, language, and intelligence.
lobes of the cerebral cortex	The frontal lobes help us to organize and predict the consequences of our behavior. It is also involved in our ability to speak language. The parietal lobes contain the somatosensory and motor areas; the temporal lobes are involved in hearing and understanding language; the occipital lobes are involved in vision.
reticular formation	This is a neural system involved in helping to arouse the cerebral cortex.

Endocrine glands and functions

Name of gland	Function
pituitary gland	the body's "master gland;" regulates the activity of the other endocrine glands
adrenal glands	involved in physical and emotional arousal
islets of Langerhans	help to regulate the level of sugar in the blood
gonads	produce sex cells and hormones important in sexual arousal
thyroid gland	helps to regulate metabolism
parathyroid glands	important in functioning of the nervous system
pineal gland	largely responsible for regulating biological rhythms such as sleep and wakefulness and menstrual cycles in females

Answers to Review At A Glance

1. brain
2. spinal
3. cord
4. neuron
5. cell body
6. nucleus
7. dendrites
8. axons
9. 100 billion
10. 1,000
11. 10,000
12. nerve
13. electrical
14. ions
15. negative
16. positive
17. semipermeable
18. polarized
19. depolarization
20. all-or-none
21. action potential
22. axon
23. Novocain
24. myelin sheath
25. neural
26. adulthood
27. multiple sclerosis
28. synapse
29. neurotransmitters
30. knob
31. dendrite
32. action potential
33. dendrite
34. neurotransmitter
35. central nervous system
36. peripheral nervous system
37. afferent
38. efferent
39. interneurons
40. somatic
41. autonomic
42. motivations
43. sympathetic
44. parasympathetic
45. ganglia
46. selectively
47. electroencephalogram
48. EEG
49. positron emission tomography
50. PET scan
51. magnetic resonance imaging
52. MRI
53. functional
54. hindbrain
55. medulla
56. pons
57. cerebellum
58. midbrain
59. thalamus
60. hypothalamus
61. limbic
62. amygdala
63. hippocampus
64. septal
65. cingulate
66. conscious
67. intelligence
68. gray
69. white
70. frontal
71. Broca's
72. aphasic
73. motor
74. frontal
75. complex
76. parietal
77. touch
78. hearing
79. Wernicke's
80. aphasia
81. occipital
82. silent areas
83. corpus callosum

84. communication	107. insulin	130. gametes
85. verbal	108. gonads	131. 23
86. spatial	109. ovaries	132. fertilization
87. split-brain	110. testes	133. zygote
88. left hemisphere	111. estrogen	134. pairs
89. emotion	112. testosterone	135. 50
90. understanding	113. thyroid	136. identical (monozygotic)
91. left	114. thyroxin	137. dominant
92. right	115. cretinism	138. recessive
93. endocrine	116. parathyroid	139. Down
94. glands	117. parathormone	140. ethical
95. hypothalamus	118. pineal	141. monozygotic
96. neurotransmitters	119. melatonin	142. adopted
97. nervous system	120. nature	143. genetic
98. pituitary	121. nurture	144. environmental
99. master gland	122. genetic	145. thought processes
100. stress	123. influence	146. ventricles
101. disease	124. genes	147. thalamus
102. adrenal	125. DNA	148. stress
103. epinephrine	126. deoxyribonucleic acid	149. genetic predisposition
104. norepinephrine	127. chromosomes	150. pregnancy
105. islets of Langerhans	128. 46	151. birth
106. glucagon	129. thousands	

Sample Answers for Short Answer Questions

1. **Explain the relationship between inheritance, genes, DNA, and chromosomes.**

    Genes are hereditary units made up of DNA (deoxyribonucleic acid). Genes are found in the nuclei of human cells. They arranged on strips called chromosomes.

2. **Distinguish between dominant and recessive traits.**

    A dominant gene will reveal its trait whenever the gene is present, whereas a recessive gene will reveal its trait only when the same recessive gene has been inherited from both parents.

3. **Describe the research methods used to help sort out the influences of nature and nurture in humans.**

    Researchers have relied on two descriptive methods. One method involves comparing traits of monozygotic (identical) twins with those of dizygotic (fraternal) twins. A second technique compares the traits of adopted children with the traits of both their biological and adoptive parents.

Multiple Choice Answers

1. The answer is *a*. While dendrites receive messages, axons help transmit messages to other neurons. The cell body of the neuron contains the nucleus, while the synapse is the area between neurons.
2. The answer is *d*. Remember that the axon "acts on" the next cell.
3. The answer is *b*. The polarized state is the resting state of the neuron, when negative ions are mostly inside and positive ions are mostly outside the cell membrane. Semipermeability refers to the fact that some, but not all, ions can pass through the membrane. When electrical charges reach the synapse, transmission across the gap occurs.
4. The answer is *b*. The process of depolarization along the membrane of a neuron allows for the massive influx of sodium ions.
5. The answer is *b*. Excitatory neurotransmitters increase the likelihood of messages crossing the synapse, and the term regulatory neurotransmitters was made up especially for this question.
6. The answer is *a*. Efferent neurons transmit messages from the central nervous system to the organs and muscles of the body, while association neurons are the neurons in the brain and spinal cord that process the information. Transmittal neurons do not, as far as I know, exist.
7. The answer is *c*. Afferent neurons carry messages from the sense organs to the central nervous system, whereas efferent neurons carry messages from the central nervous system to the organs and muscles of the body. Neurons that are neither afferent nor efferent are interneurons.
8. The answer is *a*. The central nervous system consists of the brain and the fibers of the spinal cord. All other nerves are part of the peripheral nervous system.
9. The answer is *b*. Voluntary movements are higher-order functions and are not processed by the autonomic nervous system.
10. The answer is *a*. The sympathetic nervous system generally activates, while the parasympathetic system is generally involved in calming the organs.
11. The answer is *b*. *PET* stands for positron emission topography and *MRI* stands for magnetic resonance imaging.
12. The answer is *c*. The medulla controls breathing and a variety of reflexes. The pons helps regulate balance, hearing, and some parasympathetic functions. The thalamus helps to route messages to the appropriate parts of the brain.
13. The answer is *d*. Other parts of the forebrain include the thalamus, the limbic system, and the lobes of the cerebral cortex.
14. The answer is *d*. The medulla and pons are both part of the hindbrain. The forebrain is the structure that contains the cerebral cortex.
15. The answer is *d*. The cerebellum consists of two rounded structures located in the hindbrain behind the pons. The cerebellum also plays a role in learning and memory that involve coordinated sequences of information.
16. The answer is *d*. The routing function is carried out by the thalamus.
17. The answer is *c*. Damage to the amygdala may result in a complete absence of fear or rage, although occasionally the result is uncontrollable rage.
18. The answer is *c*. Wernicke's aphasia is characterized by an inability to understand language spoken by others, although the person can speak normally. Wernicke's area is located in the left hemisphere.
19. The answer is *d*. Damage to the visual area of the occipital lobe can result in partial or even total blindness.
20. The answer is *a*. Severing the corpus callosum results in some unusual problems, discussed in the section on "split brains."
21. The answer is *d*. When information is presented to the left visual field of each eye, the information reaches the right hemisphere, which has no area controlling verbal expression. As a result, the patient is unable to identify the information.
22. The answer is *b*. Conversely, the right hemisphere is more likely to process negative emotions.
23. The answer is *b*. The hormones of the pituitary help to regulate the activities of the other glands in the endocrine system.
24. The answer is *b*. Neurotransmitters are the chemicals found in the brain.
25. The answer is *d*. The adrenals are involved in emotional arousal. The thyroid gland helps to regulate metabolism. The pituitary gland is often called the "master gland" because it helps to regulate the other glands in the endocrine system.

26. The answer is *d*. Strands of DNA contain the genetic code to make us who and what we are.
27. The answer is *a*. If both brown-eyed parents possess a recessive gene for blue eyes, and if both contribute this gene to their offspring, their child will have blue eyes.
28. The answer is *d*. Down syndrome is one of a variety of chromosomal abnormalities that results in mental retardation.
29. The answer is *a*. Dizygotic twins are no more alike genetically than siblings born at different times; monozygotic twins, however, develop from a single fertilized egg cell and are also called identical twins.
30. The answer is *d*. Both twin studies and adoption studies have allowed psychologists to begin to understand the influence of heredity on behavior. These studies are correlational in nature, however, and not based on formal experiments as described in chapter 1.
31. The answer is *d*. Dizygotic twins, by contrast, are formed from two separate ova and two sperm. Genetically, they are no more alike than siblings born at different times.
32. The answer is *c*. While research has shown that genetic factors are clearly at work, they do not explain all of the differences between people.
33. The answer is *c*. MRI images have revealed many of the dramatic differences between a normal brain and the brains of people diagnosed with schizophrenia.
34. The answer is *d*. This hypothesis is referred to as the "double-strike" theory of schizophrenia.

Answers to True-False Questions

1. T	6. F
2. T	7. T
3. F	8. F
4. F	9. T
5. T	10. F

Chapter 3 Sensation and Perception

Learning Objectives

1. Distinguish between sensation and perception and define sense organ, sensory receptor, and stimulus. (p. 74)

2. Define transduction. (p. 74)

3. Compare and contrast the absolute threshold and the difference threshold. (p. 75)

4. Explain the process of sensory adaptation. (p. 75)

5. Define psychophysics and understand Weber's law. (p. 76)

6. Understand the nature of light. (p. 78)

7. Describe how the different parts of the eye work together to produce vision. (p. 79)

8. Describe the roles played by the rods and cones in both dark adaptation and light adaptation. (p. 79)

9. Compare and contrast the trichromatic theory and the opponent-process theory of color vision, describing the evidence for each. (p. 82)

10. Understand the nature of sound. (p. 86)

11. Explain how different parts of the ear work together to produce audition (hearing). (p. 87)

12. Describe the roles played by the vestibular organ and the kinesthetic receptors in providing information about orientation and movement. (p. 91)

13. List the four different general types of skin receptors and describe the three types of stimuli that can be detected by the skin. (p. 92)

14. Explain the gate control theory of pain and describe the role played by endorphins in "runners high," acupuncture, and placebos. (p. 94)

15. Define phantom limb pain and identify its possible causes. (p. 96)

16. List the basic taste sensations and identify other factors that influence our perception of taste. (p. 99)

17. List the seven primary qualities of odors and explain the role of pheromones in regulating behavior. (p. 100)

18. Name and describe the five Gestalt principles of perceptual organization. (p. 102)

19. Describe the four kinds of perceptual constancy. (p. 103)

20. Identify the monocular cues and binocular cues of depth perception. (p. 104)

21. Distinguish between the visual illusions and describe how they are produced. (p. 106)

22. Identify how individual and cultural factors influence perception. (p. 107)

23. (From the *Application of Psychology* section) Discuss the relationship between visual perception, illusions, and art. (p. 109)

Chapter Overview

Sensation refers to the ability of the sense organs to receive messages from the outside world, while perception refers to the ability to organize and interpret these messages.

We receive external stimuli through specialized sensory receptor cells. First, sense organs receive stimuli. Next, they transduce this sensory energy into neural impulses. The neural impulses are then sent to the brain to be interpreted. The field that studies the relationships between physical stimuli and psychological sensations is called psychophysics.

The sense of sight functions by detecting light energy. The intensity of a light wave determines its brightness, while the wavelength largely determines color. The eye, which works much like a camera, is the primary sense organ for seeing. Light enters the eye through the cornea and lens and then enters the retina. Rods and cones transduce light waves into neural impulses for transportation to the brain. The 100 million rods are located throughout the retina but are not found in the fovea. Although they are active in peripheral vision and vision in dim light, they do not play a role in color vision. The 6 million cones, clustered mainly near the fovea, are involved in color vision. Two theories that explain color vision are trichromatic theory and opponent-process theory.

The sense of hearing functions by detecting sound waves. The frequency of sound waves determines pitch, while their intensity determines loudness. The outer ear collects sound waves, which vibrate the eardrum. The eardrum is connected to a series of movable bones in the middle ear. The inner ear, which contains the cochlea and the organ of Corti, transduces the sound waves' energy into neural impulses. These impulses are transported to the brain.

The sensory system also receives information about internal stimuli. For example, the vestibular organ provides information about body orientation, and the kinesthetic sense reports bodily position and movement. The various skin senses can detect pressure, temperature, and pain.

Humans also possess chemical senses, such as taste and smell. These senses respond to chemicals in the environment rather than to energy.

The interpretation of sensory neural impulses that have been transmitted to the brain is called perception. Perception is an active mental process. Gestalt principles explain many of the ways in which humans tend to organize sensory information. Individual factors, such as motivation and prior learning, also affect perception.

Key Terms Exercise

For each of the following exercises, match the key terms on the left with the correct definitions on the right. Page references to the text follow the terms so that you may refer to the text for any items you answer incorrectly or do not understand completely. You may check your responses immediately by referring to the answers that follow each exercise.

Sensation (I)

_____ 1. sense organs (p. 74)
_____ 2. sensory receptor cells (p. 74)
_____ 3. sensation (p. 74)
_____ 4. perception (p. 74)
_____ 5. stimulus (p. 74)

a. cells that translate messages into neural impulses
b. organs that receive stimuli
c. the process of organizing and interpreting information
d. any aspect of the outside world that influences our behavior.
e. the process of receiving, translating, and transmitting messages from the outside world to the brain

ANSWERS
1. b   4. c
2. a   5. d
3. e

Sensation (II)

_____ 1. transduction (p. 74)
_____ 2. absolute threshold (p. 75)
_____ 3. difference threshold (p. 75)
_____ 4. sensory adaptation (p. 75)
_____ 5. psychophysics (p. 76)
_____ 6. Weber's law (p. 76)

a. a weakened sensation resulting from prolonged presentation of the stimulus
b. the smallest magnitude of a stimulus that can be detected half of the time
c. a specialty field that studies sensory limits, sensory adaption, etc.
d. the translation of energy from one form into another
e. the amount of change in a stimulus needed to detect a difference is in direct proportion to the intensity of the stimulus
f. the smallest difference between two stimuli that can be detected half of the time

ANSWERS
1. d   4. a
2. b   5. c
3. f   6. e

Vision (I)

_____ 1. retina (p. 79)
_____ 2. rods (p. 79)
_____ 3. cones (p. 79)
_____ 4. fovea (p. 79)

a. the central spot of the retina
b. cells located in the center of the retina that code information about light, dark, and color
c. the area that contains the rods and cones
d. cells located outside the center of the retina that code information about light and dark

ANSWERS
1. c   3. b
2. d   4. a

Vision (II)

_____ 1. optic nerve (p. 80)
_____ 2. blind spot (p. 80)
_____ 3. dark and light adaptation (p. 80)
_____ 4. trichromatic theory (p. 82)
_____ 5. opponent-process theory (p. 82)

a. a theory of color vision that suggests the eye has two kinds of cones
b. changed sensitivity of the eye in response to a change in overall illumination
c. the nerve that carries messages about vision to the brain
d. a theory of color vision that suggests that the eye has three kinds of cones
e. the area where the optic nerve attaches to the retina

ANSWERS
1. c   4. d
2. e   5. a
3. b

Hearing

_____ 1. audition (p. 86)
_____ 2. eardrum (p. 87)
_____ 3. hammer, anvil, and stirrup (p. 87)
_____ 4. cochlea (p. 87)
_____ 5. basilar membrane (p. 88)
_____ 6. organ of Corti (p. 88)

a. the sense of hearing
b. a membrane in the middle ear
c. a structure of the inner ear that is filled with fluid
d. contains receptor cells that transduce sound waves into neural impulses
e. tiny bones of the middle ear
f. the organ of Corti rests upon this

ANSWERS

1. a	4. c
2. b	5. f
3. e	6. d

Body Senses, Chemical Senses, and Perception

_____ 1. vestibular organ (p. 91)
_____ 2. kinesthetic receptors (p. 91)
_____ 3. semicircular canals (p. 91)
_____ 4. gustation (p. 99)
_____ 5. olfaction (p. 99)
_____ 6. stereochemical theory (p. 100)
_____ 7. perceptual constancy (p. 103)
_____ 8. monocular and binocular cues (p. 104)

a. the theory that odor receptors are stimulated by specific molecules
b. the sense of taste
c. receptors that provide information about movement, posture, and orientation
d. structures in the inner ear that provide the brain with information about balance and movement
e. three tubes in the vestibular organ that inform the brain about tilts of the head and body
f. the sense of smell
g. visual cues that permit us to perceive distance
h. the tendency to perceive objects as being relatively unchanging

ANSWERS

1. d	5. f
2. c	6. a
3. e	7. h
4. b	8. g

Review At A Glance

(Answers to this section may be found on page 61)

Sensation: Receiving Messages about the World

Humans receive messages through their sense organs. Sense organs operate through ___(1)___ _____ _____.

These cells allow us to receive, translate, and transmit messages to the brain, a process called ___(2)___. We interpret

this information through a process called ___(3)___. Any aspect of the outside world that directly influences our behavior

is a ___(4)___. Stimuli are translated from one form of energy to another through a process called

___(5)___. Sensory receptor cells transduce sensory energy into ___(6)___ _____.

Not all sensory messages can be detected. The smallest magnitude of a stimulus that can be detected half the time is the

___(7)___ _____; the smallest difference between two stimuli that can be detected half the time is called the

___(8)___ _____. Stimuli that are presented for prolonged periods may cause weaker sensations due to ___(9)___ _____. The field that studies sensory limits and sensory adaptation is ___(10)___. The law stating that the amount of change in a stimulus needed to detect a difference is proportional to the intensity of the original stimulus is called ___(11)___ _____.

Vision: Your Human Camera

Visible light is part of a form of energy called ___(12)___ _____, which includes electricity and radio waves. Light is composed of waves that have both ___(13)___ and ___(14)___. The intensity of the light determines the ___(15)___, while the ___(16)___ determines the color we see.

Light first passes through a clear protective coating called the ___(17)___. The colored part of the eye, the ___(18)___, regulates the light passing through the pupil into the ___(19)___. The lens is held in place by ligaments that are attached to the ___(20)___ _____. This muscle regulates the image that falls on the light-sensitive ___(21)___. Two types of receptor cells in the retina are the ___(22)___ and ___(23)___. Each eye has about ___(24)___ _____ cones and about ___(25)___ _____ rods. The greatest concentration of cones is in the ___(26)___. In good light, ___(27)___ _____ is best for images focused directly on the fovea. The rods are located throughout the retina except in the center. There are four differences between rods and cones: 1) rods are largely responsible for ___(28)___ vision; 2) rods are much more sensitive to ___(29)___ than the cones; 3) rods produce images that are perceived with less ___(30)___ _____; and 4) only cones code information about ___(31)___. An area near the center of the retina contains no rods or cones and is called the ___(32)___ _____. Information in the optic nerve crosses over at the ___(33)___ _____.

The processes by which the eyes change their sensitivity to darkness or light are referred to as dark and light ___(34)___. Color is the conscious experience that results as the eye and nervous system process ___(35)___ energy. The theory that there are three kinds of cones in the retina, responding to either the red, green, or blue range of wavelength, is referred to as ___(36)___ theory. Trichromatic theory cannot explain three phenomena: ___(37)___ colors, color ___(38)___ and partial color ___(39)___.

The opponent-process theory states that the three kinds of cones stimulate two kinds of ___(40)___-mechanisms. One is the ___(41)___-_____ processing mechanism, while the other is the ___(42)___-processing mechanism. The trichromatic theory accurately describes events at the ___(43)___, while the opponent-process theory best describes the activities of ___(44)___ in the rest of the visual system.

Hearing: Sensing Sound Waves

The sense of hearing is called ___(45)___. Audition occurs when there are vibratory changes in the air known as ___(46)___. The rate of vibration of sound waves is termed the ___(47)___ of cycles; its unit of measurement is called ___(48)___. Our experience of these sound vibrations is called ___(49)___. The loudness of a sound is determined by its ___(50)___. Intensity is measured in units called ___(51)___. The complexity of a sound wave determines the ___(52)___ of a sound.

The external part of the ear, which helps to collect and localize sound, is the ___(53)___. The pinna is connected to the middle ear by the ___(54)___ auditory canal. The first structure of the middle ear is the ___(55)___. Sound waves vibrate the eardrum; this sets into movement the three bones of the middle ear, called the ___(56)___, ___(57)___, and ___(58)___. In the inner ear, a membrane called the ___(59)___ is set into motion. The vibration of the oval window creates waves in the fluid-filled ___(60)___. The pressure of these waves is relieved by the ___(61)___. The ear's sensory receptors, located in the organ of ___(62)___, are stimulated by a membrane in the cochlea called the ___(63)___. The organ of Corti then codes the messages to the brain, based on the ___(64)___ and the ___(65)___ of the sound waves. Not all sounds are transmitted from the outer ear to the cochlea; for example, we hear ourselves speak largely through bone ___(66)___ hearing. The existence of two ears helps us to ___(67)___ the origin of sounds.

Body Senses: Messages from Myself

Messages about the orientation and movement of the body come from two kinds of sense organs. The first, located in the inner ear, is the ___(68)___. This organ is composed of 1) fluid-filled sacs called the ___(69)___ and ___(70)___, which tell the brain about the body's orientation, and (2) three nearly circular tubes that inform the brain about tilts of the head and body, called the ___(71)___. The sensory receptors of each canal are located in the ___(72)___.

The ___(73)___ sense consists of individual receptors located in the skin, muscles, joints, and tendons. The skin can detect ___(74)___, ___(75)___, and ___(76)___. It contains four types of receptors: ___(77)___ nerve endings, ___(78)___ cells, tactile ___(79)___, and specialized ___(80)___ bulbs. Apparently, all four types play a role in detecting ___(81)___, while the free nerve endings are also the primary receptors for temperature and ___(82)___.

The sensitivity of the skin differs from one region to the next. The most sensitive regions are the ___(83)___, the ___(84)___, and the ___(85)___. One set of spots on the skin detects ___(86)___ and one set detects ___(87)___, but the sensation of intense ___(88)___ is created by both warm and cold spots.

Free nerve endings throughout the body serve as ___(89)___. These are receptors for stimuli that are experienced as ___(90)___ in the brain. We often experience "first and second pain" due to the existence of ___(91)___ and ___(92)___ neural pathways. No direct relationship exists between the pain stimulus and the amount of pain a person experiences. Sometimes circumstances can block pain. One theory that explains these phenomena is called the ___(93)___ theory of pain. This theory proposes that messages from ___(94)___ are allowed in or blocked from the brain by neural "gates." Pain gates allow more slow-pain neural transmission to the ___(95)___ system in three ways. First, pain messages ___(96)___ the pain gates and make them transmit slow pain messages more readily due to the action of substance P. Second, messages from the midbrain make it more likely that slow pain impulses will be carried to the ___(97)___ system. Third, when pain is prolonged, slow pain messages are carried by ___(98)___ that normally don't carry pain messages.

The pain gates appear to be operated by specialized neurons called ___(99)___ neurons. These neurons inhibit the pain neurons by using substances called ___(100)___. Women have a second pain-gate mechanism, based on the hormone ___(101)___. The opiate morphine duplicates the effects of ___(102)___. Additionally, "runner's high" appears to be the result of the release of high levels of ___(103)___. Research also suggests that the pain-reducing effects of (104) and placebo medications may be due to stimulating the body's endorphins. Research conducted on phantom limb pain has revealed that when sensory and pain neurons are cut, the corresponding ___(105)___ cortex becomes sensitive to input that activates nearby portions of the somatosensory cortex.

Chemical Senses: The Flavors and Aromas of Life

The sense of taste, called ___(106)___, and the sense of smell, called ___(107)___, respond to chemicals rather than to energy. There are approximately ___(108)___ taste buds on the tongue, each containing approximately a dozen sensory receptors called ___(109)___. The taste buds are clustered together in bumps called ___(110)___. All of our sensations of taste result from the following basic sensations: ___(111)___, sourness, ___(112)___, bitterness, and (113). We lose taste buds as we ___(114)___.

Olfactory receptor cells are located in the nasal cavity in a mucous-coated sheet called the ___(115)___. One system of classifying odors suggests that all of the complex odors and aromas of life are combinations of ___(116)__ _primary qualities. Professionals who create perfumes and other aromas, however, distinguish ___(117)___ different types of odors. Nearly all of the odors that humans can detect are ___(118)___ compounds. The theory that odor receptors can only be stimulated by molecules of a specific size and shape is called the ___(119)___ theory.

In many animals, the vomeronasal organ, located behind the olfactory epithelium, contains receptors for ___(120)___. Pheromones are released in the sweat and urine of animals are detected by the ___(121)___ organ of other animals. This process helps stimulate the release of sexual hormones, ovulation, sexual behavior, and ___(122)___ toward other animals. In humans, pheromones influence female ___(123)___ cycles.

Perception: Interpreting Sensory Messages

The process of organizing and interpreting neural energy is ___(124)___. Gestalt psychologists have described the following ways in which we organize our visual perception: 1) the center of attention and the background, called ___(125)___-_____, can be reversed; 2) things that are close together are perceived as belonging together, according to the principle of ___(126)___; 3) we tend to perceive ___(127)___ in lines and patterns; 4) similar things tend to be perceived together, according to the principle of ___(128)___; and 5) incomplete figures are perceived as wholes, according to the concept of ___(129)___.

Although raw sensations are constantly changing, we tend to perceive objects as being fairly constant and unchanging. This tendency is called ___(130)___ _____ and relates to the brightness, color, size, and shape of objects.

We are able to perceive a three-dimensional world with a two-dimensional retina because we use ___(131)___ in depth perception. Those cues that can be seen by one eye are ___(132)___ cues, while those that require both eyes are called ___(133)___ cues. The monocular cues are texture ___(134)___, linear ___(135)___, superposition, shadowing, speed of ___(136)___, aerial ___(137)___, accommodation and ___(138)___ position. The binocular cues are convergence and retinal ___(139)___.

Intentional manipulations of cues to create a perception of something that is not real are referred to as ___(140)_____. An illusion that is viewed in everyday life is the ___(141)___ illusion.

There is evidence that ___(142)___ and ___(143)___ factors play an important role in perception.

Painters often use ___(144)___ cues of depth perception to create the illusion of a ___(145)___-dimensional object.

Concept Check

Fill in the missing components of the following concept boxes. The correct answers are located in the "Answers" section at the end of the chapter.

Structures and Functions of Body Senses and Chemical Senses

Structure	Function
	inner ear structures that provide the brain with information about movement; structures are the semicircular canals, the saccule and utricle
nocioreceptors	
gate control theory of pain	
	"taste buds" on the tongue that are sensitive to sweetness, sourness, saltiness, bitterness, and fattiness
olfactory epithelium	
	organ in the nasal cavity of many animals that contains receptors to detect pheromones

Structures and Functions of the Eyes and Ears

Structure	Function
	opens and closes to control the amount of light that passes through the pupil into the lens
retina	
	located throughout the retina except in the fovea; they are largely responsible for peripheral vision and are highly sensitive to light; they cannot code information about color
cones	
	carries neural messages to the brain
pinna	
	a thin membrane in the middle ear that vibrates in response to sound waves
	a long, curled structure, filled with fluid; it is set into motion by the oval window
organ of Corti	

Extending the Chapter: Psychology, Societal Issues, and Human Diversity

These questions may be assigned to you. Whether or not they are assigned, they are designed to be challenging questions to encourage you to think independently about the material in the chapter. Many of the questions have no right or wrong answers.

From the *Applications of Psychology* section

1. Describe the ways in which successful painters use Gestalt principles of perception.

2. Discuss Leonardo da Vinci's advice for painters; how does this related to Gestalt principles of visual perception?

Psychology, Societal Issues, and Human Diversity

1. From the *Human Diversity* section of the text: describe the perception and management of pain in your culture. How did your parents and/or other caregivers respond when you were experiencing pain? Were there differing expectations based on gender or on age?

2. If future research supports human sensitivity and reactivity to pheromones, how should the production of these pheromones be regulated?

3. The perception of different foods as being tasty or disgusting is largely dependent upon one's cultural background. Describe some foods that you enjoy that others find unappetizing; likewise, what foods do you avoid that others enjoy?

4. The ease with which humans are subject to visual and other types of illusions suggests that, in reality, the world is not always the way we perceive it. What is your reaction to this statement?

Practice Quiz

The practice quiz consists of three sections: 1) Short answer questions, 2) Multiple choice questions, and 3) True-False questions. At the end of the chapter you will find suggested answers to the short answer questions, answers and explanation for the multiple choice questions, and answers to the true-false questions.

Short Answer Questions

1. List and explain five Gestalt principles of perceptual organization.

_____

_____

2. List and describe four examples of perceptual constancy.

_____

_____

3. Distinguish between monocular cues and binocular cues of depth perception. Give two examples of each.

_____

_____

Multiple Choice Questions

1. Each of the following is part of the process of sensation *except*
   a. receiving messages.
   b. translating messages.
   c. transmitting messages.
   d. interpreting messages.
   LO 1

2. Which of the following describes the process of transduction?
   a. when a friend plays the radio below your absolute threshold
   b. when light waves are converted to neural impulses
   c. when stimuli occur that are not attended to
   d. none of the above
   LO 2

3. After repeatedly asking your roommate to turn down the stereo so that you can study your psychology, you lose your temper. You rush into the living room, where your roommate indicates that the stereo *was* turned down! The amount by which the stereo was turned down was below your
   a. difference threshold.
   b. absolute threshold.
   c. sensory adaption level.
   d. in-between threshold.
   LO 3

4. The smallest magnitude of a stimulus that can be detected is called the
   a. absolute threshold.
   b. difference threshold.
   c. minimum threshold.
   d. transduction threshold.
   LO 3

5. An architect is designing apartments and wants them to be soundproof. She asks a psychologist what the smallest amount of sound is that can be heard. Her question is most related to the
   a. absolute threshold.
   b. difference threshold.
   c. Weber's law.
   d. sensory receptors.
   LO 3

6. Joe was upset when he started his car because the radio blared out loudly. Then he realized that he was the one who last played the car radio. "I didn't think I had the volume turned up so high," he thought. What phenomenon is occurring here?
   a. the absolute threshold
   b. the difference threshold
   c. sensory adaptation
   d. transduction
   LO 4

7. Weber's law
   a. refers to the ability to detect changes in the intensity of various stimuli.
   b. helps to explain the process of sensory adaptation.
   c. is useful in predicting the absolute threshold.
   d. a and b above
   LO 5

8. The brightness of a visual sensation is determined by the
   a. intensity of the light wave.
   b. frequency of the light wave.
   c. saturation of the light wave.
   d. radiation of the light wave.
   LO 6

9. In the eye, light waves are transduced into neural impulses by
    a. the cornea and the iris.
    b. the pupil and the lens.
    c. the rods and the cones.
    d. none of the above
       LO 7

10. The amount of light entering the eye is controlled by the
    a. pupil.
    b. lens.
    c. iris.
    d. fovea.
       LO 7

11. When compared with cones, rods
    a. are responsible for peripheral vision.
    b. are less sensitive to light.
    c. produce images perceived with good visual acuity.
    d. can code information about color.
       LO 8

12. Rods and cones stop firing almost completely during the process of
    a. dark adaptation.
    b. light adaptation.
    c. color vision.
    d. monochromacy.
       LO 8

13. Which of the following events is explained by the opponent-process theory of color vision?
    a. complementary colors
    b. color afterimages
    c. neuron responses
    d. all of the above
       LO 9

14. The frequency of sound waves is measured in
    a. hertz.
    b. decibels.
    c. timbre.
    d. none of the above.
       LO 10

15. The loudness of a sound depends primarily on its
    a. intensity.
    b. timbre.
    c. complexity.
    d. noise level.
       LO 10

16. The eardrum, hammer, anvil, and stirrup are located in the
    a. inner ear.
    b. middle ear.
    c. outer ear.
    d. external auditory canal.
       LO 11

17. The organ of Corti codes neural messages for the brain based on
    a. the intensity of a sound wave.
    b. the frequency of a sound wave.
    c. the pitch of a sound wave.
    d. a and b above.
       LO 11

18. In the ear, sound waves are transduced into neural messages by receptors located in the
    a. organ of Corti.
    b. hammer, anvil, and stirrup.
    c. middle ear.
    d. pinna.
       LO 11

19. Where are the sensory receptors of the vestibular organ located?
    a. cerebral cortex
    b. muscles and joints
    c. skin
    d. inner ear
       LO 12

20. Information about the location and movement of skin, muscles, joints, and tendons is provided by
    a. basket cells.
    b. kinesthetic receptors.
    c. tactile discs.
    d. specialized end bulbs.
       LO 12

21. Nocioreceptors are free nerve endings that transmit information to the brain about
    a. temperature.
    b. pressure.
    c. olfaction.
    d. pain.
       LO 13

22. Which skin receptors are the primary receptors for detecting temperature?
    a. free nerve endings
    b. specialized end bulbs
    c. tactile discs
    d. tactile epithelium
    LO 13

23. Each of the following phenomena may be explained by endorphins *except*
    a. visual acuity.
    b. "runner's high."
    c. acupuncture.
    d. placebos.
    LO 14

24. Pain gates appear to involve
    a. endorphins.
    b. estrogen in women.
    c. placebos.
    d. a and b above.
    LO 14

25. Research suggests phantom limb pain involves
    a. the hypothalamus.
    b. endorphins.
    c. the corpus callosum.
    d. the somatosensory cortex.
    LO 15

26. Each of the following is a basic taste sensation *except*
    a. spicy.
    b. sweet.
    c. sour.
    d. bitter.
    LO 16

27. Molecules responsible for each of the primary odors have a specific shape that will "fit" only one type of receptor, according to the
    a. olfactory epithelium approach.
    b. opponent-process theory of smell.
    c. integrated-key theory.
    d. stereochemical theory.
    LO 17

28. The tendency to mentally "fill in" incomplete figures is the Gestalt principle of perception called
    a. figure-ground.
    b. proximity.
    c. dissimilarity.
    d. closure.
    LO 18

29. The perception of items as containing a center and a background is referred to as the Gestalt principle of
    a. proximity.
    b. figure-ground.
    c. continuity.
    d. similarity.
    LO 18

30. We continue to perceive that a penny is round, regardless of the angle from which it is viewed. This is an example of a process called
    a. perceptual constancy.
    b. light adaptation.
    c. figure-grounding.
    d. proximity.
    LO 19

31. Each of the following is a monocular cue *except*
    a. texture gradient.
    b. aerial perspective.
    c. accommodation.
    d. convergence.
    LO 20

32. The Ames room demonstrates
    a. convergence.
    b. retinal disparity.
    c. a visual illusion.
    d. all of the above.
    LO 21

33. The moon looks bigger at the horizon than it does higher in the sky because
    a. the beams are passing through denser air, which magnifies them.
    b. it is a different color, which makes it look bigger.
    c. it appears larger in comparison to trees and buildings on the horizon.
    d. the moon's light falls on the foveas when it is low on the horizon.
    LO 21

34. According to the text, the hook-swinging ceremony is proof of
    a. the influence of motivation on perception.
    b. individual influences on perception.
    c. cultural influences on perception.
    d. none of the above.
       LO 22

35. According to the text, effective painters, drawers, and sculptors make good use of
    a. depth perception cues.
    b. visual illusions.
    c. perceptual constancy cues.
    d. all of the above.
       LO 23

True-False Questions

_____1. Each of the sense organs engages in transduction.

_____2. In the eyes, the rods are receptor cells that can detect color.

_____3. According to the trichromatic theory of color vision, the visual system has two kinds of color processors.

_____4. The eardrum is located in the inner ear.

_____5. The transduction of sound waves into neural impulses takes place in the organ of Corti.

_____6. Nocioreceptors are receptors for stimuli relating to temperature.

_____7. "Runner's high" is most likely due to the effects of endorphins.

_____8. One of the basic sensations to which the taste buds are sensitive is bitterness.

_____9. Researchers have not yet determined whether human behavior is influenced by pheromones.

_____10. Both monocular and binocular cues are involved in depth perception.

ANSWER SECTION

Concept Checks
Structures and Functions of Body Senses and Chemical Senses

Structure	Function
vestibular organ	inner ear structures that provide the brain with information about movement; structures are the semicircular canals, the saccule and utricle
nocioreceptors	receptors for stimuli that are experienced as painful in the brain
gate control theory of pain	neural gates regulate the transmission of impulses from the nocioreceptors to the brain
papillae	"taste buds" on the tongue that are sensitive to sweetness, sourness, saltiness, bitterness, and fattiness
olfactory epithelium	receptor cells at the top of the nasal cavity responsible for detecting odors
vomeronasal organ	organ in the nasal cavity of many animals that contains receptors to detect pheromones

Structures and Functions of the Eyes and Ears

Structure	Function
iris	opens and closes to control the amount of light that passes through the pupil into the lens
retina	the light-sensitive area at the back of the eye
rods	located throughout the retina except in the fovea; they are largely responsible for peripheral vision and are highly sensitive to light; they cannot code information about color
cones	concentrated in the fovea and code information light, dark, and color
optic nerve	carries neural messages to the brain
pinna	the outer ear, which is responsible for collecting sound waves
eardrum	a thin membrane in the middle ear that vibrates in response to sound waves
cochlea	a long, curled structure, filled with fluid; it is set into motion by the oval window
organ of Corti	contains the receptor cells that transduce the sound waves of the cochlear fluid into neural impulses

Answers to Review At A Glance

1. sensory receptor cells
2. sensation
3. perception
4. stimulus
5. transduction
6. neural energy
7. absolute threshold
8. difference threshold
9. sensory adaptation
10. psychophysics
11. Weber's law
12. electromagnetic radiation
13. frequency
14. intensity
15. brightness
16. wavelength
17. cornea
18. iris
19. lens
20. ciliary muscle
21. retina
22. rods
23. cones
24. 6 million
25. 125 million
26. fovea
27. visual acuity
28. peripheral
29. light
30. visual acuity
31. color
32. blind spot
33. optic chiasm
34. adaptation
35. light
36. trichromatic
37. complementary
38. afterimages
39. blindness
40. color-processing
41. yellow-blue
42. red-green
43. cones
44. neurons
45. audition
46. sound waves
47. frequency
48. hertz
49. pitch

50. intensity
51. decibels
52. timbre
53. pinna
54. external
55. eardrum
56. hammer
57. anvil
58. stirrup
59. oval window
60. cochlea
61. round window
62. Corti
63. basilar membrane
64. intensity
65. frequency
66. conduction
67. locate
68. vestibular organ
69. saccule
70. utricle
71. semicircular canals
72. cupula
73. kinesthetic
74. pressure
75. temperature
76. pain
77. free
78. basket
79. discs
80. end
81. pressure
82. pain
83. fingertips
84. lips
85. genitals
86. warmth
87. coldness
88. heat
89. nocioreceptors
90. pain
91. rapid
92. slow
93. gate control
94. nocioreceptors
95. limbic
96. sensitize
97. limbic
98. neurons

99. gate
100. endorphins
101. estrogen
102. endorphins
103. endorphins
104. acupuncture
105. somatosensory
106. gustation
107. olfaction
108. 10,000
109. taste buds
110. papillae
111. sweetness
112. saltiness
113. fattiness
114. age
115. olfactory epithelium
116. seven
117. 146
118. organic
119. stereochemical
120. pheromones
121. vomeronasal
122. aggression
123. reproductive
124. perception
125. figure-ground
126. proximity
127. continuity
128. similarity
129. closure
130. perceptual constancy
131. cues
132. monocular
133. binocular
134. gradient
135. perspective
136. movement
137. perspective
138. vertical
139. disparity
140. visual illusions
141. moon
142. individual
143. cultural
144. monocular
145. three

Sample Answers to Short Answer Questions

1. **List and explain five Gestalt principles of perceptual organization**

    The principle of figure-ground means that we organize our visual perceptions into both the center of our attention (the figure) and the indistinct background (the ground). Continuity refers to the tendency to perceive lines or patterns that follow a smooth contour as being part of a single unit. Proximity means that items that are close together are perceived as belonging together. Similarity suggests similar things are perceived as being related. Closure allows us to perceive meaning by mentally filling in missing information in order to create complete perceptions.

2. **List and describe four examples of perceptual constancy.**

    Perceptual constancy refers to our ability to perceive objects as remaining relatively unchanged in spite of changes in raw sensations. Brightness constancy allows us perceive objects as being the same brightness, even if the lighting changes. Likewise, color constancy means that we tend to perceive objects as being the same color even if lighting changes. Size constancy refers to our ability to perceive objects as being the same size, even when we view them from different distances. Shape constancy means we perceive objects as being the same shape even when we look from different angles and distances.

3. **Distinguish between monocular cues and binocular cues of depth perception. Give two examples of each.**

    Moncular cues refers to depth perception as seen by one eye, whereas binocular cues involves depth perception using both eyes. Examples of monocular depth perception include texture gradient, linear perspective, superposition, shadowing, speed of movement, aerial perspective, accommodation, and vertical position. Two binocular cues (which occur when both eyes perceive the same object) are convergence and retinal disparity.

Multiple Choice Answers

1. The answer is *d*. While choices a, b, and c are all part of the process of sensation, the process of interpreting messages is called perception.
2. The answer is *b*. The process of transduction refers to translating one form of energy to another. Thus, in order for people to see, light waves must be transduced into neural impulses.
3. The answer is *a*. The difference threshold is the smallest difference between two stimuli that can be detected half the time. Your roommate did, in fact, turn down the volume of the stereo, but the difference was so small that you could not detect it. Now, aren't you sorry that you yelled at your roomie?
4. The answer is *a*. While the absolute threshold refers to the smallest magnitude of a stimulus that can be detected, the difference threshold is the smallest difference between two stimuli that can be detected half the time.
5. The answer is *a*. The minimal amounts of stimuli that can be detected are referred to as the absolute threshold. The difference threshold refers to detecting differences between two stimuli.
6. The answer is *c*. Sensory adaptation refers to the weakened magnitude of a sensation resulting from prolonged presentation of a stimulus. Other examples include "getting used to" the cool water in a swimming pool and "getting used to" loud rock music.
7. The answer is *a*. Weber's law states that the *difference* threshold is in direct proportion to the intensity of the original stimulus. This helps to predict our ability to detect changes in stimuli. The *absolute* threshold refers to the smallest magnitude of a stimulus that can be detected.
8. The answer is *b*. While the intensity of a light is related to the brightness of the sensation, the saturation of a color is related to the variety of wavelengths that comprise the color.

9. The answer is *c*. The rods and cones are receptor cells that are found in the retina. The cornea is a protective covering on the eye's surface. The iris regulates the amount of light that enters the eye. The pupil is the opening of the iris, while the lens focuses light on the retina.

10. The answer is *c*. The colored part of the eye, the iris, opens and closes to regulate the amount of light passing through the pupil into the lens.

11. The answer is *a*. Each of the other alternatives is true of cones.

12. The answer is *a*. When we enter a dark room after being in sunlight, the rods and cones are not sensitive enough to be stimulated by the low-intensity light. The receptors thus get to rest before regaining their sensitivity to light. In light adaptation, on the other hand, the rods and cones that have been "in the dark" for a while are extremely sensitive to light.

13. The answer is *d*. According to the opponent-process theory, there are two kinds of cones in the retina that respond to light in either the red-green or yellow-blue ranges of wavelength.

14. The answer is *a*. The frequency of sound waves is measured in hertz, whereas the intensity is measured in decibels and the complexity is reflected in the timbre of a sound.

15. The answer is *a*. The intensity of a sound is by how densely compacted the air molecules are in the sound wave.

16. The answer is *b*. The middle ear transduces sound waves into mechanical energy and passes the energy on to the inner ear.

17. The answer is *d*. The intensity is coded by the number of receptors that fire, while the frequency is coded according to location in the organ of Corti and the firing of volleys of impulses by different groups of neurons.

18. The answer is *a*. The organ of Corti is located in the cochlea of the inner ear. The outer ear, called the pinna, helps to collect sound waves. The middle ear transduces sound waves into mechanical energy. The hammer, anvil, and stirrup are small bones located in the middle ear.

19. The answer is *d*. The vestibular organ of the inner ear is composed of two structures: the semicircular canals and the saccule and utricle.

20. The answer is *b*. Kinesthetic receptors are individual sensory receptors located in the skin, muscles, joints, and tendons. Basket cells, tactile discs, and specialized end bulbs are different receptors found in the skin.

21. The answer is *d*. Nocioreceptors transmit messages along two different pathways, corresponding to "first and second pain."

22. The answer is *a*. End bulbs detect skin pressure and skin pleasure and tactile discs detect pressure.

23. The answer is *a*. Endorphins have been implicated in everything from the gate control theory of pain to the experience of "runner's high," the pain-reducing effects of acupuncture, and the effects of placebos.

24. The answer is *d*. While the effect of endorphins on gate neurons has been known for some time, recent research has pointed to the importance of estrogen in helping block pain for women.

25. The answer is *d*. Research suggests that when sensory and pain neurons from **one part of the body** have been cut, the area of the **somatosensory cortex** becomes sensitive to input from parts of the body that activate nearby portions of the **somatosensory cortex**.

26. The answer is *a*. The missing basic taste sensation is saltiness.

27. The answer is *d*. All of the other choices are flights of fancy.

28. The answer is *d*. Figure-ground refers to the tendency to focus on figure, while the remainder of a stimulus is indistinct background. The principle of proximity suggests that things that are close together are usually perceived as belonging together. Dissimilarity is not a Gestalt principle.

29. The answer is *b*. The center of our attention is the figure and the rest is background, as demonstrated by the vase figure.

30. The answer is *a*. The principle of perceptual constancy in this particular example is called shape constancy. Other examples of perceptual constancy are brightness constancy, color constancy, and size constancy.

31. The answer is *d*. Both monocular and binocular cues allow us to perceive depth. Monocular cues are those that can be seen using one eye. Binocular cues require both eyes for depth perception. Convergence is an example of a binocular cue.

32. The answer is *c*. Visual illusions are astounding because they intentionally manipulate the perceptual cues we use in order to create a perception of something that is not real.

33. The answer is *c*. When the moon is seen higher in the sky, there are no objects with which to compare it.

34. The answer is *c*. The hook-swinging ceremony, a practice in which an individual perceives no pain in spite of the fact that two metal hooks are pushed through the skin of the back, indicates the powerful influence of culture on individual perception.

35. The answer is *d*. Artists use monocular cues of depth perception to create the illusion of three-dimensional objects.

Answers to True-False Questions

1. T   6. F

2. F   7. T

3. F   8. T

4. F   9. F

5. T   10. T

Chapter 4   States of Consciousness

Learning Objectives

1. Describe daydreams and explain Hilgard's concept of divided consciousness. (p. 118)

2. Identify the characteristics of the unconscious mind. (p. 119)

3. List and describe the stages of sleep. (p. 121)

4. Compare and contrast REM sleep and non-REM sleep features. (p. 121)

5. Describe what is understood about the content and meaning of dreams. (p. 123)

6. Describe the theories that seek to explain why we sleep and dream. (p. 125)

7. Identify the characteristics of the hypnotic state. (p. 127)

8. List the variables that influence individual responses to drugs; describe the risks associated with drug use. (p. 128)

9. Name the four major categories of psychotropic drugs. (p. 130)

10. Explain the effects of stimulants and compare the effects of amphetamines and cocaine. (p. 130)

11. Identify depressant drugs and compare their various effects. (p. 131)

12. Describe the effects of inhalants, hallucinogens, and marijuana. (p. 132)

13. Differentiate between act-alike and designer drugs. (p. 133)

14. (From the *Application of Psychology* section) Discuss the issues regarding legal consciousness-altering drugs. (p. 135)

Chapter Overview

Consciousness is a state of awareness. Daydreams involve focused thinking about fantasies. Divided consciousness refers to the splitting off of two conscious activities that occur simultaneously. The unconscious mind processes information without our being consciously aware.

Sleep begins as we enter a semiwakeful hypnagogic state and becomes progressively deeper as we enter dream sleep. We typically enter REM sleep four to six times each night. REM sleep, accompanied by dreams, rapid eye movement, and by an "autonomic storm," is not the only part of the dream cycle that is filled with dreams. The nature of non-REM dreams differs from REM dreams. Most of the conscious experience in dreams is visual, and most dreams have some positive or negative emotional content. Much of the content of our dreams is directly related to things going on in our waking lives, a term called day residue. Freud distinguished between the manifest content of dreams and the latent, or symbolic meaning of dreams. Sleeping and dreaming seem essential to physical and physiological health; sleep deprivation brings on fatigue, inefficiency, and irritability.

Hypnosis is sometimes used to alter consciousness and to relieve pain. Consciousness may also be altered through the use of various psychotropic drugs. These may be classified as stimulants, depressants, inhalants, and hallucinogens. Although risks differ from drug to drug, all drug users run the risk of abuse, dependence, addiction, and direct or indirect side effects.

Stimulants are drugs that activate the central nervous system. Even mild stimulants like caffeine and nicotine are physiologically addictive. Amphetamines and cocaine are other highly addictive stimulants. Depressants influence conscious activity by depressing parts of the central nervous system. Alcohol, tranquilizers, sedatives, and narcotics are all depressant drugs. Inhalants are usually toxic and often cause brain damage. Hallucinogens alter perceptions, cause hallucinations, and are often associated with bizarre or violent behavior. Psychological dependence is common with hallucinogens. Marijuana is a popular although illegal drug that produces a sense of well-being and sometimes alters perception. Health risks are also associated with the use of legal consciousness-altering drugs, such as caffeine, nicotine, and alcohol. The four stages of classic alcoholism are 1) the prealcoholic stage, 2) the prodromal stage, 3) the crucial stage, and 4) the chronic stage.

Key Terms Exercise

For each of the following exercises, match the key terms on the left with the correct definitions on the right. Page references to the text follow the terms so that you may refer to the text for any items you answer incorrectly or do not understand completely. You may check your responses immediately by referring to the answers that follow each exercise.

Consciousness

_____ 1. consciousness (p. 118)
_____ 2. daydreams (p. 118)
_____ 3. divided consciousness (p. 118)
_____ 4. unconscious mind (p. 119)

a. mental processes that occur without conscious awareness
b. a state of awareness
c. focused thinking about fantasies
d. occurs when two conscious activities that occur simultaneously are split

ANSWERS

1. b   3. d
2. c   4. a

Sleeping and Dreaming

_____ 1. hypnagogic state (p. 121)
_____ 2. myoclonia (p. 121)
_____ 3. REM sleep (p. 122)
_____ 4. day residue (p. 124)
_____ 5. stimulus incorporation (p. 124)
_____ 6. manifest content (p. 125)
_____ 7. latent content (p. 125)

a. rapid eye movement sleep, often during dreaming
b. a falling sensation that may occur during the hypnagogic state
c. a twilight state between wakefulness and sleep
d. the events that happen in a dream
e. the symbolic meaning of a dream
f. Freud's term to explain that the content of dreams is related to events taking place in our lives during the day.
g. occurs when the real-world event included in a dream is actually taking place while we are asleep

ANSWERS

1. c   5. g
2. b   6. d
3. a   7. e
4. f

Hypnosis/Altering Consciousness with Drugs

_____ 1. hypnosis (p. 127)
_____ 2. psychotropic drugs (p. 128)
_____ 3. stimulants (p. 130)
_____ 4. depressants (p. 131)
_____ 5. opiates (p. 131)
_____ 6. inhalants (p. 132)
_____ 7. hallucinogens (p. 132)

a. drugs that provide a sense of energy and well-being
b. drugs that alter perceptions
c. narcotic drugs derived from the opium poppy
d. drugs that produce relaxation, drowsiness and lowered inhibitions
e. substances that produce intoxication when inhaled
f. drugs that alter conscious experience
g. an altered state in which the individual is susceptible to suggestions

ANSWERS

1. g   5. c
2. f   6. e
3. a   7. b
4. d

Review At A Glance

(Answers to this section begin on page 77)

Wide Awake: Normal Waking Consciousness

Consciousness is a state of ___(1)___. Although other states of consciousness exist, we assume that the "real" consciousness is ___(2)___ consciousness. A state of focused thinking that involves fantasies is called ___(3)___. Freud believed that daydreams reduce the tension left by unfulfilled ___(4)___. Some researchers have found, however, that daydreams may actually ___(5)___ tension.

When our conscious awareness becomes "split" and we perform two activities that require conscious awareness at the same time, this is called ___(6)___ consciousness.

Today a number of psychologists are attempting to scientifically investigate the unconscious mind. For example, psychologists have studied what happens when we "tune out" one voice we hear and pay attention to a second voice, an experience called the ___(7)_____ phenomenon. Researchers have found that we are able to process words we hear without being ___(8)___ aware of them.

Sleeping and Dreaming: Conscious While Asleep

The sleep cycle contains several stages. After daydreaming, we generally pass into a relaxed "twilight" state called the ___(9)___ state. Occasionally we experience a sense of falling, and our body experiences a sudden jerk called a ___(10)___. Sleep researchers have distinguished ___(11)___ levels of sleep on the basis of electroencephalogram (EEG) recordings. We pass through these levels, upward and downward, many times during the night. Several times per night the sleeper enters a stage called ___(12)___ sleep. Because of eye movements during dreaming, dream sleep is often called rapid eye movement or ___(13)___ sleep. Other important physical changes also occur during sleep. One researcher has likened dream sleep to an "___(14)___ _____." REM sleep is also characterized by ___(15)___ lubrication and erection of the clitoris in females and ___(16)___ erection in males.

Research suggests the average college student spends about two hours per night in ___(17)___ sleep, divided into four to six separate episodes. The longest REM dream, about an hour, usually occurs during the ___(18)___ part of the sleep cycle.

Dreams also occur during ___(19)___ sleep. Non-REM dreams are more likely to consist of ___(20)___ impressions that are less emotional and are less likely to involve visual images. Non-REM dreams are ___(21)___ likely to be spontaneously recalled after waking than are REM dreams.

Most of the conscious experience of dreams is ___(22)___. Only about one-fourth of dream images include ___(23)___ sensations and about 20percent include bodily sensations. Dreams usually include ___(24)___ intense colors and have mostly blurry backgrounds. The dreamer has an ___(25)___ role in nearly three-fourths of dreams. About ___(26)___ of the other characters in dreams are friends, acquaintances or family members. About three-fourths of drams have ___(27)___ content, and of these, 60percent have a negative tone or a mixture of positive and negative emotions. Recurrent dreams are more likely to have ___(28)___ emotional content. ___(29)___ are slightly more likely to have positive dreams, and the characters in men's dreams are somewhat more socially restrained. Dreams fascinate us because they can be ___(30)___ and bizarre.

According to Freud, the content of dreams that is directly related to events going on in our daytime lives is called day ___(31)___. When stimuli that occur during sleep are directly incorporated into our dreams, this is called ___(32)___ _____.

According to Freud, the events we experience in a dream are the ___(33)___ content, while the symbolic meaning of the dream is the ___(34)___ content. When we miss sleep, we apparently create a "___(35)___ _____" that needs to be made up. In one experiment, no detrimental effects occurred when sleep was gradually reduced from eight to four hours per night. However, irritability and fatigue occurred when the amount of nightly sleep was ___(36)___ reduced. According to Webb, sleep serves a ___(37)___ role.

Altered States of Consciousness and Drugs

The hypnotic state usually has the following qualities: 1) a sense of deep ___(38)___, 2) alterations referred to as ___(39)___ hallucinations, (3) a loss of the sense of touch or pain referred to as hypnotic ___(40)___, 4) a sense of passing back in time called hypnotic ___(41)___ _____, and 5) hypnotic ___(42)___. In recent years, some doctors and dentists have found hypnosis to be an effective way to relieve ___(43)___.

Some factors that influence an individual's response to a drug include 1) dose and ___(44)___, 2) personal ___(45)___, 3) ___(46)___, 4) the ___(47)___ situation, and 5) ___(48)___. The risks associated with drug use include 1) the potential to cause damage or impair psychological functioning, called ___(49)___ _____; 2) a need to use the drug regularly in order to feel comfortable psychologically, called psychological __(50)__; 3) a chemical need for the drug, called physiological __(51)__; 4) powerful and potentially dangerous __(52)__ side effects; and 5) the risk of infection or other __(53)__ side effects.

Drugs that alter conscious experience are called __(54)__ drugs. The categories of psychotropic drugs are 1) drugs that increase the activity of the central nervous system, __(55)__; 2) those that reduce the activity of the central nervous system, __(56)__; 3) those that produce alterations in perceptual experience, __(57)__; and(4) those that produce a sense of intoxication when inhaled, __(58)__.

Drugs that activate motivational centers and reduce activity in inhibitory centers of the CNS are called __(59)__ (uppers). Among the most widely used stimulants are 1) the drug found in coffee, tea, and cola, __(60)__; and 2) the drug found in tobacco, __(61)__. Other stimulants that produce a sense of increased energy and a euphoric high are called __(62)__. Prolonged excessive use of amphetamines may lead to amphetamine __(63)__. A widely abused stimulant made from the leaves of the coca plant is __(64)__. Repeated use of cocaine rapidly leads to __(65)__. After the prolonged use of cocaine, the user experiences a "cocaine crash", marked by __(66)__, agitation, confusion, and exhaustion. Withdrawal from cocaine addiction is marked by intense depression, __(67)__, and craving for cocaine.

Drugs that depress parts of the central nervous system are called __(68)__. A state of relaxation is produced by the highly addictive group of depressants called __(69)__. A sense of relaxation for a briefer period is provided by __(70)__. Powerful and highly addictive depressants are called __(71)__. Narcotics such as morphine and heroin are derived from the opium poppy and are called __(72)__. Substances that are inhaled to produce a sense of intoxication, such as glue and paint, are called __(73)__.

Drugs that powerfully alter consciousness, such as LSD and mescaline, are called __(74)__. One highly dangerous hallucinogen, originally developed as an animal tranquilizer, is __(75)__.

A powerful although illegal drug that generally produces a sense of relaxation and well-being is __(76)__. Although not physically addictive, psychological __(77)__ is possible. Two special drug-related concerns involve __(78)__- and __(79)__ drugs.

Application of Psychology: The Legal Consciousness-Altering Drugs

Coffee, tea, and cola contain the powerful stimulant __(80)__. Prolonged use of caffeine, even at moderate levels, can produce physiological __(81)__. Caffeine also produces marked increases in blood pressure, especially during times of __(82)__. Most smokers begin during their teenage years, when they are vulnerable to __(83)__ and the perception of smoking as a "forbidden fruit." Most regular smokers become __(84)__. Nicotine stimulates the pleasure centers in the __(85)__ system; it also increases alertness by stimulating the __(86)__ lobes of the cortex. It also soothes the __(87)__ it creates.

A widely abused addictive depressant drug is ___(88)___. The amount of alcohol consumption that can be harmful depends on the person and the ___(89)___. Also, the potential harmful effects can affect job performance, relationships, and personal ___(90)___. Drinking during pregnancy has been linked to ___(91)_____ syndrome in infants Alcohol can rapidly result in psychological ___(92)___ and physiological ___(93)___.

Concept Checks

Fill in the missing components of the following concept box. The correct answers are located in the "Answers" section at the end of the chapter.

Sleeping and Dreaming

Concept	Description
hypnagogic state	
	a machine that measures electrical brain activity
REM sleep	
	dreams are brief, less emotional and less visual
	a Freudian term referring to the large part of dream content related to events taking place in our lives during the day
stimulus incorporation	

Psychoactive Drugs

Type of drug	Effect	Examples
stimulants	increase activity of motivational centers and decrease activity of inhibitory centers of the CNS	
depressants	depress parts of the CNS	
inhalants		glue, cleaning fluid, and paint.
	powerfully alter consciousness by altering perceptual experiences	LSD and mescaline.
designer drugs	produce a dreamlike high	

Extending the Chapter: Psychology, Societal Issues, and Human Diversity

These questions may be assigned to you. Whether or not they are assigned, they are designed to be challenging questions to encourage you to think independently about the material in the chapter. Many of the questions have no right or wrong answers.

I. From the *Applications of Psychology* section

1. Discuss the impact of advertising on the use of caffeine, alcohol, and nicotine by young people in the United States. Provide concrete examples from radio, television, and print media. How should these media be further regulated? If not, why?

2. What justification exists for some dangerous consciousness-altering drugs to be legal, whereas most consciousness-altering drugs are illegal?

II. Psychology, Societal Issues, and Human Diversity

1. Why do humans generally find great attraction to altered states of consciousness?

2. Some altered states of consciousness are associated with religious ceremonies. How can our society continue to celebrate diversity and honor religious freedom while still regulating consciousness-altering drugs?

3. Why do you think hypnosis is not more widely used as a substitute anesthesia in surgical procedures?

4. (From the *Human Diversity* section of the text) What factors account for the differing rates of drug use among different racial and ethnic groups?

5. What impact do the anti-smoking campaigns have on young would-be smokers? Design a research study to generate answers.

Practice Quiz

The practice quiz consists of three sections: 1) Short answer questions, 2) Multiple choice questions, and 3) True-False questions. At the end of the chapter you will find suggested answers to the short answer questions, answers and explanation for the multiple choice questions, and answers to the true-false questions.

Short Answer Questions

1. What are the characteristics of hypnosis?

_____

_____

2. List and describe the risks associated with drug use.

_____

_____

3. List and describe the categories of psychotropic drugs.

_____

_____

Multiple Choice Questions

1. According to Freud, which state of consciousness helps to reduce the tension of unmet needs and wishes?
   a. hypnagogic state
   b. divided consciousness
   c. daydreaming
   d. REM state
   LO 1

2. Driving long distances while thinking about other events is an example of
   a. REM sleep.
   b. the unconscious mind.
   c. myoclonia.
   d. divided consciousness.
   LO 1

3. The ability to focus on one voice and tune out other voices has been labeled
   a. the cocktail party phenomenon.
   b. divided consciousness.
   c. the hypnagogic state.
   d. REM state.
   LO 2

4. According to researchers, voices that we "tune out" may nevertheless be processed _____.
   a. consciously
   b. unconsciously
   c. in a hypnagogic state
   d. in a state of flowing consciousness
   LO 2

5. Myoclonia is experienced in which stage of sleep?
   a. hypnagogic stage
   b. light sleep
   c. deep sleep
   d. REM sleep
   LO 3

6. How many hours per night does the average college student spend dreaming?
   a. 1
   b. 2
   c. 4
   d. 6
   LO 3

7. Which of the following may occur during REM sleep?
   a. movement of the eyes
   b. increased blood flow to the brain
   c. irregular breathing
   d. all of the above
   LO 4

8. The difference between REM and non-REM dreams is that
   a. non-REM dreams have more imagery.
   b. REM dreams are less frequent.
   c. non-REM dreams have bizarre content.
   d. non-REM dreams are closer to normal. thinking
   LO 4

9. According to Freud, the symbolic meaning of dreams is called the
   a. manifest content.
   b. latent content.
   c. hypnagogic content.
   d. reality content.
   LO 5

10. According to Webb, we sleep
    a. to restore our bodies.
    b. because we are not well adapted to night time darkness.
    c. to synthesize protein in our brains.
    d. because we need to dream.
    LO 6

11. Which of the following is *not* a characteristic of the hypnotic experience?
    a. hypnotic hallucinations
    b. hypnotic analgesia
    c. hypnotic control
    d. hypnotic repression
    LO 7

12. An individual's response to a drug can be affected by
    a. dose and purity of the drug.
    b. the individual's personal characteristics.
    c. the social situation.
    d. all of the above.
    LO 8

13. Richard finds that he feels comfortable psychologically only when he can smoke marijuana daily. He shows evidence of
    a. drug abuse.
    b. psychological dependence.
    c. physiological addiction.
    d. severe emotional problems.
    LO 8

14. Painful withdrawal symptoms and increased tolerance for larger and larger doses of a drug are characteristic of
    a. marijuana abuse.
    b. cocaine abuse.
    c. psychological addiction.
    d. physiological addiction.
    LO 8

15. Each of the following is a stimulant *except*
    a. alcohol.
    b. caffeine.
    c. amphetamines.
    d. cocaine.
    LO 9

16. Each of the following activates motivational centers of the central nervous system *except*
    a. stimulants.
    b. amphetamines.
    c. cocaine.
    d. opiates.
    LO 10

17. Which of the following is a withdrawal symptom of a cocaine addict?
    a. chills
    b. sweats
    c. agitation
    d. high blood pressure
    LO 10

18. Each of the following is considered to be addictive *except*
    a. sedatives.
    b. tranquilizers.
    c. narcotics.
    d. hallucinogens.
    LO 11

19. Each of the following is a potential side effect of prolonged marijuana use *except*
   a. damage to the chromosomes of reproductive cells.
   b. reverse tolerance.
   c. a decrease in the efficiency of cognitive processing.
   d. a decrease in the action of male sex hormones.
   LO 12

20. Drugs such as MDA and MDMA (ecstasy) are considered to be
   a. look-alike drugs.
   b. act-alike drugs.
   c. designer drugs.
   d. depressants.
   LO 13

21. Alcohol is considered to be
   a. a depressant, because it frequently leaves drinkers feeling depressed.
   b. a stimulant, because it makes the drinker less inhibited.
   c. a depressant, because it depresses inhibitory mechanisms in the brain.
   d. both a stimulant and a depressant.
   LO 14

True-False Questions

_____ 1. According to Freud, daydreams help us to reduce tension in our lives.

_____ 2. The electroencephalograph is a measure of brain activity used in measuring stages of sleep.

_____ 3. When we sleep, dreams occur only when we are in REM.

_____ 4. Body temperature appears to follow a circadian rhythm.

_____ 5. Nicotine is considered a stimulant.

_____ 6. While under hypnosis, some individuals report hypnotic analgesia.

_____ 7. Unlike most stimulants, cocaine is not an addictive drug.

_____ 8. Amphetamines can produce intense psychological dependence.

_____ 9. Morphine, heroin, and codeine are all derived from the opium poppy.

_____ 10. Hallucinogens are considered highly addictive.

ANSWER SECTION

Concept Checks

Sleeping and Dreaming

Concept	Description
hypnagogic state	relaxed state between wakefulness and sleep
EEG (electroencephalogram)	a machine that measures electrical brain activity
REM sleep	rapid eye movement sleep, often accompanies dreaming
non-REM sleep	dreams are brief, less emotional and less visual
day residue	a Freudian term referring to the large part of dream content related to events taking place in our lives during the day
stimulus incorporation	stimuli that occur during sleep wind up in our dreams

Sleep phenomena

Concept	Description
nightmares	terrifying dreams that occur during REM
night terrors	individual awakens in a state of panic; occurs during non-REM sleep
sleepwalking	walking and other complicated activities that occur during non-REM sleep
insomnia	two major varieties are sleep-onset and early-awakening
narcolepsy	a rare disorder in which the individual unexpectedly falls deeply asleep
sleep apnea	sudden interruption of breathing during sleep

Psychoactive Drugs

Type of drug	Effect	Examples
stimulants	increase activity of motivational centers and decrease activity of inhibitory centers of the CNS	amphetamines and cocaine
depressants	depress parts of the CNS	sedative, tranquilizers and narcotics
inhalants	a sense of intoxication when inhaled	glue, cleaning fluid, and paint
hallucinogens	powerfully alter consciousness by altering perceptual experiences	LSD and mescaline
designer drugs	produce a dreamlike high	MDA and MDMA (ecstasy)

Answers to Review At A Glance

1.	awareness	33.	manifest	65.	addiction
2.	waking	34.	latent	66.	depression
3.	daydreams	35.	sleep debt	67.	agitation
4.	needs	36.	abruptly	68.	depressants
5.	create	37.	protective	69.	sedatives
6.	divided	38.	relaxation	70.	tranquilizers
7.	cocktail party	39.	hypnotic	71.	narcotics
8.	consciously	40.	analgesia	72.	opiates
9.	hypnagogic	41.	age regression	73.	inhalants
10.	myoclonia	42.	control	74.	hallucinogens
11.	four	43.	pain	75.	phencyclidine (PCP)
12.	dream	44.	purity	76.	marijuana
13.	REM	45.	characteristics	77.	dependence
14.	autonomic storm	46.	expectations	78.	act-alike
15.	vaginal	47.	social	79.	designer
16.	penile	48.	moods	80.	caffeine
17.	REM	49.	drug abuse	81.	addiction
18.	last	50.	dependence	82.	stress
19.	non-REM	51.	addiction	83.	peer pressure
20.	fragmentary	52.	direct	84.	addicted
21.	less	53.	indirect	85.	limbic
22.	visual	54.	psychotropic	86.	frontal
23.	auditory	55.	stimulants	87.	discomfort
24.	few	56.	depressants	88.	alcohol
25.	active	57.	hallucinogens	89.	situation
26.	half	58.	inhalants	90.	health
27.	emotional	59.	stimulants	91.	fetal alcohol
28.	negative	60.	caffeine	92.	dependence
29.	Men	61.	nicotine	93.	addiction
30.	creative	62.	amphetamines		
31.	residue	63.	psychosis		
32.	stimulus incorporation	64.	cocaine		

Sample Answers to Short Answer Questions

1. What are the characteristics of hypnosis?

According to the text, the hypnotic state typically has the following characteristics: 1) relaxation; 2) hypnotic hallucinations; 3) hypnotic analgesia; 4) hypnotic age regression; and 5) hypnotic control.

2. List and describe the risks associated with drug use.

According to the text, the risks are: 1) drug abuse; 2) psychological dependence; 3) physiological addiction, tolerance, and withdrawal; 4) direct side effects, ranging from numbness to brain damage; and 5) indirect side effects, such as infection.

3. List and describe the categories of psychotropic drugs.

Psychotropic drugs may be categorized as: 1) stimulants, which increase the activity of motivational centers and decrease the activity of inhibitory centers in the central nervous system; 2) depressants, which reduce activity in the CNS; 3) inhalants; 4) hallucinogens; 5) marijuana; and 6) act-alike and designer drugs.

Multiple Choice Answers

1. The answer is *c*. Freud's explanation of daydreaming, however, fails to explain the fact that many daydreams *create* rather than release tension.
2. The answer is *d*. According to Hilgard, our conscious awareness becomes split, and we simultaneously perform two activities requiring conscious awareness.
3. The answer is *a*. The label results from the fact that this phenomenon often occurs at parties.
4. The answer is *b*. Researchers have found that even words that were "ignored" can be processed without conscious awareness.
5. The answer is *a*. The hypnagogic stage is the relaxed "twilight" state between wakefulness and sleep. Occasionally, while in this state, we suddenly feel as though we are falling and our body experiences a sudden jerking movement called a myoclonia.
6. The answer is *b*. While the length of the dreams vary, the longest is usually about an hour and typically occurs during the last part of the sleep cycle.
7. The answer is *d*. REM sleep, which occurs while we dream, occurs during an "autonomic storm." Dreams also occur during non-REM sleep.
8. The answer is *d*. Non-REM dreams are more likely to be brief, less emotional, and are less likely to involve visual images.
9. The answer is *b*. Freud believed that the latent content contained the true meaning of a dream. The manifest content was the obvious, but superficial, meaning of the dream.
10. The answer is *b*. Webb believes sleep provides a protective rather than a restorative role.
11. The answer is *d*. While hypnotic repression does not exist, hypnotic age regression (in which a subject feels that he is experiencing an earlier time in his life) does exist.
12. The answer is *d*. In addition to the factors listed in the question, the expectations that we have of the drug's effects and the mood at the time of taking the drug can also affect the response to the drug.
13. The answer is *b*. Psychological dependence occurs when the individual needs to use the drug to feel comfortable psychologically. Drug abuse occurs when it causes biological damage or impaired psychological or social functioning. Physiological addiction occurs when the body begins to require the presence of the drug and the user begins to experience withdrawal symptoms in the drug's absence.
14. The answer is *d*. A "psychological addiction" is referred to as dependence.
15. The answer is *a*. Whereas choices Bb, c, and d, are stimulants, that is, drugs that activate the nervous system, alcohol is a depressant.
16. The answer is *d*. Opiates are considered to be depressants.
17. The answer is *c*. Depression is another characteristic of withdrawal for the cocaine addict.
18. The answer is *d*. Sedatives, tranquilizers, and narcotics are recognized as highly addictive drugs. Hallucinogens can alter perceptual experiences but are not generally considered to be addictive.
19. The answer is *a*. Among other problems created by the prolonged use of marijuana are a weakening of the body's immune system and an increased risk of lung cancer.
20. The answer is *c*. Designer drugs are those that have been designed by chemists so recently that they have not yet been classified as illegal.
21. The answer is *c*. Although alcohol does make drinkers less inhibited, and it can reduce tension and anxiety, its classification as a depressant refers to its effect on the nervous system.

Answers to True-False Questions

1. F   6. T

2. T   7. F

3. F   8. T

4. T   9. T

5. T   10. F

Chapter 5   Basic Principles of Learning

Learning Objectives

1. Identify the key features of the definition of learning. (p. 142)

2. Identify the significant elements in Pavlov's study of classical conditioning; for example, association. (p. 144)

3. Define classical conditioning and its terminology, including UCS, UCR, CS, and CR. (p. 145)

4. Identify applications of classical conditioning and their importance. (p. 147)

5. Identify and define the processes involved in operant conditioning. (p. 149)

6. Understand how positive reinforcement is influenced by timing and consistency. (p. 150)

7. Distinguish between primary reinforcement and secondary reinforcement. (p. 151)

8. Compare and contrast the four schedules of reinforcement: fixed ratio, variable ratio, fixed interval, and variable interval. (p. 152)

9. Understand the process of shaping. (p. 153)

10. Define negative reinforcement, and compare escape conditioning to avoidance conditioning. (p. 155)

11. List the dangers of using punishment and identify guidelines for the appropriate use of punishment. (p. 156)

12. Understand the differences between classical and operant conditioning. (p. 158)

13. Distinguish between stimulus discrimination and stimulus generalization. (p. 158)

14. Identify how extinction occurs. (p. 161)

15. Understand how spontaneous recovery and disinhibition are related to extinction. (p. 162)

16. Compare the cognitive and connectionist interpretations of learning. (p. 164)

17. Know the characteristics of place learning, latent learning, and insight learning. (p. 164)

18. Define modeling and explain the roles of vicarious reinforcement and vicarious punishment in learning. (p. 166)

19. Know how biological factors affect learning, including learned taste aversions. (p. 167)

20. (From the *Application of Psychology* section) Explain how people sometimes "learn the wrong things." (p. 169)

Chapter Overview

"Learning" refers to any relatively permanent change in behavior brought about through experience. One type of learning is called classical conditioning. In this type of learning, a previously neutral stimulus called a conditioned stimulus (CS) is paired with an unconditioned stimulus (UCS) that elicits an unlearned or unconditioned response (UCR). Eventually, the CS comes to elicit a conditioned response (CR) that is identical or very similar to the UCR. Classical conditioning occurs because of the association in time of a neutral stimulus and a stimulus that already elicits the response. Contemporary research indicates that classical conditioning may play a role in resistance to disease and sexual arousal.

Operant conditioning is a form of learning in which the consequences of behavior lead to changes in the probability of its occurrence. Positive reinforcements increase the probability of a response. Two important issues involving the use of positive reinforcement are timing and consistency.

Primary reinforcers, such as food and water, are innately reinforcing; secondary reinforcers are learned. There are four different schedules of reinforcement, each resulting in different patterns of behavior. The schedules are fixed ratio, variable ratio, fixed interval, and variable interval. Shaping refers to the process of reinforcing behaviors that are progressively more similar to the target response. Negative reinforcement occurs when the reinforcing consequence is 1) the removal of a negative event, also called escape conditioning, or 2) the avoidance of a negative event, also called avoidance conditioning. Punishment is a negative consequence of a behavior that reduces the frequency of the behavior. Stimulus discrimination occurs when a response is more likely in the presence of a specific stimulus than in the presence of other stimuli. Stimulus generalization has occurred when an individual responds to similar but different stimuli.

When a learned response stops occurring because the aspect of the environment that originally caused the learning has changed, the process is called extinction. Extinction is often slowed because of spontaneous recovery and disinhibition.

Psychologists disagree about whether learning results from neural connections between specific stimuli and specific responses or whether learning is a change in cognition. Research that supports the cognitive view includes Tolman's studies of place learning and latent learning, Köhler's studies of insight learning, and Bandura's research on modeling. The ability of humans to learn from experience is not limitless; it is influenced in a number of ways by biological factors.

Superstitious behavior is an example in which operant conditioning can lead to learning the "wrong" things.

Key Terms Exercise

For each of the following exercises, match the key terms on the left with the correct definitions on the right. Page references to the text follow the terms so that you may refer to the text for any items you answer incorrectly or do not understand completely. You may check your responses immediately by referring to the answers that follow each exercise.

Classical and Operant Conditioning

_____ 1. learning (p. 142)
_____ 2. classical conditioning (p. 147)
_____ 3. operant conditioning (p. 149)
_____ 4. positive reinforcement (p. 149)
_____ 5. fixed ratio schedule (p. 151)
_____ 6. variable ratio schedule (p. 152)
_____ 7. fixed interval schedule (p. 152)
_____ 8. variable interval schedule (p. 153)

a. a schedule in which the reinforcer is given following the first response after a predetermined amount of time

b. learning in which the consequences of behavior lead to changes in the probability of its occurrence

c. a schedule in which the reinforcer is given following the first response after a variable amount of time

d. a schedule in which the reinforcer is given after a varying number of responses have been made

e. any consequence of a behavior that leads to an increase in the probability of its occurrence

f. a relatively permanent change in behavior brought about through experience

g. a schedule in which the reinforcer is given only after a specified number of responses

h. a form of learning in which a previously neutral stimulus is paired with an unconditioned stimulus to elicit a conditioned response that is very similar to the unconditioned response

ANSWERS
1. f   5. g
2. h   6. d
3. b   7. a
4. e   8. c

Operant Conditioning

_____ 1. shaping (p. 154)
_____ 2. negative reinforcement (p. 155)
_____ 3. punishment (p. 156)
_____ 4. extinction (p. 161)

a. when a learned response stops occurring due to removing the original source of learning
b. positively reinforcing behaviors that successively become more similar to desired behaviors
c. a negative consequence that leads to a reduction in the frequency of the behavior that produced it
d. reinforcement that comes from the removal or avoidance of a negative event as a consequence of a behavior

ANSWERS

1. b	3. c
2. d	4. a

Spontaneous Recovery, Disinhibition and Theoretical Interpretations of Learning

_____ 1. spontaneous recovery (p. 162)
_____ 2. disinhibition (p. 162)
_____ 3. cognitive map (p. 164)
_____ 4. modeling (p. 166)
_____ 5. superstitious behavior (p. 169)

a. a temporary increase in the strength of an extinguished response caused by an intense but unrelated stimulus
b. an inferred mental awareness of the structure of a physical space or related elements
c. learning based on observation of the behavior of another
d. a temporary increase in the strength of a conditioned response that is likely to occur during extinction after the passage of time
e. behavior that is reinforced when a reinforcing stimulus accidentally follows a response

ANSWERS

1. d	4. c
2. a	5. e
3. b	

Who Am I?

Match the psychologists on the left with their contributions to the field of psychology on the right. Page references to the text follow the names of the psychologists so that you may refer to the text for further review of these psychologists and their contributions. You may check your responses immediately by referring to the answers that follow.

_____ 1. Ivan Pavlov (p. 142)
_____ 2. John B. Watson (p. 147)
_____ 3. B. F. Skinner (p. 154)
_____ 4. Edward C. Tolman (p. 164)
_____ 5. Wolfgang Köhler (p. 166)
_____ 6. Albert Bandura (p. 166)

a. I believe that modeling is an important aspect of learning.
b. I observed insight learning in my friend Sultan.
c. I was an American behaviorist who taught little Albert to fear white rats.
d. I believed that rats were capable of place learning and latent learning and could form cognitive maps.
e. I was a Russian physiologist who believed that conditioning was a form of learning through association.
f. My name is associated with superstitious reinforcement, schedules of reinforcement, and a learning apparatus.

ANSWERS
1. e   4. d
2. c   5. b
3. f   6. a

Review At A Glance
(Answers to this section may be found on page 95)

Definition of Learning

In psychology, any relatively permanent change in behavior brought about by experience is referred to as ___(1)___.

Classical Conditioning: Learning by Association

The scientific study of classical conditioning began around the turn of the century with an accidental discovery made by a Russian physiologist named Ivan ___(2)___. While studying the role of saliva in digestion, Pavlov observed that his laboratory dogs began to ___(3)___ even before an attendant placed food in their mouths. The sight of the attendant had come to elicit the same ___(4)___ to food. Pavlov considered ___(5)___ to be the association in time of a neutral stimulus and a stimulus that elicits the response. The key phrase in classical conditioning is the "___(6)___ in _____" of the two stimuli. The ___(7)___ and the timing of the association are both important.

A stimulus that can elicit a response without any learning is called a ___(8)___, or ___(9)___ _____. An unlearned, inborn reaction to the unconditioned stimulus is referred to as a ___(10)___, or ___(11)___ _____. A stimulus that is originally unable to elicit a response but acquires the ability to do so through classical conditioning is a ___(12)___, or ___(13)___ _____. When the previously unconditioned response can be elicited by the conditioned stimulus, it is called a ___(14)___, or ___(15)___ _____.

Responding to the mere sight of a needle as if you were actually being injected is brought about by ___(16)___ _____. Classical conditioning is defined as a form of learning in which a previously ___(17)___ stimulus (CS) is followed by a stimulus (UCS) that elicits an ___(18)___ response (UCR). As a result, the ___(19)___ stimulus comes to elicit a response, the CR, that is similar to the UCR. Classical conditioning is considered a form of learning because an old behavior can be elicited by a new ___(20)___. Classical conditioning does not depend upon the ___(21)___ of the individual that is being conditioned.

The experiment conducted by ___(22)___ and Rayner on "Little Albert" demonstrated the classical conditioning of ___(23)___. A method for reversing a classically conditioned response is called ___(24)___. Research suggests that classical conditioning plays a role in the functioning of the body's ___(25)___ system. Other researchers have explored the role of classical conditioning in ___(26)___ _____.

Operant Conditioning: Learning from the Consequences of Your Behavior

People often change the frequency with which they do things based on the ___(27)___ of their actions. Learning from the consequences of behavior is called ___(28)___ _____. When the consequences of a behavior tend to increase its occurrence, this is called ___(29)___ _____. Teachers helped a girl overcome her shyness by praising her only when she played with another child. In this case, the consequence of playing with other children was positive, and the frequency of her behavior ___(30)___. To ensure that positive reinforcement was responsible for the changes in behavior, the teachers stopped reinforcing her for playing with peers in the ___(31)___ phase of the research, and then reinforced her again in the fourth phase.

In operant conditioning, the behavior that becomes more frequent is the ___(32)___ response, and the positive consequence of that response is the positive ___(33)___. There are two important issues in the use of reinforcement: 1) the greater the delay between the response and the reinforcer, the slower the learning; this is called ___(34)___ _____ _____; and (2) for learning to take place, positive reinforcement should be given ___(35)___; Reinforcers that do not have to be acquired through learning, such as food, water, and physical activity, are called ___(36)___ reinforcers. In contrast, reinforcers that are learned are ___(37)___ reinforcers.

Positive reinforcers may not always follow every response but may occur on a variety of ___(38)___. Two schedules are based on the number of ___(39)___. When a reinforcer is given only after a specified number of responses, it is called a ___(40)___ _____ schedule. If a reinforcer is given after a varying number of responses has been made, it is a ___(41)___ _____ schedule. Two additional schedules are based on the passage of ___(42)___. When a reinforcer follows the first response occurring after a predetermined amount of time, it is termed a ___(43)___ _____ schedule. When reinforcement is given to the first response after a varying amount of time, it is a ___(44)___ _____ schedule.

If the response to be reinforced is not likely to occur, a technique can be used that reinforces responses that are progressively more similar to the desired response. This is called the method of successive ___(45)___, or ___(46)___. Many animal learning laboratories use a special learning apparatus called a ___(47)___ box.

Sometimes the reinforcing consequence removes or avoids a negative event. This situation is called ___(48)___ _____. One form of negative reinforcement occurs when the behavior causes a negative event to stop; this is referred to as ___(49)___ _____. Another form of negative reinforcement occurs when the behavior causes something not to happen when it otherwise would have happened; this is called ___(50)___ _____.

If the consequence of a behavior is negative and, as a result, the frequency of a behavior decreases, the behavior has been ___(51)___. Although punishment can be an effective method of reducing the frequency of the behavior, there are several dangers in using punishment. For example, punishment is often ___(52)___ to the punisher. Punishment also may have a generalized ___(53)___ effect on the individual. Punishment is often painful and may lead the person who is punished to dislike or to act ___(54)___ toward the punisher. Punishers may find an increase in the behavior they are trying to punish, a result known as the ___(55)___ ___. Finally, even when punishment is effective in suppressing inappropriate behavior, it does not teach the individual how to act more ___(56)___ instead.

The following guidelines are suggested for the use of punishment: 1) do not use ___(57)___ punishment; 2) reinforce ___(58)___ behavior to take the place of the inappropriate behavior you are trying to eliminate; 3) do not punish people; punish specific ___(59)___ instead; 4) do not mix punishment with ___(60)___ for the same behavior; 5) once you have begun to punish, do not ___(61)___ ___.

Classical and operant conditioning differ in three primary ways: 1) classical conditioning involves an ___(62)___ between two stimuli, while operant conditioning involves an association between a response and the resulting ___(63)___; 2) classical conditioning usually involves ___(64)___ involuntary behavior, while operant conditioning usually involves more complicated ___(65)___ behaviors; and 3) in classical conditioning the individual does not have to do anything for the CS or the UCS to be presented, but in operant conditioning the reinforcement is ___(66)___ on the response.

As part of adapting to the world, most responses are more likely to occur in the presence of some stimuli than in the presence of others; this is called stimulus ___(67)___. The stimulus in which the response is reinforced is referred to as the ___(68)___ ___, while the stimulus in which the response is never reinforced is called ___(69)___. The opposite of stimulus discrimination is stimulus ___(70)___, which refers to the fact that similar stimuli tend to elicit the same response.

Extinction: Learning When to Quit

The process by which a learned response stops because of a change in the part of the environment that originally caused the learning is termed ___(71)___. In classical conditioning, a CR will be extinguished if the CS is presented repeatedly, but the ___(72)___ is no longer paired with it. In operant conditioning, extinction results from a change in the ___(73)___ of behavior. The extinction of operantly conditioned behavior is affected by the reinforcement schedule and the type of reinforcement, according to the ___(74)___ ___ effect. Responses learned through ___(75)___ ___ are the most difficult responses to extinguish. Avoidance responses can be extinguished by using ___(76)___ ___.

Extinction often proceeds irregularly if some intense but unrelated stimulus occurs, the extinguished response may temporarily return; this is termed ___(77)___.

Theoretical Interpretations of Learning

One view of learning suggests that during the learning process ___(78)___ connections are made between specific stimuli and specific responses. Another view holds that learning involves changes in ___(79)___. Edward C. Tolman concluded that laboratory rats who chose to take a shortcut to reach a goal had actually learned a ___(80)___ of the location of the goal. In another experiment, Tolman concluded that a group of unreinforced rats had learned as much about the location of a goal as a reinforced group. This type of unreinforced learning is called ___(81)___.

Wolfgang Köhler provided additional evidence for the cognitive view with his research on chimpanzees. When presented with a problem, the chimps would not reach a solution gradually; rather, they developed a sudden cognitive change called ___(82)___. Albert Bandura has demonstrated the importance of learning by observation, referred to as ___(83)___. We are more likely to imitate a model whose behavior we see reinforced; this is called ___(84)___ _____. On the other hand, we are less likely to imitate a model whose behavior we see punished; this is termed ___(85)___ _____.

Biological Factors in Learning

Learning is influenced in a number of ways by ___(86)___ factors. Apparently, people are biologically prepared to learn some kinds of ___(87)___ more readily than others. Also, people seem to be highly prepared to learn to avoid certain kinds of foods; this is called ___(88)___ _____ _____.

Application of Psychology: Learning the Wrong Things

Skinner has suggested that ___(89)___ are learned through flukes in positive reinforcement.

Concept Checks

Fill in the missing components of the following concept boxes. The correct answers are located in the "Answers" section at the end of the chapter.

Classical conditioning

Term	Definition	Example from Pavlov's experiment
	stimulus that can elicit the response without any learning	meat powder
unconditioned response (UCR)		salivation
conditioned stimulus (CS)	a stimulus that eventually can elicit responses as a result of being paired with an unconditioned stimulus	
	a response similar or identical to the UCR that is elicited by a conditioned stimulus	salivation (in response to the CS)

Operant conditioning

Term	Clue	Examples
	innately reinforcing	food, water
	reinforcement learned through classical conditioning	school grades, money
	reinforcers given after a specified number of responses	wages earned by "piece" work
	reinforcers given after a varying number of responses	gambling, sales commissions
	reinforcers given after a specified period of time	visits by members of Congress to their constituents
	reinforcers given after a varying amount of time	fishing
	successive approximations	learning motor skills, cleaning up bedrooms, and so on
	removal or avoidance of a negative event	causing a negative event to stop or causing something negative not to occur

Extending the Chapter: Psychology, Societal Issues, and Human Diversity

These questions may be assigned to you. Whether or not they are assigned, they are designed to be challenging questions to encourage you to think independently about the material in the chapter. Many of the questions have no right or wrong answers.

I. From the *Application of Psychology* section

1. What examples of superstitious behavior have you personally observed?

II. Psychology, Societal Issues, and Human Diversity

1. Culture exerts a tremendous impact on childrearing practices. Discuss attitudes about punishment in your culture. How do these ideas compare with the suggestions found in the text?

2. How might a student develop a variety of classically and operantly conditioned responses to college classes?

3. If you have a pet (or know someone who does), in what ways have you conditioned your pet's behavior? How has your pet conditioned *your* behavior?

4. Research topic: Much research has been conducted on where in the brain memory is stored, processed, retrieved, and so on. Find and evaluate an article on this topic.

Practice Quiz

The practice quiz consists of three sections: 1) Short answer questions, 2) Multiple choice questions, and 3) True-False questions. At the end of the chapter you will find suggested answers to the short answer questions, answers and explanation for the multiple choice questions, and answers to the true-false questions.

Short Answer Questions

1. List three ways in which classical and operant conditioning differ.

_____

_____

2. Distinguish among place learning, latent learning, and insight learning.

_____

_____

3. Define modeling and discuss its importance in human learning.

_____

_____

Multiple Choice Questions

1. Which of the following is/are part of the definition of learning?
   a. change in behavior
   b. relatively permanent
   c. brought about by experience
   d. all of the above
   LO 1

2. Pavlov's initial interest in classical conditioning was stimulated when he observed his research dogs salivating at the sight of
   a. food.
   b. the attendants.
   c. saliva.
   d. the food dish.
   LO 2

3. In classical conditioning, an unlearned, inborn reaction to an unconditioned stimulus is a(n)
   a. unconditioned stimulus.
   b. conditioned stimulus.
   c. unconditioned response.
   d. conditioned response.
   LO 3

4. In Pavlov's classic experiment, meat powder was the
   a. unconditioned stimulus.
   b. unconditioned response.
   c. conditioned stimulus.
   d. conditioned response.
   LO 3

5. Classical conditioning apparently plays a role in the development of
   a. resistance to disease.
   b. allergic reactions.
   c. sexual arousal.
   d. all of the above.
   LO 4

6. Irrational fears that are thought to be caused by classical conditioning are called
   a. psychosomatic illnesses.
   b. avoidance behaviors.
   c. phobias.
   d. stimulus discrimination.
   LO 4

7. Learning that results from the consequences of behaviors is called
   a. extinguished conditioning.
   b. operant conditioning.
   c. classical conditioning.
   d. positive conditioning.
   LO 5

8. Which of the following BEST describes the law of effect?
   a. A conditioned stimulus will produce a conditioned response.
   b. The consequence of a response determines whether the response will be repeated.
   c. Reinforcers should be given immediately after a response.
   d. Behaviors will be elicited if the conditioned response is strong.
   LO 5

9. If positive reinforcement is not given within a short time following the response, learning will proceed slowly. This phenomenon is called
   a. delay of reinforcement.
   b. extinction.
   c. conditioned response.
   d. consistency.
   LO 6

10. Reinforcers that are innately reinforcing, such as food, water, and warmth are called
    a. primary reinforcers.
    b. secondary reinforcers.
    c. extinguished reinforcers.
    d. superstitious reinforcers.
    LO 7

11. If a child is rewarded for appropriate behavior every 15 minutes, what type of schedule is being used?
    a. fixed ratio
    b. variable ratio
    c. fixed interval
    d. variable interval
    LO 8

12. Salespeople who are paid exclusively by commission are reinforced on which type of schedule?
    a. fixed ratio
    b. fixed interval
    c. variable ratio
    d. variable interval
    LO 8

13. If you wanted to teach a chicken to "play" the piano, you should
    a. wait for a musically inclined chicken to show up.
    b. extinguish piano-playing behavior.
    c. use shaping.
    d. use negative reinforcement.
    LO 9

14. Behavior that is reinforced because it causes a negative event to stop is called
    a. shaping.
    b. punishment.
    c. escape conditioning.
    d. avoidance conditioning.
    LO 10

15. Both escape conditioning and avoidance conditioning are forms of
    a. superstitious behavior.
    b. positive reinforcement.
    c. negative reinforcement.
    d. secondary reinforcement.
    LO 9

16. Which of the following is suggested as a guideline for the use of punishment?
    a. Do not use physical punishment.
    b. Do not give punishment mixed with rewards.
    c. Make it clear to the individual which behavior is being punished.
    d. All of the above.
    LO 10

17. If the consequence of a behavior is negative and the frequency of that behavior decreases, the behavior has been
    a. positively reinforced.
    b. negatively reinforced.
    c. disinhibited.
    d. punished.
    LO 11

18. Which of the following is correct?
    a. Classical conditioning usually involves reflexive behavior, while operant conditioning usually involves more complicated, spontaneous behavior.
    b. Classical conditioning usually involves more complicated, spontaneous behavior, while operant conditioning involves reflexive behavior.
    c. In classical conditioning, the reinforcement is contingent on the behavior of the learner.
    d. In operant conditioning the UCS and CS occur independently of the learner's behavior.
    LO 12

19. John loves to receive mail. Over the years, he has learned to tell the difference between the sound of the mail truck and the other cars and trucks that pass his house. What process is at work here?
    a. stimulus discrimination
    b. stimulus generalization
    c. extinction
    d. negative reinforcement
    LO 13

20. After Little Albert was conditioned to fear a white rat, he also displayed fear responses to a white rabbit and a white coat. This is an example of
    a. stimulus generalization.
    b. stimulus discrimination.
    c. variable interval reinforcement.
    d. superstitious behavior.
    LO 13

21. When Sandy's disruptive classroom behavior stops because the teacher and other students no longer pay attention to the behavior, the process is called
    a. stimulus discrimination.
    b. extinction.
    c. stimulus generalization.
    d. punishment.
    LO 14

22. Behaviors that have been reinforced on a variable schedule are more difficult to extinguish than those that have been continuously reinforced. This is known as
    a. the partial reinforcement effect.
    b. an extinction schedule.
    c. shaping.
    d. avoidance conditioning.
    LO 14

23. The most difficult responses of all to extinguish are those learned through
    a. positive reinforcement.
    b. variable schedules.
    c. escape conditioning.
    d. avoidance conditioning.
    LO 14

24. Behaviors that appear to be extinguished may return when some dramatic, but unrelated, stimulus event occurs. This is called
    a. spontaneous recovery.
    b. stimulus generalization.
    c. stimulus discrimination.
    d. external disinhibition.
    LO 15

25. What do spontaneous recovery and disinhibition have in common?
    a. The UCS becomes neutral.
    b. The UCR is diminished.
    c. An extinguished response returns.
    d. A response is generalized.
    LO 15

26. The neural-connection view of learning is supported by which of the following?
    a. place learning
    b. latent learning
    c. insight learning
    d. none of the above
    LO 16

27. Köhler's research with Sultan supports which theoretical view of learning?
    a. insight learning
    b. latent learning
    c. place learning
    d. modeling
    LO 17

28. Those who are concerned about the effects that televised aggression has on children are likely to focus on
    a. insight learning.
    b. latent learning.
    c. place learning.
    d. modeling.
    LO 18

29. Modeling demonstrates the importance of _____ in learning.
    a. secondary reinforcers
    b. biological factors
    c. preparedness
    d. cognition
    LO 18

30. Learned taste aversion is a form of
    a. operant conditioning.
    b. classical conditioning.
    c. insight learning.
    d. none of the above.
    LO 19

31. The fact that fish cannot fly and owls cannot learn to swim is an indication of
    a. lack of adequate reinforcement.
    b. their lack of experience.
    c. the laziness of these creatures.
    d. the effects of biological limits.
    LO 19

32. Occasionally, behavior is reinforced when the reinforcing stimulus accidentally follows the response. This is referred to as
    a. classical conditioning.
    b. a primary reinforcer.
    c. extinction.
    d. superstitious behavior.
    LO 20

True-False Questions

_____1 In classical conditioning, a stimulus that comes to elicit responses by being paired with an unconditioned stimulus is called a conditioned stimulus.

_____2. The infamous "Little Albert" experiment demonstrated the power of operant conditioning.

_____3. Food and water are examples of secondary reinforcement.

_____4. Gambling is a behavior that is typically rewarded on a fixed schedule.

_____5. Another term for shaping is "the method of successive approximations."

_____6. Escape conditioning and avoidance conditioning are two types of negative reinforcement.

_____7. In classical conditioning, the reinforcing consequence is contingent upon the occurrence of the response.

_____8. Stimulus discrimination applies more to laboratory animals than to humans.

_____9. The ability to form cognitive maps is consistent with the cognitive rather than the connectionist point of view.

_____10. According to Bandura and others, modeling is a powerful type of learning.

ANSWER SECTION
Concept Check

Classical conditioning

Term	Definition	Example from Pavlov's experiment
unconditioned stimulus (UCS)	stimulus that can elicit the response without any learning	meat powder
unconditioned response (UCR)	an unlearned, inborn reaction to an unconditioned stimulus	salivation
conditioned stimulus (CS)	a stimulus that eventually can elicit responses as a result of being paired with an unconditioned stimulus	metronome
conditioned response	a response similar or identical to the UCR that is elicited by a conditioned stimulus	salivation (in response to the CS)

Operant conditioning

Term	Clue	Examples
primary reinforcer	innately reinforcing	food, water
secondary reinforcer	reinforcement learned through classical conditioning	school grades, money
fixed ratio schedule	reinforcers given after a specified number of responses	wages earned by "piece" work
variable ratio schedule	reinforcers given after a varying number of responses	gambling, sales commissions
fixed interval schedule	reinforcers given after a specified period of time	visits by members of Congress to their constituents
variable interval schedule	reinforcers given after a varying amount of time	fishing
shaping	successive approximations	learning motor skills, cleaning up bedrooms, and so on
negative reinforcement	removal or avoidance of a negative event	causing a negative event to stop or causing something negative not to occur

Answers to Review At A Glance

1. learning	31. reversal	61. back out
2. Pavlov	32. operant	62. association
3. salivate	33. reinforcer	63. stimuli
4. reflexive response	34. delay of reinforcement	64. reflexive
5. classical conditioning	35. consistently	65. voluntary
6. association/time	36. primary	66. contingent
7. frequency	37. secondary	67. discrimination
8. UCS	38. schedules	68. discriminative stimulus
9. unconditioned stimulus	39. responses	69. S^{delta}
10. UCR	40. fixed ratio	70. generalization
11. unconditioned response	41. variable ratio	71. extinction
12. CS	42. time	72. UCS
13. conditioned stimulus	43. fixed interval	73. consequences
14. CR	44. variable interval	74. partial reinforcement
15. conditioned response	45. approximations	75. avoidance learning
16. classical conditioning	46. shaping	76. spontaneous recovery
17. neutral	47. Skinner	77. disinhibition
18. unlearned	48. negative reinforcement	78. neural
19. conditioned	49. escape conditioning	79. cognition
20. stimulus	50. avoidance conditioning	80. cognitive map
21. behavior	51. punished	81. latent learning
22. Watson	52. reinforcing	82. insight
23. fear	53. inhibiting	83. modeling
24. counterconditioning	54. aggressively	84. vicarious reinforcement
25. immune	55. criticism trap	85. vicarious punishment
26. sexual arousal	56. appropriately	86. biological
27. consequences	57. physical	87. fears
28. operant conditioning	58. appropriate	88. learned taste aversion
29. positive reinforcement	59. behaviors	89. superstitions
30. increased	60. rewards	

Sample Answers to Short Answer Questions

1. List three ways in which classical and operant conditioning differ.

Three differences are: 1) classical conditioning involves an association between two stimuli, whereas operant conditioning involves an association between a response and the consequence that follows the response; 2) classical conditioning involves reflexive behaviors, whereas operant conditioning usually involves more complicated, voluntary behaviors; and 3) in classical conditioning, the individual doesn't actually have to do anything for the CS or UCS to be presented, whereas in operant conditioning, the reinforcement occurs only if the learner actually makes a response.

2. Distinguish among place learning, latent learning, and insight learning.

Place learning, demonstrated by Tolman's research, occurs as learners form a cognitive map, and supports the cognitive view of learning. Latent learning, also demonstrated by Tolman, is learning that occurs in the absence of any apparent reinforcement, and also supports the cognitive view of learning. Insight learning, demonstrated by Köhler's research, refers to a sudden cognitive change that helps a learner to solve a problem. Insight learning is additional support for the cognitive view of learning.

3. Define modeling and discuss its importance in human learning.

Modeling is learning based on observation of others. Its significance is that we don't have to directly experience everything in the world in order to become conditioned. For example, a healthy respect of bees can be learned by watching another person receive a bee sting.

Multiple Choice Answers

1. The answer is *d*. Note that the definition of learning is restricted to *relatively* permanent, as opposed to temporary, changes in behavior.
2. The answer is *b*. The dogs had learned to associate the attendants with the food—the stimulus of the attendant came to elicit the response of salivation.
3. The answer is *c*. In the first phase of classical conditioning, the unconditioned stimulus produces an unconditioned response.
4. The answer is *a*. Since the meat powder is a stimulus that brought about a response (salivation) without any prior conditioning, it is called an unconditioned stimulus.
5. The answer is *d*. Assuming you answered this question correctly, before you proceed, be sure that you understand *how* these various responses are classically conditioned.
6. The answer is *c*. Some psychologists believe that phobias care learned when a neutral stimulus is paired with a fear-inducing stimulus.
7. The answer is *b*. The term *operant* is derived from the word *operate*. That is, when our behavior operates on the world, it produces consequences for us. These consequences determine whether or not we will continue the behavior.
8. The answer is *b*. The law of effect, postulated by Thorndike, became the basis for operant conditioning.
9. The answer is *a*. Another important issue in the use of positive reinforcement is the need to be consistent in the delivery of the positive reinforcement.
10. The answer is *a*. Secondary reinforcers, on the other hand, are learned. They take on their reinforcing value through classical conditioning. As an example, consider the process by which money became a powerful reinforcer for you.
11. The answer is *c*. If the reward is based on the passage of a fixed amount of time it is a fixed interval schedule.
12. The answer is *c*. Variable versus fixed refers to the predictability of the reinforcer. That is, variable reinforcers reward on an unpredictable schedule. Ratio refers to the number of behaviors, while interval refers to the amount of time. Thus, a variable ratio implies that the rewards are unpredictable and based on the number of behaviors. A fixed interval schedule, on the other hand, produces a predictable reinforcer after a set amount of time.
13. The answer is *c*. Shaping is a technique that can produce complex behavior by reinforcing behaviors that are successively more similar to the desired behavior. Shaping is also called the method of successive approximations.
14. The answer is *c*. Both escape conditioning and avoidance conditioning are examples of negative reinforcement. Avoidance conditioning is reinforcing because it prevents something negative from happening.
15. The answer is *c*. Negative reinforcement occurs when the reinforcing consequence removes or avoids a negative event.
16. The answer is *d*. In addition to the guidelines mentioned in the question, the text discusses dangers in the use of punishment. These include the fact that the punishment is often reinforcing to the punisher, the generalized inhibiting effect on the individual receiving the punishment, and the criticism trap.
17. The answer is *d*. Punishment and negative reinforcement are often confused. Be sure that you understand the differences between them.
18. The answer is *a*. This is an important question, since it requires you to understand the fundamentals of both classical and operant conditioning. If the answer made sense to you, congratulations! If you struggled with the question, you might wish to review the sections on classical and operant conditioning. Many students find that they need to spend some extra time with this material.
19. The answer is *a*. While stimulus discrimination elicits different responses to different stimuli (at a traffic signal we "go" on green and "stop" on red), stimulus generalization elicits the same response to similar stimuli (we "go" on all green lights regardless of where they are located).

20. The answer is *a*. Little Albert's fear response had generalized to other similar objects. Had he *not* reacted fearfully to these stimuli, he would have demonstrated discrimination.

21. The answer is *b*. Extinction refers to the process of unlearning a learned response due to the removal of the original source of learning. In this instance, Sandy's behavior was conditioned and maintained by the teacher and the other members of the class. When they began to ignore the behavior, they effectively removed the original source of learning.

22. The answer is *a*. Think of examples of specific behaviors that have been partially reinforced and that are difficult to extinguish.

23. The answer is *d*. The person making the response never knows whether or not the stimulus has been removed so the individual persists in making the response.

24. The answer is *d*. In contrast to external disinhibition, spontaneous recovery is likely to occur during extinction and doesn't require the occurrence of a dramatic event. When you suddenly spot your former "significant other" in the mall (the one you thought you were "over") and experience a conditioned emotional response, you have just experienced spontaneous recovery.

25. The answer is *c*. Both spontaneous recovery and disinhibition remind us that the road to extinction is not always smooth.

26. The answer is *d*. Place learning, latent learning, and insight learning are all examples of the cognitive approach to learning.

27. The answer is *a*. Köhler's research suggested that Sultan learned because of a cognitive change—new insight into the problems he was presented.

28. The answer is *d*. Modeling refers to learning based on the observation of another's behavior. In this case, the actors on television may be modeling extremely aggressive behavior.

29. The answer is *d*. Modeling, or learning by observing others, can be an extremely efficient way to learn. Modeling underscores the importance of cognitive factors in learning.

30. The answer is *b*. Learned taste aversion occurs when we develop a negative reaction to a particular taste because it has been associated with nausea or illness.

31. The answer is *d*. Biological limits also constrain human learning.

32. The answer is *d*. Superstitious behavior is often described as being "resistant to extinction." Can you explain why this is so?

Answers to True-False Questions

1. T	6. T
2. F	7. F
3. F	8. F
4. F	9. T
5. T	10. T

Chapter **6**   **Memory**

Learning Objectives

1.   Identify the operations involved in the information-processing view of memory and describe the three-stage theory of memory. (p. 174)

2.   Know the characteristics of the sensory register. (p. 174)

3.   Define short-term memory and understand how its life span and capacity can be influenced. (p. 175)

4.   Discuss the ways in which long-term memory differs from short-term memory. (p. 177)

5.   Describe the three kinds of long-term memory: procedural, episodic, and semantic. (p. 178)

6.   Understand how information is organized in long-term memory. (p. 178)

7.   Identify the serial position effect and the tip-of-the-tongue phenomenon.. (p. 180)

8.   Distinguish between deep and shallow processing in the levels of processing model and understand the role of elaboration. (p. 180)

9.   Distinguish among the four major theories of forgetting: decay theory, interference theory, schema theory, and motivated forgetting. (p. 183)

10.   Recognize and understand synaptic theories of memory. (p. 189)

11. Distinguish between anterograde amnesia and retrograde amnesia. (p. 191)

12. (From the *Application of Psychology* section) Discuss the results of research relating eyewitness testimony and memory. (p. 194)

Chapter Overview

The stage theory of memory states that human memory consists of three stages: 1) the sensory register, which holds an exact image of each sensory experience for a very brief interval until it can be fully processed; 2) short-term memory, which holds information for approximately 30 seconds (information will fade from short-term memory unless the material is rehearsed; the capacity of short-term memory is 7 ± 2 items, but this can be increased by organizing the material into larger chunks); and 3) long-term memory, which indexes information and stores it primarily in terms of its meaning.

The three kinds of long-term memory are procedural, episodic, and semantic. Procedural memory is memory for skills and other procedures. Episodic memory refers to memory for specific experiences that can be defined in terms of time and space, while semantic memory refers to memory for meaning.

The organization of memory in LTM has been characterized as an associative network. One network model is called the spreading activation model. Researchers have investigated the serial position effect and the tip-of-the-tongue phenomenon.

An alternative to the stage model is the levels of processing model, which views the differences between short-term and long-term memory in terms of degree rather than separate stages.

Psychologists have identified four ways in which forgetting occurs: 1) decay theory, which states that forgetting occurs simply because time passes; 2) interference theory, which states that forgetting occurs because other memories interfere with retrieval (Interference may occur from memories that were formed by prior learning, called proactive interference, or from memories that were formed by later learning, called retroactive interference.); 3) schema theory, which holds that memory changes over time to become more consistent with our beliefs, knowledge and expectations; and 4) repression, the process by which memories that are upsetting or threatening may be forgotten.

The biological basis of memory is called the memory trace or engram. A theory that has been proposed to explain the biological nature of memory is synaptic facilitation, which views learning as a change in the synapses.

Amnesia is a major memory disorder. Anterograde amnesia, caused by damage in the hippocampus, is an inability to store and/or retrieve new information. Retrograde amnesia is the inability to retrieve old, long-term memories.

Research suggests that eyewitness testimony and recall may be inaccurate because of biased questioning or the characteristics of the eyewitnesses.

Key Terms Exercise

For each of the following exercises, match the key terms on the left with the correct definitions on the right. Page references to the text follow the terms so that you may refer to the text for any items you answer incorrectly or do not understand completely. You may check your responses immediately by referring to the answers that follow each exercise.

Memory (I)

_____ 1. encode (p. 174)
_____ 2. stage theory of memory (p. 174)
_____ 3. sensory register (p. 174)
_____ 4. short-term memory (STM) (p. 175)
_____ 5. rehearsal (p. 175)
_____ 6. long term memory (p. 177)

a. the first stage of memory that briefly holds exact images until they can be processed
b. the second stage of memory that can store five to nine bits of information
c. mental repetition in order to retain information in short-term memory
d. a storehouse for information that must be kept for long periods of time
e. a theory of memory based on the idea that we store information in three separate but linked memories
f. to represent information in some form in the memory system

ANSWERS
1. f   4. b
2. e   5. c
3. a   6. d

Memory (II)

_____ 1. procedural memory (p. 178)
_____ 2. semantic memory (p. 178)
_____ 3. episodic memory (p. 178)
_____ 4. serial position effect (p. 180)
_____ 5. levels of processing model (p. 180)

a. memory for experiences that can be defined in terms of space and time
b. memory for meaning without reference to time and place of learning
c. memory for skills and other procedures
d. immediate recall of a list of items is better for items at the beginning and end of the list
e. states the distinction between short-term and long-term memory is a matter of degree

ANSWERS
1. c   4. d
2. b   5. e
3. a

Forgetting/Biological Basis of Memory

_____ 1. decay theory (p. 184)
_____ 2. interference theory (p. 184)
_____ 3. schema theory (p. 185)
_____ 4. repression (p. 187)
_____ 5. engram (p. 189)
_____ 6. synaptic facilitation (p. 189)
_____ 7. anterograde amnesia (p. 191)
_____ 8. retrograde amnesia (p. 192)

a.   a memory trace that is the biological basis of memory
b.   the theory that forgetting occurs when similar memories interfere with storing and retrieving information
c.   neural activity causes structural changes in the synapses which lead to more efficient learning and memory
d.   Freud's theory that forgetting occurs because the conscious mind pushes unpleasant information into the unconscious
e.   the theory that forgetting occurs as the memory trace fades over time
f.   a memory disorder characterized by the inability to store new information in memory
g.   memory disorder characterized by an inability to retrieve old, long-term memories
h.   information stored in LTM sometimes changes over time to become consistent with our beliefs, knowledge and expectations

ANSWERS

1. e	5. a
2. b	6. c
3. h	7. f
4. d	8. g

Review At A Glance
(Answers to this section are found on page 111)

Three Stages of Memory: An Information-Processing View

Most recent theories of memory borrow a concept used in computer design called ___(1)_____. Raw sensory information is represented, or ___(2)___, in some form in the memory system. Selected information is transferred to a more permanent memory storage by ___(3)___ mechanisms. As information is needed, it is ___(4)___ from memory, although some is lost or becomes irretrievable.

The stage theory assumes that we have a ___(5)___-_____ memory. The first of these stages is the ___(6)_____, which holds images until they can be processed. Visual information is retained for about ___(7)___ second(s), while auditory information can be retained as an echo for as long as ___(8)___ seconds.

The second stage of memory, called ___(9)___-_____ memory, stores information for less than ___(10)_____ unless it is renewed by mental repetition, also called ___(11)___. Although information in short-term memory can be stored in many forms, humans seem to prefer transforming information into sounds or ___(12)_____. The capacity of short-term memory, as described by George Miller, is ___(13)___ bits of information. Short-term memory also serves as our ___(14)___ memory. Research suggests that it takes us about ___(15)___ of a second to examine each item in our short-term memory. Miller calls the units of memory ___(16)___. The capacity of short-term memory can be expanded by using techniques called ___(17)_____.

Information is stored for long periods of time in ___(18)___-_____ memory. Long-term memory differs from short-term memory in several important ways. Unlike short-term memory, where information can be scanned, the vast

amount of information in long-term memory is organized by being ___(19)___, and information is retrieved by using
___(20)___. In contrast to short-term memory, which stores information in terms of physical qualities, information in long-term memory is primarily stored in terms of its meaning, also referred to as ___(21)___. Many psychologists believe that information in long-term memory is not just durable, but it is actually ___(22)___. Finally, while STM is primarily stored in the ___(23)___ lobes of the cerebral cortex, information in LTM is first integrated in the ___(24)___ and then permanently stored in the language and perception areas of the ___(25)___.

There appears to be different types of long-term memory. Memory for skills, such as how to ride a bicycle, is called ___(26)___ memory. Memory associated with meaning is called ___(27)___ memory. Information about specific experiences is stored in ___(28)___ memory. Some psychologists include semantic memory and episodic memory under the heading ___(29)___ memory.

Organization in LTM helps facilitate the retrieval of information from the vast amount stored in the LTM. The organization of memory has been characterized as an ___(30)___ network. An influential network model is called the ___(31)___ model.

The superior recall for items at the beginning and end of a serial list is called the ___(32)___ effect. Research on the tip-of-the-tongue phenomenon suggests we are able to recall about ___(33)___ the items within a minute or so.

An alternative approach to the stage model, called the ___(34)___ model, suggests that there is only one memory store beyond the sensory register. This model suggests that information will be kept only briefly if it is processed at a ___(35)___ level, but will be kept longer if processed at a ___(36)___ level. Information can be deeply processed by creating more associations between the new memory and existing memories, a technique called ___(37)___. Research suggests that a good way to promote elaboration is to relate the information to ___(38)___.

Forgetting and Why it Occurs

Forgetting occurs because memories that are not used fade over time, according to the ___(39)___ theory. Although it appears that the passage of time is a cause of forgetting in the sensory register and ___(40)___-___ memory, the decay theory does not appear to explain forgetting in ___(41)___-___ memory.

Forgetting in long-term memory occurs because other memories interfere with the retrieval of information, according to the ___(42)___ theory. Interference is most likely to occur when memories are ___(43)___. Interference due to prior learning is ___(44)___ interference, while interference created by later learning is ___(45)___ interference.

A theory that information stored in LTM changes over time to become more consistent with our beliefs, knowledge and expectations is called ___(46)___ theory. Research suggests distortions occur during the process of ___(47)___. Current versions of schema theory are based on the distinction between ___(48)___ and semantic memory.

Sigmund Freud's explanation for forgetting, that the conscious mind pushes unpleasant information into unconsciousness, is called ___(49)___. More recent research indicates that ___(50)___ emotional arousal can actually lead to better recall than neutral experiences. Our memories for intensely negative events, however, tend to be disorganized and ___(51)___. Vivid memories for emotional events, called ___(52)___ memories, also tend to be distorted.

Biological Basis of Memory: The Search for the Engram

The physical change in the nervous system that occurs when we learn something has been referred to as the memory trace or ___(53)___. Hebb's theory, synaptic facilitation, suggests that learning is due to a physical change at the ___(54)___. A classical conditioning study conducted on ___(55)___ _____ has provided support for Hebb's theory. More recent research suggests changes in synapses are based on changes in their proteins for ___(56)___, but not for ___(57)___. Research indicates that events that create negative emotional arousal tend to stimulate the region of the brain called the ___(58)___, which helps to improve ___(59)___. Negative emotional arousal also inhibits the ___(60)___. Inhibition of the hippocampus appears to result in ___(61)___ for emotionally charged memories.

An inability to consciously retrieve new information from long-term memory is found in the memory disorder called ___(62)___ _____. Anterograde amnesia usually does not affect the ability to acquire ___(63)___ memories, but seems to destroy some ___(64)___ memories. Researchers believe that this condition is caused by damage in the forebrain structure called the ___(65)___. Individuals who are unable to retrieve old, long-term memories are experiencing ___(66)___ _____. Both retrograde and anterograde amnesia are experienced by individuals with ___(67)___ _____. This disorder is caused by the prolonged loss of the vitamin ___(68)___ from the diet of chronic alcoholics. Individuals with Korsakoff's syndrome often engage in ___(69)___.

Application of Psychology: Eyewitness Testimony and Memory

Research suggests that eyewitness testimony and recall may be inaccurate due to biased ___(70)___. Eyewitnesses also are inaccurate when the "look but do not ___(71)___." Allport's research has confirmed that stereotypes and ___(72)___ affect the accuracy of eyewitness testimony. With regard to repressed memories of sexual and physical abuse in childhood, a number of studies indicate that some of these memories may be ___(73)___.

Concept Checks

Fill in the missing components of the following concept boxes. The correct answers are located in the "Answers" section at the end of the chapter.

Stages of memory

Concept	Characteristics
	first stage of memory; holds images until they can be processed
short-term memory	
	information is indexed and stored primarily in terms of meaning; retrieval assisted by the use of cues
procedural memory	
	memory associated with meaning, such as word knowledge
episodic memory	

Theories of Forgetting

Theory of forgetting	Explanation
	memories that are not used fade over time
Interference theory	
Schema theory	
	Painful memories are pushed into the unconscious

Extending the Chapter: Psychology, Societal Issues, and Diversity

These questions may be assigned to you. Whether or not they are assigned, they are designed to be challenging questions to encourage you to think independently about the material in the chapter. Many of the questions have no right or wrong answers.

I.   From the *Applications of Psychology* section

1. Discuss the memory-related factors leading to inaccurate eyewitness testimony.

2. What have researchers learned about the relationship between stereotypes and eyewitness testimony?

3. Describe the results of research on the recall of repressed memories of sexual and physical abuse.

4. What suggestions would you make to improve the accuracy of eyewitness testimony?

II. Psychology, Societal Issues, and Diversity

1. If you were trying to help another student improve her study skills, what ideas from this chapter would you suggest?

2. If memory-enhancing and memory-blocking drugs are found to be effective in the future, how should these be regulated?

3. (From the *Human Diversity* section of the text) In what ways does culture influence memory? (Hint: Consider the methods used to memorize as well as the content of memory.)

Practice Quiz

The practice quiz consists of three sections: 1) Short answer questions, 2) Multiple choice questions, and 3) True-False questions. At the end of the chapter you will find suggested answers to the short answer questions, answers and explanation for the multiple choice questions, and answers to the true-false questions.

Short Answer Questions

1. Describe the three-stage theory of memory.

_____

_____

2. What is the serial position effect?

_____

_____

3. Explain the levels of processing model of memory.

_____

_____

Multiple Choice Questions

1. Which of the following is *not* a stage in the information-processing model of memory?
   a. short-term memory
   b. long-term memory
   c. episodic memory
   d. sensory register
   LO 1

2. According to the information-processing model, attention serves as a
   a. temporary memory buffer.
   b. control mechanism.
   c. retrieval mechanism.
   d. sensory register.
   LO 1

3. The sensory register has all of the following characteristics *except*
   a. Visual information lasts about a quarter of a second.
   b. It holds an exact image of each sensory experience.
   c. Auditory information lasts about 4 seconds.
   d. The capacity is 7 ± 2 bits of information.
   LO 2

4. Which of the following BEST describes the memory capacity of the sensory register?
   a. Capacity is limited on the average to 7 chunks of information.
   b. There is the potential for partial recall of everything ever experienced in episodic memory.
   c. It is designed to hold an exact image of the sensory experience.
   d. It depends on the effort put into the process of attention.
   LO 2

5. Suppose that you call the information operator to find a friend's phone number. When you dial your friend's number, you get a busy signal. Later, when you start to dial the number again, you realize you have forgotten it. This experience probably occurred because the phone number was only temporarily stored in your
   a. short-term memory.
   b. long-term memory.
   c. sensory register.
   d. none of the above.
   LO 3

6. One technique to help overcome the limited capacity of STM is called
   a. chunking.
   b. rehearsal.
   c. working memory.
   d. semantic codes.
   LO 3

7. Working memory is a special function of
   a. the sensory register.
   b. short-term memory.
   c. long-term memory.
   d. any of the above.
   LO 3

8. The phone number discussed in question #5 probably could have been remembered for a longer period if you had practiced
   a. chunking.
   b. repression.
   c. rehearsal.
   d. *a and c.*
   LO 3

9. Each of the following is true regarding differences between STM and LTM *except*
   a. information in LTM is indexed.
   b. information in STM is stored in terms of physical qualities.
   c. information in LTM may be permanent.
   d. information in LTM s primarily stored in the frontal lobes of the cortex.
   LO 4

10. Although short-term memory stores information in terms of physical qualities, long-term memory stores information in terms of
    a. acoustic codes.
    b. semantic codes.
    c. attitudes.
    d. all of the above.
    LO 4

11. You remember some specific football plays from the first half of last week's game; this is
    a. episodic memory.
    b. procedural memory.
    c. semantic memory.
    d. all of the above.
    LO 5

12. What do episodic and semantic memories have in common?
    a. They are forms of working memory.
    b. They are easily described in words.
    c. They can easily be retrieved.
    d. They are forms of procedural memory.
    LO 5

13. Memories of how to ride a bicycle or how to ski are examples of
    a. semantic memory.
    b. procedural memory.
    c. declarative memory.
    d. episodic memory.
    LO 5

14. Which characteristic of long-term memory facilitates the retrieval of information?
    a. unlimited capacity
    b. the organization of material
    c. the chunking of information
    d. the ability of long-term memory to store procedural information
    LO 6

15. Which concept states that memories are linked together through experience?
    a. semantic memory
    b. reconstructive memory
    c. associative network
    d. serial forgetting
    LO 6

16. When you get to the grocery store, you realize you left your shopping list at home. According to the serial position effect, the items on the list you are most likely recall are
    a. at the beginning of the list.
    b. in the middle of the list.
    c. at the end of the list.
    d. *a* and *c*
    LO 7

17. The "tip-of-the-tongue phenomenon appears to be caused by a problem in
    a. retrieval.
    b. engrams.
    c. storage.
    d. repression.
    LO 7

18. The process of reading material and relating it to previous learning or to your own life is called
    a. rehearsal.
    b. consolidation.
    c. elaboration.
    d. chunking.
    LO 8

19. The levels of processing model states that deep processing involves greater _____ than shallow processing.
    a. rehearsal
    b. engrams
    c. consolidation
    d. elaboration
    LO 8

20. Which theory suggests that forgetting is caused by a fading memory trace?
    a. schema theory
    b. repression
    c. decay theory
    d. interference theory
    LO 9

21. The expression "You can't teach an old dog new tricks" would support which theory of forgetting"?
    a. repression
    b. retroactive interference
    c. proactive interference
    d. pass interference
    LO 9

22. After having the same phone number for years, you move and get a different, but similar, phone number. Retroactive interference would be demonstrated by your difficulty in remembering
    a. the new phone number.
    b. the old phone number.
    c. either phone number.
    d. your new address.
    LO 9

23. Research on memories that become distorted to fit our schema indicates that this process occurs during
    a. the formation of memories.
    b. the process of retrieval.
    c. proactive inhibition.
    d. repression.
    LO 9

24. Mike thinks of himself as a good fisherman. His friends have noticed that every time he tells the story about the "big one" he caught a few years ago, he seems to remember the fish as larger and larger, and the experience as more and more dramatic. Mike's behavior is consistent with which theory of forgetting?
    a. decay
    b. interference
    c. schema
    d. repression
    LO 9

25. The theory of forgetting that suggests that the conscious mind pushes information into the unconscious is called
    a. decay.
    b. schema theory.
    c. interference.
    d. repression.
    LO 9

26. The vivid recall of a negative emotional experience is called a
    a. flashbulb memory.
    b. flashback.
    c. reconstructive flash.
    d. none of the above
    LO 9

27. According to Hebb, the process that creates unique patterns of neural activity that reverberate through neural loops, thus making synapses more efficient, is called
    a. the engram.
    b. anterograde amnesia.
    c. the memory loop.
    d. synaptic facilitation.
    LO 10

28. Simple forms of learning, such as classical conditioning of the gill withdrawal reflex in the sea snail, appear to physically take place
    a. in the creature's hippocampus.
    b. only in creatures without a brain.
    c. at the synaptic level.
    d. outside of the nervous system.
    LO 10

29. An inability to store and/or retrieve new information in long-term memory is characteristic of
    a. RNA.
    b. anterograde amnesia.
    c. retrograde amnesia.
    d. retroactive amnesia.
    LO 11

30. A key brain structure that is often damaged in patients with anterograde amnesia is the
    a. hippocampus.
    b. cerebral cortex.
    c. hypothalamus.
    d. amygdala.
    LO 11

31. Korsakoff's syndrome
    a. is caused by prolonged thiamine deficiency.
    b. is characterized by anterograde and retrograde amnesia.
    c. is characterized by confabulation.
    d. all of the above
    LO 11

32. Each of the following is suggested to improve the quality of eyewitness testimony *except*
    a. present a "blank lineup" first.
    b. present people in a lineup one at a time.
    c. do not tell the eyewitness whether he or she. has identified the right person
    d. present a "blank lineup" last.
       LO 12

33. The text cites the kidnapping of Jean Piaget as an example of
    a. the accuracy of childhood memories.
    b. the way in which memories gradually change over time.
    c. remembering a childhood event that never actually occurred.
    d. the emotional trauma caused by early childhood events.
       LO 12

34. According to the work of Loftus and others in the area of eyewitness testimony,
    a. eyewitnesses are likely to repress traumatic information.
    b. eyewitnesses are strongly influenced by decay theory.
    c. eyewitnesses are not easily misled.
    d. eyewitnesses can be misled when they are asked misleading questions.
       LO 12

True-False Questions

_____1. In the three stage theory of memory, the first stage is called short-term memory.

_____2. One method to improve the capacity of short-term memory is called chunking.

_____3. Short-term memory and long-term memory appear to be stored in the same areas of the brain.

_____4. One type of declarative memory is called procedural memory.

_____5. According to the serial position effect, memory for items at the beginning of a list are better than memory for the middle items of a list.

_____6. According to the levels of processing model, creating more associations leads to greater elaboration.

_____7. According to schema theory, forgetting occurs when similar memories interfere with the retrieval of information.

_____8. Research suggests that even flashbulb memories can become distorted or forgotten.

_____9. According to many researchers, changes in the synapses of the brain contain the biological bases of memory.

_____10. A forebrain structure believed to play an important role in long-term memory is the engram.

ANSWER SECTION

Concept Checks

Stages of memory

Concept	Characteristics
sensory register	first stage of memory; holds images until they can be processed
short-term memory	also called working memory; can hold 5 to 9 bits of information briefly
long-term memory	information is indexed and stored primarily in terms of meaning; retrieval assisted by the use of cues
procedural memory	memory for skills, such as riding a bicycle
semantic memory	memory associated with meaning, such as word knowledge
episodic memory	memory for specific experiences, such as your first day on campus

Theories of Forgetting

Theory of forgetting	Explanation
decay theory	Memories that are not used fade over time
interference theory	Other memories interfere with recall; proactive interference is created by prior learning, and retroactive interference is created by later learning.
schema theory	Memories become more consistent with our beliefs, knowledge, and expectations over time.
motivated forgetting	Painful memories are pushed into the unconscious.

Answers to Review At A Glance

1. information processing	26. procedural	51. confused
2. encoded	27. semantic	52. distorted
3. control	28. episodic	53. engram
4. retrieved	29. declarative	54. synapse
5. three-stage	30. associative	55. sea snails
6. sensory register	31. spreading activation	56. LTM
7. 1/4	32. serial position	57. STM
8. 4	33. half	58. amygdala
9. short-term	34. levels of processing	59. recall
10. 30 seconds	35. shallow	60. hippocampus
11. rehearsal	36. deeper	61. disorganization
12. acoustic codes	37. elaboration	62. anterograde amnesia
13. 7 ± 2	38. yourself	63. procedural
14. working	39. decay	64. declarative
15. .04	40. short-term	65. hippocampus
16. chunks	41. long-term	66. retrograde amnesia
17. chunking strategies	42. interference	67. Korsakoff's syndrome
18. long-term	43. similar	68. thiamine
19. indexed	44. proactive	69. confabulation
20. cues	45. retroactive	70. questioning
21. semantic codes	46. schema	71. see
22. permanent	47. retrieval	72. prejudices
23. frontal	48. episodic	73. erroneous
24. hippocampus	49. repression	
25. cerebral cortex	50. negative	

Sample Answers for Short Answer Questions

1. Describe the three-stage theory of memory.

According to this approach, the first stage, called the sensory register, holds a replica of the sensory input for a brief interval, while relevant information is selected for further processing. The second stage, short-term memory, holds information for about 30 seconds, unless the information is rehearsed. Long-term memory holds information primarily in terms of its meaning; these memories appear to be stored permanently.

2. What is the serial position effect?

This refers to the superior recall of items at the beginning and end of a list of items, compared with those items listed in the middle.

3. Explain the levels of processing model of memory.

This model represents an alternative to the three-stage theory of memory. It assumes there is only one type of memory beyond the sensory register. The durability of this information depends upon how well the information is processed as it is being encoded. Generally, the more deeply information is processed, the longer the memory will be kept. Deep processing involves greater elaboration, which refers to creating more associations between the new memory and existing memories.

Multiple Choice Answers

1. The answer is *c*. According to the Atkinson-Shriffin stage theory of memory, the three stages of memory are each separate, but linked. Episodic memory refers to memory about specific experiences in life.
2. The answer is *b*. Other control mechanisms are storage and retrieval.
3. The answer is *d*. The capacity mentioned in *d* refers to the capacity for short-term memory.
4. The answer is *c*. The seven chunks of information response is associated with short-term memory.
5. The answer is *a*. Presumably, since the information was not rehearsed, the phone number faded after a short period of time.
6. The answer is *a*. Chunking is the process of putting more than one bit of information into a unit, thereby expanding the capacity of STM.
7. The answer is *b*. This function further limits the already small capacity of short-term memory.
8. The correct answer is *d*. Chunking is a method of putting bits of information together. For example, you might chunk the first three numbers of the phone number. People frequently do this with their social security numbers. Instead of remembering it as nine individual numbers, we tend to remember it as a chunk of three numbers followed by a chunk of two numbers followed by a chunk of four numbers. A second approach for remembering the phone number is to mentally rehearse it. A third technique, not mentioned in the question, is to use a phone with an "automatic redial."
9. The answer is *d*. Information in LTM is first held in the hippocampus and then permanently stored in the language and perception areas of the cortex.
10. The correct answer is *b*. Although short-term memory is usually stored in terms of the sights, sounds, and touch of experiences, long-term memory primarily stores information in terms of meaning.
11. The answer is *a*. Episodic memory stores information about specific experiences. Procedural memory is memory for skills, such as riding a bicycle. Semantic memory is memory about the meaning of words.
12. The answer is *b*. Both episodic and semantic memory are considered to be types of declarative memory.
13. The answer is *b*. Procedural memory refers to our memory of motor movements and skills.
14. The answer is *b*. While LTM appears to have unlimited capacity, this characteristic does not facilitate the retrieval of information. The chunking of information is a process carried about by the short-term memory. Finally, the ability of LTM to store procedural information does not facilitate the retrieval of information.
15. The answer is *c*. According to this view, memories form links that we use to think about information we have stored in memory.
16. The answer is *d*. The serial position effect has important implications for everything from the manner in which evidence is presented in a trial to how you can most effectively prepare for an exam.
17. The answer is *a*. The tip-of-the-tongue phenomenon suggests the information is stored, but for some reason, we're not pressing the right mental "buttons" to retrieve it.
18. The answer is *c*. Elaboration is the process of creating more associations between the new memory and existing memories.
19. The answer is *d*. Elaboration refers to the creation of more associations between a new memory and existing memories. When you tie in the concepts you are reading about in your psychology text to events in your own life, you are elaborating.
20. The answer is *c*. Decay theory suggests that the change in the brain that occurs after something is learned gradually fades unless the material is rehearsed.
21. The answer is *c*. The expression implies that any attempt to teach a dog would be interfered with by the dog's prior learning; proactive interference suggests that prior learning interferes with later learning. Retroactive interference suggests that something learned later interferes with something previously learned.
22. The answer is *b*. Retroactive interference refers to interference created by later learning.
23. The answer is *b*. Distortions of memory most likely occur when we try to remember things, that is, during the process of retrieval.
24. The answer is *c*. Schema theory, unlike decay theory, suggests that, over time, memory changes to become more consistent with our beliefs, knowledge and expectations. Over time, Mike's memory may become distorted to become consistent with his belief that he is a good fisherman.
25. The answer is *d*. Repression is Freud's theory. It is often used synonymously with the term *motivated forgetting*.

26. The answer is *a*. Although flashbulb memories can be recalled in vivid detail, they are nonetheless subject to the normal processes of forgetting.
27. The answer is *d*. This process implies that some forms of learning may be "remembered" at the synapse.
28. The answer is *c*. This finding supports Hebb's notion of synaptic facilitation.
29. The answer is *b*. Retrograde amnesia is the disorder characterized by an inability to retrieve old, long-term memories. Interestingly, in both anterograde and retrograde amnesia, there is little or no disruption to STM.
30. The answer is *a*. Isn't it interesting that the hippocampus keeps turning up as a key brain structure throughout this chapter?
31. The answer is *d*. Confabulation may be thought of as an exaggerated version of reconstructive distortion.
32. The answer is *d*. Research suggests if a "blank lineup" is presented first, the perpetrator is identified more accurately in a second lineup.
33. The answer is *c*. As an adult, Piaget remembered some of the details of his kidnapping as a child. As it turned out, however, he never was kidnapped. He had created the memories he later "remembered."
34. The answer is *d*. Loftus and others have shown that misleading questions presented to eyewitnesses can actually cue the recall of items that were not present.

Answers to True-False Questions

1. F
2. T
3. F
4. F
5. T
6. T
7. F
8. T
9. T
10. F

Chapter 7   Cognition, Language, and Intelligence

Learning Objectives

1.   Define cognition and know its three primary facets. (p. 202)

2.   Distinguish between the basic and prototypical characteristics of natural concepts. (p. 204)

3.   Define problem solving and recognize the three major types of cognitive operations involved in problem solving. (p. 206)

4.   Distinguish among the following problem-solving strategies: trial-and-error, algorithmic, and heuristic. (p. 208)

5.   Distinguish between the representativeness heuristic and the availability heuristic. (p. 208)

6.   Discuss the importance of framing and emotional factors in decision making. (p. 209)

7.   Define creativity and distinguish between convergent thinking and divergent thinking. (p. 209)

8.   Define language, including the meaning of semantic content, the distinction between the surface structure of language and the deep structure of language, and the generative property of language. (p. 211)

9.   Distinguish among phonemes, morphemes, and syntax. (p. 212)

10.   Understand the Whorfian hypothesis and recognize its significance. (p. 213)

11.   Know the research results regarding the language capabilities of animals. (p. 213)

12. Define intelligence and compare the position of psychologists who view intelligence as a general ability to those who view it as several specific abilities. (p. 215)

13. Distinguish between fluid intelligence and crystallized intelligence. (p. 217)

14. Identify intelligence tests and discuss how they are useful. (p. 218)

15. Understand the concept of intelligence quotient and distinguish between ratio IQ and deviation IQ. (p. 219)

16. List the characteristics of good intelligence tests. (p. 222)

17. Define tacit intelligence and describe its relationship to general intelligence. (p. 222)

18. Identify the factors that contribute to an individual's intelligence. (p. 223)

19. Recognize the importance of intelligence scores in modern society. (p. 224)

20. Discuss possible reasons for the recent rise in intelligence test scores. (p. 225)

21. Identify the race-ethnic differences in intelligence and achievement scores and describe the controversies and policy implications raised by the publication of *The Bell Curve*. (p. 229)

22. (From the *Application of Psychology* section) Identify techniques to help improve critical thinking. (p. 232)

Chapter Overview

"Cognition" refers to the process by which information is obtained through the senses, transformed through the processes of perception and thinking, stored and retrieved through the processes of memory, and used in the processes of problem solving and language.

The basic units of thinking are called concepts. Concepts are categories of things, events, or qualities linked together by some common feature or features. Not all concepts are equally easy to learn; some are more natural than others. Natural concepts are both basic and prototypical.

Problem solving is the use of information to reach a goal that is blocked. Problem solving uses cognitive operations, which include formulating the problem, understanding the elements of the problem, and generating and evaluating alternative solutions. Algorithmic and heuristic operations are two types of cognitive strategies used to solve problems. Two heuristics are the representativeness heuristic and the availability heuristic. Creative problem solving requires the ability to think in flexible and unusual ways, called divergent thinking; problem solving that is more logical and conventional is called convergent thinking.

Language is a symbolic code used in human communication. The meaning that is communicated is called the semantic content of language. Human language is highly efficient and generative; an infinite set of utterances can be made using a finite set of elements and rules. These rules are referred to as syntax. Phonemes are the smallest units of sound, while morphemes are the smallest units of meaning in a language.

Psychologists have long been interested in the relationship between language and thought. The Whorfian or linguistic relativity hypothesis states that the structure of language influences thinking. Controversy continues over whether animals are able to understand syntax.

"Intelligence" refers to the cognitive abilities of an individual to learn from experience, to reason well, and to cope effectively with the demands of daily living. Some psychologists believe that intelligence is a single factor, while others view intelligence as many different kinds of intellectual abilities. Gardner suggests there are seven independent types of intelligence. Fluid intelligence is the ability to learn new strategies to solve new kinds of problems, whereas crystallized intelligence is the ability to use previously learned skills to solve familiar problems. The intelligence quotient (IQ) is obtained by dividing an individual's mental age by his or her chronological age. This approach to calculating intellectual ability has been replaced by the deviation IQ, which compares individual scores to a normal distribution. Useful IQ tests must be standardized, objective, reliable, valid, and evaluated against proper norms. Some researchers have focused on "everyday intelligence," also called tacit intelligence. An individual's level of intelligence is determined both by inherited and environmental factors. Some researchers believe that intelligence scores have risen dramatically over the past several generations. The publication of *The Bell Curve* has sparked controversy concerning the relationship between heredity and intelligence, and the impact of intelligence on economic well-being.

By increasing one's mental efforts, improving problem formulation and breaking out of mental sets, it is possible to improve one's critical thinking skills.

Key Terms Exercise

For each of the following exercises, match the key terms on the left with the correct definitions on the right. Page references to the text follow the terms so that you may refer to the text for any items you answer incorrectly or do not understand completely. You may check your responses immediately by referring to the answers that follow each exercise.

Concepts and Problem Solving

_____ 1. cognition (p. 202)
_____ 2. concepts (p. 202)
_____ 3. mental set (p. 207)
_____ 4. algorithms (p. 208)
_____ 5. heuristics (p. 208)
_____ 6. convergent thinking (p. 210)
_____ 7. divergent thinking (p. 210)

a. categories of objects or events that are linked together by some common feature or features
b. efficient problem solving strategies that do not guarantee a correct solution
c. intellectual process through which information is obtained, transformed, stored, and used
d. loosely organized, unconventional thinking
e. logical, conventional thinking
f. patterns of reasoning that guarantee finding a correct solution
g. a habitual way of viewing a problem

ANSWERS

1. c	5. b
2. a	6. e
3. g	7. d
4. f	

Language

_____ 1. language (p. 211)
_____ 2. semantic content (p. 211)
_____ 3. surface structure (p. 211)
_____ 4. deep structure (p. 211)
_____ 5. phoneme (p. 212)
_____ 6. morpheme (p. 212)
_____ 7. syntax (p. 212)
_____ 8. linguistic relativity hypothesis (p. 213)

a. the underlying structure that contains a statement's meaning
b. the meaning in symbols such as language
c. the smallest unit of meaning in a language
d. a symbolic code used in communication
e. the smallest unit of sound in a language
f. the grammatical rules of a language
g. the superficial structure of a statement
h. the idea that the structure of a language influences thinking

ANSWERS

1. d	5. e
2. b	6. c
3. g	7. f
4. a	8. h

Intelligence I

_____ 1. intelligence (p. 215)
_____ 2. fluid intelligence (p. 217)
_____ 3. crystallized intelligence (p. 218)
_____ 4. intelligence quotient (p. 219)
_____ 5. normal distribution (p. 221)
_____ 6. standardization (p. 222)

a. a numerical value of intelligence derived from an intelligence test
b. methods for administering tests in the same way to all individuals
c. the cognitive ability of an individual to learn from experience, to reason well, and to cope with the demands of daily living
d. the ability to learn or invent new strategies to deal with new problems
e. the ability to use previously learned skills to solve familiar problems
f. a symmetrical pattern of scores in which most scores are clustered near the center

ANSWERS

1. c	4. a
2. d	5. f
3. e	6. b

Intelligence II

_____ 1. norms (p. 222)
_____ 2. objectivity (p. 222)
_____ 3. reliability (p. 222)
_____ 4. validity (p. 222)
_____ 5. tacit intelligence (p. 223)

a. the practical knowledge and skills needed to deal with everyday problems
b. similarity in test scores even if the test is administered at different times or by different examiners
c. the extent to which a test measures what it's supposed to measure
d. scoring a test question so that the same score is produced regardless of who does the scoring
e. standards used as the basis of comparison for test scores

ANSWERS

1. e	4. c
2. d	5. a
3. b	

Who Am I?

Match the psychologists on the left with their contributions to the field of psychology on the right. Page references to the text follow the names of the psychologists so that you may refer to the text for further review of these psychologists and their contributions. You may check your responses immediately by referring to the answers that follow each exercise.

_____ 1. Benjamin Whorf (p. 213)
_____ 2. Sir Francis Galton (p. 215)
_____ 3. Alfred Binet (p. 218)
_____ 4. David Wechsler (p. 218)
_____ 5. Howard Gardner (p. 217)

a. I developed intelligence scales for children and adults.
b. I developed the first useful intelligence test (in France).
c. I believe there are seven independent types of intelligence, including artistic and athletic.
d. It's my belief that language influences thinking.
e. My writings in the late 1800s helped popularize the concept of intelligence.

ANSWERS
1. d   4. a
2. e   5. c
3. b

Review At A Glance
(Answers to this section may be found on page 130)

Definition of Cognition

The intellectual processes through which information is obtained, transformed, stored, retrieved, and used is ___(1)___. Cognition processes ___(2)___; it is active and it is ___(3)___.

Concepts: The Basic Units of Thinking

Categories of objects and events linked together by common features are called ___(4)___. Some concepts are easier to learn than others; these are ___(5)___ concepts. Natural concepts have two primary characteristics: they are ___(6)___ and ___(7)___. Basic concepts have a medium degree of ___(8)___. In contrast, a high degree of inclusiveness is found in ___(9)___ concepts, and a low degree of inclusiveness is found in ___(10)___ concepts. Among the important characteristics of basic concepts are 1) they share many common ___(11)___; 2) they share similar ___(12)___; 3) they often share motor ___(13)___; and 4) they are easily ___(14)___.
The second defining characteristic of natural concepts is that they are good examples, or ___(15)___.

Problem Solving: Using Information to Reach Goals

The cognitive process that uses information to reach a goal that is blocked is called ___(16)___ _____. There are three major steps in problem solving: 1) ___(17)___ the problem, 2) understanding and ___(18)___ the elements of the problem, and 3) ___(19)___ and evaluating alternative solutions.

A habitual way of viewing a problem is called a ___(20)___ _____. Three types of cognitive strategies are used in problem solving: 1) trial-and-error, 2) a type in which every possible solution is examined and which guarantees a solution, called an ___(21)___, and 3) a shortcut strategy that increases the probability of finding a correct solution, but doesn't guarantee a correct solution, known as ___(22)___. A heuristic that involves making judgments about the unknown on the assumption that it is similar to what we already know is called the ___(23)___ heuristic. Another strategy, that involves reasoning based on information that is available in memory, is called the ___(24)___ heuristic. Decision-making is also influenced by the way a problem or question is presented; this is called ___(25)___. According to the text, both cognitive and ___(26)___ factors influence our decision making.

The ability to produce novel and socially valued products or ideas is ___(27)___. Thinking that is logical and conventional is called ___(28)___ thinking, while thinking that is loosely organized, only partially directed, and unconventional is called ___(29)___ thinking. Most formal education emphasizes ___(30)___ thinking. Divergent thinking produces answers that must be evaluated ___(31)___

Language: Symbolic Communication

Language is a symbolic code used in communication. The meaning that is communicated is referred to as ___(32)___ _____. Noam Chomsky has distinguished between the superficial structure of a statement, called ___(33)___ _____, and the underlying structure that contains the statement's meaning, called ___(34)___ _____. Human language is a highly ___(35)___ system. Language gives us the ability to create an infinite number of utterances from a fixed set of elements and rules; this is called the ___(36)___ property of language. The smallest unit of sound in a language is a ___(37)___, while the smallest unit of meaning in a language is a ___(38)___. The rules of a language are called ___(39)___. Differences exist between rules of syntax and the ___(40)___ rules of grammar. The hypothesis that the structure of a language influences thinking, proposed by Benjamin Whorf, is called the ___(41)___ hypothesis. Linguistic relativity has led us to substitute some ___(42)___-_____ terms for some terms that were masculine.

Unlike bees which are able to communicate only in ways that are limited by inheritance, human language is ___(43)___ and must be learned through interactions with ___(44)___ speakers. Human languages can generate an ___(45)___ number of unique and novel utterances. The experiences of Washoe and Koko suggest that chimps are able to learn to use ___(46)___. Researchers, however, question whether chimps' use of language exhibits an understanding of ___(47)___.

Intelligence: The Sum Total of Cognition

The abilities of an individual to learn from experience, to reason well, and to cope well with daily life is

___(48)___. Sir Francis Galton popularized the notion of intelligence in the late 1800s. He believed intelligence is

inherited and is composed of a single ___(49)___ factor. Charles Spearman uses the term ___(50)___ to refer to this

general factor, but other psychologists believe intelligence is a collection of many separate abilities. Louis Thurstone, for

example, devised a test to measure ___(51)___ different abilities, while J. P. Guilford believes intelligence is made up of

___(52)___ different abilities. According to Howard Gardner, there are ___(53)___ independent types of intelligence.

Other psychologists distinguish between the ability to learn or invent new strategies to solve a new problem, called

___(54)___ intelligence, and the ability to use previously learned skills to solve familiar problems, called

___(55)___ intelligence.

Around 1900, Alfred ___(56)___ became the first person to develop a useful measure of intelligence. Binet's test was

refined by Lewis ___(57)___ of Stanford University. A similar intelligence test was also developed by David ___(58)___

. Intelligence tests are designed to be a ___(59)___ of some of the cognitive abilities that constitute intelligence. They

are useful in predicting the performance of individuals in situations that require

___(60)___.

IQ scores are calculated by dividing a subject's ___(61)___ age by this ___(62)___ age and multiplying the result

by ___(63)___. Binet's approach, which calculates the ___(64)___ IQ, is no longer used in contemporary intelligence

tests.

A newer approach to measuring intellectual ability, termed the ___(65)___ IQ, assumes that the scores of large

numbers of individuals who take an intelligence test will fall in a ___(66)___ distribution. Most scores will be clustered

around the ___(67)___, and as scores deviate from the average they become progressively less common. Using this

approach, the average intelligence score is set at ___(68)___.

Good intelligence tests, as well as other psychological tests, are characterized by 1) ___(69)___, so that tests are given

the same way to all who take the test; 2) ___(70)___, in which the test is given to a large representative sample of the

population; 3) ___(71)___, so that there is little or no ambiguity as to what constitutes a correct answer; (4) ___(72)___,

so that the scores obtained would be the same if administered on two different occasions or by two different examiners;

and (5) ___(73)___, so that a test measures what it is supposed to measure.

The practical knowledge and skills needed to deal with everyday problems is called ___(74)___ intelligence. Tacit

intelligence is related to general intelligence in the following three ways: 1) those who have very low levels of general

intelligence usually do not have highly developed ___(75)___ intelligence; 2) it is unlikely that those with limited

___(76)___ intelligence will succeed in highly complex areas of general intelligence; and 3) those with highly developed

general intelligence are more likely to have good ___(77)___ knowledge across many different areas.

Research both on twins and on persons adopted at birth confirm the importance of ___(78)___ in determining IQ.

Another important factor in intelligence appears to be one's intellectual ___(79)___.

A strong correlation exists between IQ and success in ___(80)___ and in ___(81)___. Intelligence predicts success in occupations because: 1) many occupations require advanced ___(82)___; 2) those with higher intelligence are easier to ___(83)___; and 3) those with higher intelligence tend to perform better in ___(84)___ jobs.

In many countries, evidence suggests that intelligence score have ___(85)___ dramatically over the past few generations. Among the possible explanations for these finds are: 1) improved health and ___(86)___; 2) increases in levels of ___(87)___; 3) fewer ___(88)___ per family; 4) increases in environmental ___(89)___; and 5) in the United States, dramatic changes in the lives of person of ___(90)___. The last several decades have seen a narrowing of the gap of intellectual and academic scores between ___(91)___ groups in the U. S. The changes have occurred since the end of official ___(92)___ in the U.S.

A book about intelligence, called *The Bell Curve*, suggested that North American society is moving toward a ___(93)___, in which genetics would increasingly determine one's intelligence. The book further contends that society is headed towards ___(94)___ decline. Although critics and research dispute many of the book's ideas, the book raises important questions about the role of ___(95)___ merit in our society.

Application of Psychology: Improving Critical Thinking

According to the text, improved critical thinking skills can result from increased ___(96)___ effort, improved ___(97)___ formulation and by breaking out of unproductive ___(98)___ _____. A type of mental set in which we have difficulty in seeing new uses for objects is called ___(99)___ _____. One recommendation to avoid errors in reasoning is to avoid ___(100)___ thinking. Critical thinking can also be made more effective by ___(101)___ one's critical thinking. A general strategy for problem solving includes the following steps: 1) formulate the problem; 2) generate all possible ___(102)___; 3) eliminate poor solutions; 4) examine the ___(103)___ of the remaining solutions; 5) generate ways to implement the solution; and 6) ___(104)___ the solution.

Concept Checks

Fill in the missing components of the following concept boxes. The correct answers are located in the "Answers" section at the end of the chapter.

Thinking

Concept	Definition
algorithm	
	making judgments about the unknown on the assumption that it is similar to what is already known
availability heuristic	
convergent thinking	
	loosely organized, unconventional thinking

Differing Views of Intelligence

Theorist	Concept
Galton, Spearman, Wechsler	
	there are seven independent types of intelligence
	developed the first useful intelligence test

Characteristics of Good Intelligence Tests

Characteristic	Definition
	all individuals are administered the test the same way
	standards used as the basis of comparison for scores on a test
objectivity	
reliability	
validity	

Extending the Chapter: Psychology, Societal Issues, and Human Diversity

These questions may be assigned to you. Whether or not they are assigned, they are designed to be challenging questions to encourage you to think independently about the material in the chapter. Many of the questions have no right or wrong answers.

I.   From the *Application of Psychology* section

1.   Select a problem you recently tried to solve, and demonstrate how using the material in the text might have improved the quality of the solution.

2.   What is the most useful idea regarding critical thinking that you read in this section?

II.   Psychology, Societal Issues, and Human Diversity

1.   Describe the research conducted on the Cree (found in the *Human Diversity* section in the text). How do their notions of intelligence compare with your own ideas about intelligence?

2.   Describe the ways in which our society rewards and punishes divergent thinkers.

3.   Does society place too much emphasis on intelligence test scores? In what ways does society overemphasize these scores?

4.   To what extent is racism and sexism a result of racist and sexist language? How can and how should this type of language be "regulated?"

5.   Inasmuch as intellectually gifted children represent a potentially important resource for our society, how should public policy be designed to nurture such abilities in children?

Practice Quiz

The practice quiz consists of three sections: 1) Short answer questions, 2) Multiple choice questions, and 3) True-False questions. At the end of the chapter you will find suggested answers to the short answer questions, answers and explanation for the multiple choice questions, and answers to the true-false questions.

Short Answer Questions

1. Describe the characteristics of "basic" concepts, according to Rosch.

_____

_____

2. Distinguish between convergent and divergent thinkers.

_____

_____

3. Distinguish between phonemes and morphemes and describe the importance of syntax.

_____

_____

Multiple Choice Questions

1. Which of the following is an important characteristic of cognition?
   a. Cognition processes information.
   b. Cognition is active.
   c. Cognition is functional.
   d. all of the above
   LO 1

2. According to Eleanor Rosch, basic concepts
   a. are very inclusive.
   b. are difficult to name.
   c. share many common attributes.
   d. rarely share similar shapes.
   LO 2

3. Rosch's research with the Dani tribe of New Guinea supports the notions that
   a. natural concepts are good prototypes.
   b. natural concepts are basic.
   c. natural concepts are confusing for many people.
   d. there are very few natural concepts.
   LO 2

4. Which of the following represents the proper sequence of cognitive operations involved in problem solving?
   a. generate and evaluate solutions, formulate the problem, understand the elements
   b. understand the elements, generate and evaluate solutions, formulate the problem
   c. formulate the problem, generate and evaluate solutions, understand the elements
   d. formulate the problem, understand the elements, generate and evaluate solutions
   LO 4

5. Amy is trying to solve a problem by using a strategy that guarantees a correct solution. The technique she is using is
   a. algorithms.
   b. trial-and-error.
   c. heuristics.
   d. framing.
   LO 4

6. Voting for a candidate based on having heard her on TV rather than on having systematically studied the viewpoints of all the candidates is problem solving based on
   a. algorithms.
   b. convergence.
   c. divergence.
   d. heuristics.
   LO 4

7. Which problem solving method involves reasoning based on information that is available in memory?
   a. trial-and-error
   b. algorithms
   c. the availability heuristic
   d. the representativeness heuristic
   LO 4

8. Framing refers to
   a. the decision to use heuristics or algorithms.
   b. the usefulness of trial-and-error.
   c. artificial intelligence.
   d. the way a question or problem is posed.
   LO 6

9. People who are creative tend to use
   a. convergent thinking.
   b. divergent thinking.
   c. subordinate thinking.
   d. little or no thinking.
   LO 7

10. Which of the following contains the underlying meaning in a statement?
    a. deep structure
    b. surface structure
    c. phonemes
    d. syntax
    LO 9

11. The grammatical rules of a language are referred to as
    a. morphemes.
    b. syntax.
    c. phonemes.
    d. surface structure
    LO 8

12. When we say that language is generative, we mean that
    a. it is passed down from generation to generation.
    b. novel language utterances generate new thoughts.
    c. there is no limit to what can be said.
    d. dialects change over several generations.
    LO 8

13. Which of the following is the correct sequence used by children in language development?
    a. morphemes, phonemes, and then syntax
    b. syntax, phonemes, and then morphemes
    c. phonemes, morphemes, and then syntax
    d. syntax, morphemes, and then phonemes
    LO 9

14. The Whorfian hypothesis
    a. was strongly supported by Rosch's research with the Dani tribe.
    b. was not supported by Rosch's research.
    c. was not supported by research regarding labels for personality types and their influence on how we think about people.
    d. is just the opposite of the linguistic relativity hypothesis.
    LO 10

15. According to the linguistic relativity hypothesis
    a. you should be careful about the language you use around your relatives.
    b. the surface structure is usually the same as the deep structure.
    c. the structure of a language may influence the way individuals think.
    d. other species have demonstrated fairly sophisticated language.
    LO 10

16. Although apes have been taught American Sign Language (ASL), many researchers contend
    a. they can't communicate with each other.
    b. they rarely express their emotions.
    c. they show little evidence of understanding syntax.
    d. they are unable to teach other apes ASL.
    LO 11

17. The term g refers to the idea that intelligence
    a. is made of genetically inherited abilities.
    b. may be grouped into subcategories.
    c. has a basic general component.
    d. was developed by Sir Francis Galton.
       LO 12

18. According to Gardner, which of the following is a type of intelligence?
    a. linguistic
    b. spatial
    c. kinesthetic
    d. all of the above
       LO 12

19. Which type of intelligence is useful in developing new strategies to solve new problems?
    a. linguistic
    b. kinesthetic
    c. fluid
    d. crystallized
       LO 13

20. Each of the following is true regarding intelligence tests *except*
    a. the first tests were developed by Binet.
    b. there is widespread agreement concerning the definition of intelligence.
    c. intelligence tests do a good job of predicting success in school.
    d. intelligence tests use a small sample of some of the cognitive abilities that comprise intelligence.
       LO 14

21. Joe has a mental age of 10 and a chronological age of 8. His ratio IQ score is
    a. 80
    b. 100
    c. 120
    d. 125
       LO 15

22. According to the deviation IQ approach, the average score on an IQ test is
    a. 90
    b. 100
    c. 110
    d. 125
       LO 15

23. When a test measures what it claims to measure it is
    a. valid.
    b. reliable.
    c. standardized.
    d. objective.
       LO 16

24. Every time Sally took the SAT tests, her scores were exactly the same. This means the SAT tests have a high degree of _____ for Sally.
    a. standardization
    b. reliability
    c. validity
    d. meaning
       LO 16

25. The ability to solve everyday problems is referred to as
    a. crystallized intelligence.
    b. fluid intelligence.
    c. kinesthetic intelligence.
    d. tacit intelligence.
       LO 17

26. Research conducted with twins as well as with adopted children has tended to support the influence of which factor on intelligence?
    a. environment
    b. learning
    c. heredity
    d. none of the above
       LO 18

27. According to the text, a strong positive correlation exists between IQ and success in
    a. education.
    b. tacit knowledge.
    c. occupations.
    d. *a* and *c* above.
       LO 19

28. Each of following is suggested as a possible reason for the recent increase in intelligence scores *except*
    a. improved health and nutrition.
    b. smaller families.
    c. greater selectivity in marriage partners.
    d. greater environmental complexity.
       LO 20

29. Research indicates dramatic increases in recent generations in what type of intelligence?
    a. fluid
    b. crystallized
    c. spatial
    d. emotional
    LO 20

30. According to the authors of *The Bell Curve*
    a. intelligence will become less important in our society as computers do more and more work.
    b. technology is helping to shrink the gap between rich and poor.
    c. IQ is a poor predictor of success in school.
    d. the future will see a widening gap between those who are intelligent and affluent people and those who are less intelligent and less affluent.
    LO 21

31. Each of the following is an effective strategy for improving critical thinking *except*
    a. break out of unproductive mental sets.
    b. try to engage in more heuristic thinking.
    c. increase your mental effort.
    d. try to formulate the problem in two different ways.
    LO 22

32. Functional fixedness is an example of
    a. critical thinking.
    b. algorithmic reasoning.
    c. an unproductive mental set.
    d. a technique to improve problem formulation.
    LO 24

True-False Questions

_____1. According to Rosch, natural concepts are good prototypes.

_____2. Heuristics are useful since they guarantee a solution to a problem.

_____3. The way a question is framed can strongly influence the answer.

_____4. Language is generative, which means it is passed down from generation to generation.

_____5. The kind of thinking most likely to be rewarded in school is divergent thinking.

_____6. The grammatical rules of language are called syntax.

_____7. Researchers are in basic agreement that animal language shows syntax.

_____8. According to Gardner, there are seven independent types of intelligence.

_____9. The ratio IQ is the type most commonly used today.

_____10. Traditional IQ tests do a good job of measuring tacit intelligence.

ANSWER SECTION

Concept Checks

Thinking

Concept	Definition
algorithm	pattern of reasoning that guarantees a correct solution
representativeness heuristic	making judgments about the unknown on the assumption that it is similar to what is already known
availability heuristic	reasoning on the basis of information already available in memory
convergent thinking	logical, conventional thinking that focuses on a problem
divergent thinking	loosely organized, unconventional thinking

Differing Views of Intelligence

Theorist	Concept
Galton, Spearman, Wechsler	intelligence is a single factor
Gardner	there are seven independent types of intelligence
Binet	developed the first useful intelligence test

Characteristics of Good Intelligence Tests

Characteristic	Definition
standardization	all individuals are administered the test in the same manner
norms	standards used as the basis of comparison for scores on a test
objectivity	the same score is achieved regardless of who does the scoring
reliability	test produces similar scores even if it administered on different occasions or by different examiners
validity	test measures what it is supposed to measure

Answers to Review At A Glance

1. cognition
2. information
3. useful
4. concepts
5. natural
6. basic
7. prototypical
8. inclusiveness
9. superordinate
10. subordinate
11. attributes
12. shapes
13. movements
14. named
15. prototypes
16. problem solving
17. formulating
18. organizing
19. generating
20. mental set
21. algorithm
22. heuristics
23. representativeness
24. availability
25. framing
26. emotional
27. creativity
28. convergent
29. divergent
30. convergent
31. subjectively
32. semantic content
33. surface structure
34. deep structure
35. efficient

36. generative
37. phoneme
38. morpheme
39. syntax
40. prescriptive
41. linguistic relativity
42. gender-neutral
43. flexible
44. fluent
45. infinite
46. language
47. syntax
48. intelligence
49. general
50. g
51. seven
52. 150
53. seven
54. fluid
55. crystallized
56. Binet
57. Terman
58. Wechsler
59. sample
60. intelligence
61. mental
62. chronological
63. 100
64. ratio
65. deviation
66. normal
67. average
68. 100
69. standardization
70. norms

71. objectivity
72. reliability
73. validity
74. tacit
75. tacit
76. general
77. practical
78. heredity
79. environment
80. education
81. occupation
82. education
83. train
84. complex
85. risen
86. nutrition
87. education
88. children
89. complexity
90. color
91. race-ethnic
92. segregation
93. meritocracy
94. genetic
95. intellectual
96. mental
97. problem
98. mental sets
99. functional fixedness
100. heuristic
101. monitoring
102. solutions
103. consequences
104. implement

Sample Answers for Short Answer Questions

1. **Describe the characteristics of "basic" concepts, according to Rosch.**

According to Rosch, some concepts are more natural than others. One characteristic of natural concepts is that they are basic. Basic concepts have a medium degree of inclusiveness. They also share many common attributes. Members of basic concepts also share similar shapes, they often share similar movements and basic concepts are easily named.

2. Distinguish between convergent and divergent thinkers.

Convergent thinkers use logic and facts and stay focused on a problem until a solution is found. Convergent thinking is considered conventional and is generally emphasized in formal education. Divergent thinking, in contrast, is loosely organized and unconventional. Generally, divergent thinkers are considered creative.

3. Distinguish between phonemes and morphemes and describe the importance of syntax.

A phoneme is the smallest unit of sound in a language. A morpheme is the smallest unit of meaning in a language. An individual phoneme might not convey meaning unless it is combined with other phonemes. Syntax refers to the grammatical rules of a language. These rules are understood by the speakers of a language and allow an infinite number of utterances to be made.

Multiple Choice Answers

1. The answer is *d*. While cognition is involved in virtually every aspect of psychology, it is an integral part of thinking, language, and intelligence.
2. The answer is *c*. Natural concepts are both basic and prototypical. Basic concepts have a medium degree of inclusiveness, share many common attributes, share similar shapes, often share motor movements, and *are easily named*. The second quality of natural concepts is that they are good prototypes; that is, they are good examples. Generally, natural concepts are easily learned.
3. The answer is *a*. Members of the Dani tribe learned the names of primary colors more easily than other colors, suggesting that some color concepts are more prototypical, that is, more natural, than others.
4. The answer is *d*. Following this strategy may help you to improve your own problem-solving abilities.
5. The answer is *a*. The use of algorithms is a time-consuming strategy, which makes them ideal for computer use.
6. The answer is *d*. Heuristics involve using "short-cut" strategies to solve problems; basing one's vote on having seen one candidate on TV is an example of a "short-cut."
7. The answer is *c*. The representativeness heuristic refers to making judgments about the unknown by assuming it is similar to what we already know. Trial-and-error randomly tires to solve problems, and algorithms are systematic patterns of reasoning that guarantee finding a solution.
8. The answer is *d*. Research strongly suggests that the way a question is framed can dramatically impact decision making.
9. The answer is *b*. While convergent thinking is logical, conventional, and focused, divergent thinking is unconventional and loosely organized.
10. The answer is *a*. According to Chomsky, the superficial spoken or written structure of a statement is the surface structure, while the underlying meaning of the statement is held by the deep structure.
11. The answer is *b*. These rules allow an infinite number of utterances to be generated. Phonemes are the individual units of sound in a language, whereas morphemes are smallest units of meaning in a language. The surface structure of a language is the spoken or written structure of a communication.
12. The answer is *b*. The generative property of language gives us the potential for an unlimited number of utterances from a finite set of rules and elements.
13. The answer is *c*. Children first babble in the sounds of their language (phonemes), then progress to morphemes, and finally acquire syntactic rules.
14. The answer is *b*. The Whorfian hypothesis (also called the linguistic relativity hypothesis) was supported by research regarding labels and their impact on how we think about people, but was NOT supported by Rosch's study on the Dani tribe.
15. The answer is *c*. The linguistic relativity hypothesis is also referred to as the Whorfian hypothesis.
16. The answer is *d*. According to researchers, the chimps fail to use language to comment on the world and they do not understand syntax. This contradicts the findings of Patterson, who has taught Koko over 600 signs.
17. The answer is *c*. The concept of g is Spearman's notion that intelligence is a single broad concept. Other psychologists, from Thurstone to Gardner, view intelligence as a collection of several independent abilities.

18. The answer is *d*. Gardner suggests there are seven independent types of intelligence; in addition to those listed in the question, the others are logical-mathematical, musical, interpersonal, and intrapersonal.
19. The answer is *c*. Crystallized intelligence is the ability to use previously learned skills to solve familiar problems. Linguistic and kinesthetic intelligence are two examples of Gardner's multiple intelligence.
20. The answer is *b*. Although psychologists may agree about some of the components of intelligence, there is little agreement about a precise definition.
21. The answer is *d*. Using the IQ formula (IQ = MA/CA X 100), 10/8 = 1.25 X 100 = 125.
22. The answer is b. The deviation IQ is based on the properties of the normal distribution curve, sometimes called the bell curve.
23. The answer is *a*. Reliability implies that the scores would be the same if the test was repeated. A test that is standardized is administered the same way to all who take the test. An objective test has agreed-upon right and wrong answers.
24. The answer is *b*. Whereas reliability means the scores are similar when taken on more than one occasion, validity means the test measures what it is supposed to measure.
25. The answer is *d*. Tacit intelligence refers to practical knowledge that is not typically taught in school.
26. The answer is *c*. While the environment is also widely recognized as an important factor in intelligence, the question asked about the research conducted specifically with twins and adopted children.
27. The answer is *d*. According to the text, the correlation between IQ and these variables is about as high as between people's heights and weights.
28. The answer is *c*. The text does not cite evidence that people are more selective in their marriage partners.
29. The answer is *a*. Results from the Raven Progressive Matrices Test strongly support the notion of increases in fluid intelligence.
30. The answer is *d*. The authors of *The Bell Curve* suggest intelligence cannot be modified and that intellectual differences are widening the gap between the "haves" and the "have-nots" in our society.
31. The answer is *b*. Actually, the text recommends trying to *avoid* heuristic reasoning.
32. The answer is *c*. Functional fixedness occurs when we focus our thinking about the elements in a problem on their habitual uses. The text recommends trying to break out of functional fixedness to improve one's critical thinking.

Answers to True-False Questions

1. T   6. T

2. F   7. F

3. T   8. T

4. F   9. F

5. F   10. F

Chapter 8   Developmental Psychology

Learning Objectives

1. Discuss the interplay of nature and nurture in development and describe the role of maturation.   (p. 238)

2. Define imprinting and discuss the importance of critical periods. (p. 239)

3. From the Harlows' research, discuss the role of early experiences on development. (p. 241)

4. Describe the significance of individual variation in development. (p.241)

5. Identify the characteristics common to stage theories of development. (p. 243)

6. Discuss Kohlberg's three levels of moral reasoning: premoral, conventional, and principled. (p. 244)

7. Identify and describe Gilligan's three levels of moral reasoning: individual survival, self-sacrifice, and equality. (p. 244)

8. Compare and contrast Gilligan's and Kohlberg's theories. (p. 246)

9. Describe Erikson's stage theory of personality development and list the stages of personality development. (p. 247)

10. Differentiate between the developmental stages termed the "neonatal period" and "infancy." (p. 250)

11. Identify the cognitive, emotional, and social aspects of development during infancy. (p. 251)

12. Identify the cognitive, emotional, and social aspects of development during early childhood. (p. 252)

13. Identify the cognitive, emotional, and social aspects of development during middle childhood. (p. 254)

14. Explain the changes that occur in physical development during puberty, including primary and secondary sex characteristics, menarche, and the adolescent growth spurt. (p. 256)

15. Identify the characteristics of formal operational thinking and adolescent egocentrism. (p. 257)

16. Discuss the research results on adolescent social and emotional development. (p. 258)

17. Identify the physical and cognitive aspects of development in adulthood. (p. 260)

18. Recognize aspects of emotional and social development in adulthood. (p. 261)

19. Contrast Erikson's and Levinson's views of adult personality development (p. 262)

20. Define *climacteric* and know how it affects men and women. (p. 265)

21. Identify the controversies associated with the stage theories of adulthood. (p. 266)

22. Describe the biological and psychological changes that are involved in aging and recognize the factors associated with "happy aging" and longevity. (p. 267)

23. (From the *Application of Psychology* section) Identify the following: Baumrind's discipline styles, the "two-way street" of parenting, and common discipline mistakes. (p. 269)

24. (From the *Application of Psychology* section) Discuss the results of research on sociocultural factors in parenting and the research regarding day care, divorce, and parenting. (p. 270)

Chapter Overview

Psychologists differ on the issue of how much our development is biologically determined (nature) or is shaped by the learning environment (nurture). Today, most psychologists believe that nature and nurture combine to influence our actions, thoughts, and feelings.

Research on imprinting in some animals shows that experiences during critical periods of early development can have long-lasting effects on behavior. Research conducted by the Harlows on the effects of early deprivation in monkeys showed the lasting effects of early social deprivation. Opinions are divided regarding the effects of abnormal early experiences in humans.

Stage theorists believe that all children pass through the same qualitatively different stages in the same order. For example, Piaget identified four stages of cognitive development from infancy to adulthood. According to Piaget, the process of assimilation adds new information to existing concepts, or schemas, that results in quantitative changes in a child's cognitions. The process of changing schemas in qualitative ways to incorporate new experiences is called accommodation. Piaget's four stages include 1) the sensorimotor stage (birth to 2 years), during which an infant conceptualizes the world in terms of schemas that incorporate sensory information and motor activities; 2) the preoperational stage (2 to 7 years), during which children can think in mental images, but exhibit egocentric thinking; 3) the concrete operational stage (7 to 11 years), during which children increase their ability to reason logically; and 4) the formal operational stage (11 years on), during which an individual uses full adult logic and can understand abstract concepts.

Kohlberg's theory of moral development is concerned with the logical process of arriving at answers to moral dilemmas. Kohlberg's theory proposes the following levels of moral development: 1) the premoral level, when the child has no sense of morality as adults understand the term; 2) the conventional level, when a child's moral view is based on what others will think of him or her; and 3) the principled level, when individuals judge right and wrong according to ethical principles rather than by the consequences of the actions.

Gilligan suggests that females progress through three stages of moral development: 1) morality as individual survival, 2) morality as self-sacrifice, and 3) morality as equality.

Erikson's theory of personality development suggests that individuals experience eight stages or crises, the outcomes of which will partly determine the future course of personality development. The development of the child proceeds through the following periods: 1) the neonatal period, the first two weeks of life marking the transition from the womb to independent life; 2) infancy, a time of rapid change in physical, perceptual, cognitive, linguistic, social, and emotional development; 3) early childhood, a period of great improvements in the coordination of small and large muscle groups; and 4) middle childhood, during which physical growth is slowed, but important cognitive changes occur, such as the ability to conserve and decenter.

Adolescence is the development period from the onset of puberty until the beginning of adulthood. The production of sex hormones in puberty triggers biological changes known as the primary sex characteristics. Menarche, the fist menstrual period, occurs in American females at about 12 years and 6 months, while males produce sperm about two years later. Within each sex, there is wide variation in the age at which puberty begins. Secondary sex characteristics appear in both sexes during puberty. The adolescent growth spurt lasts for slightly more than a year in early adolescence. In late adolescence weight gain is common due to a decline in the basal metabolism rate. For both sexes different parts of the body grow at different rates, weight and physique change in irregular ways, and many adolescents experience skin problems. According to Piaget, the formal operational stage, which is characterized by the ability to use abstract concepts, occurs in some individuals by about age 11. Peers replace the family as the most important influence on the adolescent. Adolescent emotions are characterized by an increase in parent-child conflict, more mood changes and an increase in risky behavior.

Adulthood is not a single phase of life. Challenges involving love, work, and play continue throughout adulthood. Psychologists disagree about whether the changes in adulthood are the result of programmed stages of biological development or are reactions to significant life events, such as starting a job, retiring, marriage, the birth of children, and so on.

Intelligence appears stable throughout adulthood in healthy adults. Some relatively positive personality changes that occur for many people during adulthood include becoming more insightful, dependable, and candid. Also, whereas women become less traditional shortly after marriage, men gradually become less traditional the longer they are married.

Erikson's developmental theory refers to early adulthood as the stage of intimacy vs. isolation. It is a time during which many individuals enter committed loving relationships. Erikson calls middle adulthood the stage of generativity vs. stagnation, the goal of which is to find meaning in work and family lives.

The period from the late 60s and beyond is referred to by Erikson as the stage of integrity vs. despair. According to Erikson, older adults who see meaning in their lives continue to live a satisfying existence.

Psychological variables associated with happy aging are whether one stays engaged in life's activities and whether one believes the myths about old age.

According to Baumrind, the three types of parental discipline styles are authoritarian, permissive, and authoritative. Children and parents are affected by each other's behavior. Research suggests that day-care children do not differ from those raised by others in their own homes in terms of physical health, emotional or intellectual development, or attachment.

Key Terms Exercise

For each of the following exercises, match the key terms on the left with the correct definitions on the right. Page references to the text follow the terms so that you may refer to the text for any items you answer incorrectly or do not understand completely. You may check your responses immediately by referring to the answers that follow each exercise.

Nature, Nurture, and Maturation

_____ 1. development (p. 237)	a. a time period in development that is qualitatively different from the periods that come before and after
_____ 2. maturation (p. 238)	
_____ 3. imprinting (p. 239)	
_____ 4. critical period (p. 239)	b. the more-or-less predictable changes in behavior associated with increasing age
_____ 5. early experiences (p. 241)	
_____ 6. stage (p. 243)	
	c. a biologically determined period during which certain forms of learning can take place most easily
	d. a form of early learning that takes place in some animals
ANSWERS	
1. b 4. c	e. systematic physical growth of the body
2. e 5. f	f. experience occurring early in development, believed by some to have lasting effects
3. d 6. a	

Development in Infancy and Childhood (I)

_____ 1. neonatal period (p. 250)
_____ 2. sensorimotor stage (p. 250)
_____ 3. object permanence (p. 251)
_____ 4. attachment (p. 252)
_____ 5. separation anxiety (p. 252)

a. the first 2 weeks of life following birth
b. the psychological bond between infants and caregivers
c. the period of cognitive development from birth to 2 years
d. the distress expressed by infants when they are separated from their caregivers
e. the understanding that objects continue to exist even after they are removed from view

ANSWERS
1. a   4. b
2. c   5. d
3. e

Development in Infancy and Childhood (II)

_____ 1. preoperational stage (p. 253)
_____ 2. egocentric (p. 253)
_____ 3. animism (p. 253)
_____ 4. transductive reasoning (p. 253)
_____ 5. concrete operational stage (p. 255)
_____ 6. conservation (p. 255)

a. the period of cognitive development from ages 2 to 7
b. the belief that inanimate objects are alive
c. the period of cognitive development from ages 7 to 11
d. the concept that quantity does not change just because superficial features have changed
e. self-centered thinking, characteristic of preoperational children
f. errors in inferring cause and effect relationships

ANSWERS
1. a   4. f
2. e   5. c
3. b   6. d

Adolescence

_____ 1. adolescence (p. 256)
_____ 2. puberty (p. 256)
_____ 3. formal operational stage (p. 257)
_____ 4. adolescent egocentrism (p. 258)

a. characterized by the ability to use abstract concepts
b. imaginary audience, the personal fable, hypocrisy, and pseudostupidity
c. the point at which the individual is physically capable of sexual reproduction
d. the period from the onset of puberty until the beginning of adulthood

ANSWERS
1. d   3. a
2. c   4. b

Who Am I?

Match the psychologists on the left with their contributions to the field of psychology on the right. Page references to the text follow the names of the psychologists so that you may refer to the text for further review of these psychologists and their contributions. You may check your responses immediately by referring to the answers that follow each exercise.

_____ 1. Konrad Lorenz (p. 239)
_____ 2. Harry and Margaret Harlow (p. 241)
_____ 3. Jean Piaget (p. 244)
_____ 4. Lawrence Kohlberg (p. 244)
_____ 5. Carol Gilligan (p. 246)
_____ 6. Erik Erikson (p. 247)

a. While studying geese, I observed imprinting.
b. My stage theory focuses on the development of moral reasoning, especially in boys.
c. My theory focuses on personality development and assumes that people pass through eight important stages.
d. Our studies of early social deprivation led to some surprising results.
e. I studied children extensively and proposed an important theory of cognitive development.
f. My research showed that the moral development of girls is different from that of boys.

ANSWERS
1. a   4. b
2. d   5. f
3. e   6. c

Review At A Glance
(Answers to this section may be found on page 150)

Preview: Development

The more-or-less predictable changes in behavior throughout our lives are described as the process of ___(1)___. The field of psychology that focuses on development across the lifespan is ___(2)___ psychology.

Nature, Nurture, and Maturation: Molding or Unfolding?

Most contemporary psychologists believe that behavior and developmental changes are controlled both by biological factors, called ___(3)___, and the psychological environment, called ___(4)___.

The most important biological factor in development is the systematic physical growth of the body, including the nervous system; this process is called ___(5)___. Research conducted with infants on toilet training supports the importance of ___(6)___.

Early Experience and Critical Periods

Konrad Lorenz has observed that goslings will follow any moving object that they are exposed to after hatching. He called this behavior ___(7)___. Imprinting can occur only during a brief period of a bird's life, called the ___(8)___

_____.

Harry and Margaret Harlow's research with monkeys focused on the effects of early __(9)__ deprivation. Infant monkeys were raised in complete __(10)__ for the first few months of life and never lived with a __(11)__. When the monkeys reached adulthood and were placed in cages with normal monkeys, the Harlows noticed that their behavior was distinctly __(12)__. When the mother-deprived monkeys became mothers themselves, they (13) their own infants. Opinions among psychologists are divided regarding the effects of abnormal early experiences among __(14)__.

Normal development is highly variable in two respects: 1) the differences __(15)__ children in their development and(2) the differences __(16)__ individual children in the rates at which they move from one developmental period to the next.

Stage Theories of Development

Psychologists who believe that behavior goes through a series of abrupt changes are called __(17)__ theorists. They believe that the changes occurring from one stage to the next are __(18)__ different, while changes that occur within each stage are __(19)__ different. Stages are believed to be __(20)__ programmed, and all children pass through the same stages in the same order. A well-known stage theory is Piaget's theory of __(21)__ development.

The stage theories of Kohlberg and Gilligan focus on the development of __(22)__ reasoning. According to Kohlberg, we pass through three major levels in the development of moral reasoning. The first level, in which children make moral judgment to obtain rewards and avoid punishment, is called the __(23)__ level. At the second level, moral decisions are based on what others, particularly parents, will think of them; this level is referred to as the __(24)__ level. At the third level, called the __(25)__ level, decisions are based on ethical principles rather than the consequences. According to Kohlberg, __(26)__ people reach a stage in which they reason mostly in principled ways. Gilligan has claimed that Kohlberg's theory does not always accurately describe the moral development in __(27)__. According to Gilligan, female moral development centers on the needs of people rather than on __(28)__. Gilligan's theory suggests that moral development progresses from morality as individual __(29)__, to morality as __(30)__-_____, and finally to morality as __(31)__.

Erik Erikson's theory, which focuses on developing relationships with people, describes major turning points or __(32)__ that all people experience. According to Erikson, the outcome of these crises will help determine future __(33)__ development.

Development in Infancy and Childhood

We are all in a constant change throughout our lives; the change is called __(34)__. The first two weeks of life are termed the __(35)__ period. When stimulated on the cheek, the neonate engages in the __(36)__ reflex. Apparently, neonates cannot see beyond about __(37)__ inches from their eyes.

At 2 weeks of age, the baby is called an ___(38)___. Infancy is characterized by rapid ___(39)___ development and rapid change in all ___(40)___. According to Piaget, the infant is in the ___(41)___ stage. From about 2 weeks on, the infant begins to interact ___(42)___ with its environment. According to Piaget, later in the sensorimotor stage, the child understands that objects exist even when they are out of sight; this is called ___(43)___ _____.

By 9 months, infants begin to understand some nouns. By age 2, the infant can communicate in word combinations called ___(44)___ speech.

At 2 months of age, the infant engages in true social behavior—___(45)___ at their caregivers. The emotion of ___(46)___ appears around four months. Shyness, fear of strangers, and fear of separation from caregivers begins between ___(47)___ to _____ months. Infants between 6 and 9 months also show fear and avoidance of Gibson's ___(48)___ cliff.

In early childhood, from ages 2 to 7, the child's physical growth is less explosive. According to Piaget, the child has entered the ___(49)___ stage. At the age of 2, most children can think in ___(50)___ images. The preoperational child's thought is self-centered, or ___(51)___, and the young child believes that inanimate objects are alive, a trait called (52)___. The preoperational child also makes errors in understanding cause-and-effect relationships, called ___(53)___ reasoning. The preoperational stage is also characterized by dramatic growth in ___(54)___.

The sequence of development in a child's play activities is: 1) playing alone, called ___(55)___ play; 2) playing near other children, called ___(56)___ play; and 3) playing with others, or ___(57)___ play. By the age of 2, most boys and girls have begun to act in ___(58)___-_____ ways.

The elementary school years occur while the child is in Piaget's ___(59)___ _____ stage. Children in this stage are able to use most adult concepts, with the exception of ___(60)___ concepts. They can order objects according to size and weight, called ___(61)___, and they understand that logical propositions can be reversed, called ___(62)___. Children in this stage also understand that the quantity of objects does not change if the shape or other superficial features have changed; this concept is called ___(63)___. Piaget has stated that conservation is possible when a child can think of more than one thing at a time, referred to as the ability to ___(64)___. Although ties to parents remain important, after age 7 friendships with ___(65)___ become more important to children. Friendship groups, called ___(66)___, also emerge during this stage.

Adolescent Development

Adolescence begins with the onset of ___(67)___. The hormones produced at puberty trigger a series of changes that lead to ___(68)___ and menstruation in females and to the production of ___(69)___ _____ in males; these are called the ___(70)___ _____ _____. The first menstrual period, called ___(71)___, begins at about 12 years and 6 months in females. Sperm cell production in males begins about ___(72)___ years later. For males and females, the more obvious physical changes occurring during puberty, such as lowering of the voice in males and development of the breasts in females, are called ___(73)___ _____ _____. Around the onset of puberty, adolescents experience a rapid increase in height and weight that is referred to as the ___(74)___ _____ _____.

At about age 11, some adolescents demonstrate an ability to use abstract concepts, which Piaget calls the ___(75)___ _____ stage. Adolescents often possess a self-centered type of thinking which Elkind has termed ___(76)___ _____. The primary characteristic of this type of thinking is that the adolescent feels that he or she is the focus of everyone's attention; this is termed the ___(77)___ _____. Adolescents may also feel that their problems are unique, which Elkind calls the ___(78)___ _____. Another characteristic of adolescent egocentrism involves criticizing others for actions and traits that they find acceptable in themselves, called ___(79)___. A final characteristic, involving oversimplified logic, is called ___(80)___.

Socially, the adolescent experiences a shift in orientation from parents to ___(81)___. Although most adolescents are relatively happy and well adjusted, three areas in which adolescents have greater problems are conflicts with ___(82)___, more dramatic shifts in ___(83)___, and increases in ___(84)___ behavior.

Adulthood

The body begins slow physical decline after ___(85)___ adulthood. Declines occur in the senses, especially ___(86)___, hearing and ___(87)___. Throughout adulthood, from the twenties to the seventies, small but steady increases occur in the knowledge of ___(88)___ and word ___(89)___. Research suggests that older adults perform as well as younger adults on tasks involving learning and ___(90)___ about concepts. Older adults do better than younger adults on tasks involving ___(91)___ meaning and wise decision making. Finally, older adults do less well than younger adults on tasks involving ___(92)___ reasoning and divergent thinking. Some facets of personality change more across the adult life span than others. For example, enjoyment of others and enjoyment of excitement are fairly stable throughout adulthood, while the desire for ___(93)___ and ___(94)___ are more subject to change.

Some psychologists believe that adulthood consists of a series of ___(95)___ of development. Stage theories of adulthood have been proposed by ___(96)___ and Levinson. These stages differ from the stages of child development in that 1) not every adult is believed to go through every stage, 2) the order of the stages can ___(97)___ for some individuals, and 3) the timing of the stages is not controlled by ___(98)___ maturation. Erikson refers to early adulthood as the stage of ___(99)___ vs. ___(100)___. According to Levinson, early adulthood consists of three briefer stages: 1) creating an adult manner of working and living independently characterize the ___(101)___ to early adulthood; (2) reevaluating one's start into adult life occurs in the ___(102)___ _____ _____; and 3) working hard toward one's goals characterizes the culmination of ___(103)___ _____.

Middle adulthood is characterized by shifting from a focus on who we are ___(104)___ to thinking about who we ___(105)___. Erikson believes that the challenges of middle adulthood are to find ___(106)___ in our activities. He calls this stage ___(107)___ _____ _____. Levinson describes four brief stages of middle adulthood. The first of these stages reaches a peak in the early forties and is sometimes a period of anguish; it is called the ___(108)___. A period of calm and stability follows, called entering ___(109)___ _____. Another period of reassessment occurs for most individuals in the age 50 ___(110)___, followed by another stable period from about age 55 to 65, called the culmination of ___(111)___ ___ _____.

The ___(112)___, which begins around age 45, is marked by a loss of the capacity to reproduce in women and by a decline in the reproductive capacity of men. In women, the end of menstruation is called the ___(113)___. Research suggests that the difficulties of menopause experienced by some women may be influenced by their ___(114)___. According to Erikson, individuals in their late 60s and beyond are in the stage called ___(115)___ vs. ___(116)___.

Among the criticisms of the stage theories are: 1) the early studies tended to focus more on ___(117)___ ; 2) the theories need to take into account cultural ___(118)___ and historical changes; and 3) not all developmentalists view adulthood as a series of ___(119)___.

Aging is partly a biological process, but it involves many ___(120)___ aspects as well. Two keys to happy aging are 1) staying ___(121)___ in life's activities and 2) ignoring ___(122)___ about old age. Research found that people rated as having a ___(123)___, dependable and ___(124)___ personality in childhood experienced greater longevity. Those who were rated as "___(125)___" in childhood tended to die at a younger age.

Application of Psychology: Parenting

According to Baumrind, parental discipline styles are of three types: 1) the ___(126)___ parent provides strict rules with little discussion of the reasons for the rules; 2) the ___(127)___ parent gives the child few rules and rarely punishes misbehavior; and 3) the ___(128)___ parent is an authority figure to the child, but explains and discusses rules. According to Baumrind, middle class white children of ___(129)___ parents are happier and better behaved. However, that style may not be best in all American cultures.

According to Richard Bell and others, children affect their ___(130)___ behavior as much as parents affect their ___(131)___ behavior. According to O'Leary, the most common discipline mistakes made by ineffective parents are lax discipline, reinforcement of ___(132)___ behavior, verbosity, and ___(133)___.

Sociocultural factors are important in understanding differences in parenting. For example, collectivistic cultures are more likely to emphasize the well-being of the ___(134)___ and the larger culture, whereas ___(135)___ cultures place more emphasis on individual achievement.

Research suggests that there are generally no differences between children in ___(136)___ _____ and children being raised by parents in their own home in terms of their physical health, emotional or intellectual development, or attachment. Furthermore, children whose parents divorce may experience ___(137)___ _____, but usually the disruptions are for a relatively brief period of time.

Concept Checks

Fill in the missing components of the following concept boxes. The correct answers are located in the "Answers" section at the end of the chapter.

Developmental Theories

Theorist	Developmental Areas	Proposed Stages
Piaget	cognitive	
	moral	premoral, conventional, and principled reasoning
Gilligan	moral	
	social	eight stages or crises, the outcome of which will determine future personality development

Developmental Concepts

Term	Definition
imprinting	
critical period	
	a term that applies to the infant in the first two weeks of life
cooperative play	
	occurring during puberty, ovulation and menstruation in females and the production of mature sperm in males
	development of the breast and hips in females; growth of the testes, broadening shoulders, and so on in males; growth of pubic hair and body hair in both sexes
climacteric	

Extending the Chapter: Psychology, Societal Issues, and Human Diversity

These questions may be assigned to you. Whether or not they are assigned, they are designed to be challenging questions to encourage you to think independently about the material in the chapter. Many of the questions have no right or wrong answers.

I.   From the *Applications of Psychology* section

1.   Describe the advantages and disadvantages of each of Baumrind's discipline styles. Include both the child's perspective and the parent's perspective in your answer.

2.   Describe examples of sociocultural factors in parenting that you have observed.

II.   Psychology, Societal Issues, and Human Diversity

1.   How much freedom should a parent have to discipline a child? How can society balance the right of a parent to discipline a child with the duty to protect the rights of the child?

2.   What steps should our society take to minimize the difficulties associated with adolescence?

3.   Given the increasing reliance on day care centers, to what extent should our society increase the regulation of day care center operations, employees, and so on?

4.   Should researchers engage in efforts to expand the upper limits of the human lifespan? Why or why not?

5.   (From the *Human Diversity* section of the text) Discuss the choices parents must make when they have a child who cannot hear.

Practice Quiz

The practice quiz consists of three sections: 1) Short Answer questions, 2) Multiple choice questions, and 3) True-False questions. At the end of the chapter you will find suggested answers to the short answer questions, answers and explanation for the multiple choice questions, and answers to the true-false questions.

Short Answer Questions

1.   Describe the development of cognitive abilities during the preoperational stage.

_____

_____

2.   List and describe the characteristics of adolescent egocentrism.

_____

_____

3. Distinguish between the theories of moral development proposed by Kohlberg and Gilligan.

_____

_____

Multiple Choice Questions

1. The debate among psychologists regarding the relative contributions of environment and heredity to the developmental process is called
   a. the critical period.
   b. the nature-nurture controversy.
   c. the stage controversy.
   d. behaviorism.
   LO 1

2. Research on toilet training conducted with identical twins illustrates the importance of which developmental factor?
   a. maturation
   b. imprinting
   c. nurture
   d. genetics
   LO 1

3. Lorenz observed that after hatching, baby goslings will follow any moving object to which they are exposed. He called this behavior
   a. maturation.
   b. exprinting.
   c. imprinting.
   d. follow-the-leader.
   LO 2

4. Research conducted by the Harlows underscores the profound importance of
   a. imprinting.
   b. maturation.
   c. early experience.
   d. all of the above.
   LO 3

5. With regard to variation in development, the text asserts that
   a. different children develop at different rates.
   b. children vary in their *own* rate of development from one period to the next.
   c. little variation exists between children beyond the age of seven.
   d. a and b above.
   LO 4

6. Each of the following is a belief of stage theorists *except*
   a. as children progress through the stages, the differences between children are qualitative.
   b. as children progress through the stages, the differences are quantitative.
   c. children pass through the same stages in the same order.
   d. stages are biologically programmed to unfold.
   LO 5

7. According to Kohlberg, at what level of moral development would a child most likely be concerned about pleasing his parents and teachers?
   a. the preconventional level
   b. the premoral level
   c. the conventional level
   d. the principled level
   LO 6

8. According to Gilligan, a woman in the most advanced stage of moral development experiences morality as
   a. individual survival.
   b. self-sacrifice.
   c. inequality.
   d. equality.
   LO 7

9. Which theorist is most likely to suggest that important gender differences exist in moral development?
   a. Gilligan
   b. Kohlberg
   c. Piaget
   d. Erikson
   LO 8

10. The stage during which Erikson believes a child learns to meet the demands imposed by society is
    a. basic trust vs. mistrust.
    b. autonomy vs. shame and doubt.
    c. industry vs. inferiority.
    d. identity vs. role confusion.
    LO 9

11 A child who failed to learn multiplication and division in grade school did not successfully complete which of Erikson's stages of personality development?
    a. autonomy vs. shame and doubt
    b. integrity vs. despair
    c. industry vs. inferiority
    d. initiative vs. guilt
    LO 9

12. The neonatal period refers to the first
    a. 2 hours of life.
    b. 2 days of life.
    c. 2 weeks of life.
    d. 2 months of life.
    LO 10

13. What BEST distinguishes the infancy stage from other stages of development?
    a. Physical growth is most rapid in the first year.
    b. Cognitive growth is 5 times greater than in any other developmental stage
    c. Emotions are fully developed before the next developmental stage.
    d. It is the only stage that has no emotional development.
    LO 10

14. Which of the following is *not* developed during the infancy period?
    a. object permanence
    b. telegraphic speech
    c. separation anxiety
    d. transductive reasoning
    LO 11

15. Which of the following is characteristic of the preoperational child?
    a. the child is egocentric
    b. the child uses transductive reasoning
    c. the child is capable of abstract thought
    d. *a* and *b* above
    LO 12

16. Which of the following describes the correct developmental sequence of play?
    a. parallel play, solitary play, cooperative play
    b. solitary play, cooperative play, parallel play
    c. solitary play, parallel play, cooperative play
    d. cooperative play, solitary play, parallel play
    LO 12

17. Friendship groups or cliques begin to develop during which of the stages of cognitive development?
    a. preoperational
    b. concrete operational
    c. sensorimotor
    d. formal operational
    LO 13

18. The recognition that the volume of water remains the same whether it is in a short, wide beaker, or a long, narrow beaker is called
    a. reversibility.
    b. conservation.
    c. decentering.
    d. formal operations.
    LO 13

19. Which of the following is *not* a primary sex characteristic?
    a. ovulation in females
    b. lowering of the voice in males
    c. menstruation in females
    d. production of sperm in males
    LO 14

20. The concepts of liberty and justice can be understood by an adolescent who
    a. has achieved the concrete operational stage.
    b. has achieved the formal operational stage.
    c. does not exhibit pseudostupidity.
    d. does not exhibit hypocrisy.
    LO 15

21. Debbie, an adolescent, feels that she is the only person in the world who has ever had a crush on the boy who sits next to her, argued with her parents, and had complexion problems. Which component of adolescent egocentrism is she experiencing?
    a. imaginary audience
    b. personal fable
    c. hypocrisy
    d. pseudostupidity
    LO 15

22. In which of the following areas do adolescents have more challenges when compared with younger and older individuals?
    a. parent-child conflicts
    b. mood changes
    c. risky behavior
    d. all of the above
    LO 16

23. Which of the following cognitive abilities improves throughout adulthood?
    a. reasoning about everyday problems
    b. knowledge of facts and word meanings
    c. abstract problem solving and divergent thinking
    d. general recall
    LO 17

24. Compared to individuals in their 20s, individuals in their 70s showed declines in
    a. knowledge of word meanings.
    b. understanding mathematical concepts.
    c. solving life problems.
    d. fluid intelligence.
    LO 17

25. Adult personalities are likely to change in each of the following areas *except*
    a. enjoyment of being with other people.
    b. becoming more dependable.
    c. becoming more candid.
    d. becoming more accepting of life's hardships.
    LO 18

26. Jerry, age 67, and Al, age 65, are acquaintances. Jerry feels his life is meaningful and enjoys his existence, but he has noticed that Al has lately withdrawn and sees his life as a "bunch of unmet goals." These individuals illustrate which of Erikson's stages?
    a. basic trust vs. mistrust
    b. intimacy vs. isolation
    c. generativity vs. stagnation
    d. integrity vs. despair
    LO 18

27. Hank, age 47, has recently changed careers and has joined a health club. His behavior falls into which of Levinson's stages?
    a. entering middle adulthood
    b. midlife transition
    c. age 50 transition
    d. settling down
    LO 19

28. Each of the following is true regarding the climacteric *except*
    a. it eventually leads to menopause in women.
    b. it is characterized by a decline in the reproductive capacity of men.
    c. about half of women experience discomfort during menopause.
    d. there are widespread psychological and sexual effects in men.
    LO 20

29. Common myths about menopause include
    a. the body will rapidly age after menopause.
    b. menopause is associated with an increase in illness.
    c. sexual interest decreases after menopause.
    d. all of the above.
    LO 20

30. Each of the following has been a criticism of stage theories of development *except*:
    a. They are difficult to understand.
    b. They don't account for gender differences.
    c. Few cross-cultural studies of stage theories exist.
    d. The stage approach is not universally accepted.
    LO 21

31. In the Terman study, which personality factor was MOST associated with early death?
    a. conscientiousness
    b. cheerfulness
    c. dependability
    d. truthfulness
    LO 22

32. According to the text, happy aging is associated with staying engaged in life's activities and
    a. being cheerful.
    b. focusing on charitable activities.
    c. ignoring the myths of old age.
    d. being financially comfortable.
    LO 22

33. According to Baumrind, the best behaved and happiest children have parents who use what style of parenting?
    a. authoritarian
    b. permissive
    c. authoritative
    d. disciplinarian
    LO 23

34. The "two-way street" concept in childrearing suggests that
    a. both mothers *and* fathers need to accept responsibility for childrearing.
    b. parents need to be consistent in their childrearing approaches with *all* their children.
    c. children act as important influences on their siblings.
    d. children's behavior affects their parents' behavior just as parents' behavior affects their children's behavior.
    LO 23

35. According to research comparing children in day-care centers versus children raised by mothers in their own homes, the biggest differences were found in the children's
    a. physical health.
    b. intellectual development.
    c. attachment.
    d. none of the above
    LO 24

True-False Questions

_____1. Researchers have observed imprinting in human infants.

_____2. Neonate is the term applied to the newborn during the first two weeks of life.

_____3. According to Piaget, object permanence is a significant accomplishment during the sensorimotor stage.

_____4. Animism and transductive reasoning are characteristics of the concrete operational stage.

_____5. Adolescents rarely engage in egocentric behavior, since most adolescents have achieved formal operational reasoning.

_____6. Early and middle adulthood is marked by improvements in crystallized intelligence.

_____7. According to Erikson, middle adulthood is the stage of integrity vs. despair.

_____8. The Terman study found that those who were rated as being "cheerful" children tended to die at earlier ages.

_____9. According to Baumrind, the authoritarian parent encourages independence by explaining rules, and rarely uses punishment.

_____10. According to O'Leary, common discipline mistakes include lax parenting, verbosity, and overreactivity.

ANSWER SECTION

Concept Checks

Developmental Theories

Theorist	Developmental Areas	Proposed Stages
Piaget	cognitive	sensorimotor, preoperational, concrete operational, and formal operational
Kohlberg	moral	premoral, conventional, and principled reasoning
Gilligan	moral	morality as individual survival, morality as self-sacrifice, and morality as equality
Erikson	social	eight stages or crises, the outcome of which will determine future personality development

Developmental Concepts

Term	Definition
imprinting	a form of early learning that occurs in goslings and other animals; imprinting can occur only during a critical period
critical period	a biologically determined period in the life of some animals during which certain forms of learning can take place most easily
neonate	a term that applies to the infant in the first two weeks of life
cooperative play	characteristic of the end of Piaget's preoperational stage, this type of play involves cooperation between two or more children; this type of play occurs after a stage of solitary play and parallel play
primary sex characteristics	occuring during puberty, ovulation and menstruation in females and the production of mature sperm in males
secondary sex characteristics	development of the breast and hips in females; growth of the testes, broadening shoulders, and so on in males; growth of pubic hair and body hair in both sexes
climacteric	period between about ages 45 and 60, characterized by a loss of capacity to reproduce in women and a decline of reproductive capacity in men

Sample Answers for Short Answer Questions

1. Describe the development of cognitive abilities during the preoperational stage.

The preoperational stage begins around the age of 2 and lasts until the age of 7. The young child's thinking is characterized by egocentrism, in which the child views himself as the center of the universe. One example of egocentric thinking is animism, the belief that inanimate objects are alive. Another characteristic is transductive reasoning, that is, errors in thinking about cause-and-effect relationships. Toward the end of this stage, the child has begun to grasp logical operations and engages in fewer cause-and-effect errors.

2. List and describe the characteristics of adolescent egocentrism.

Adolescent egocentrism is Elkind's concept for explaining some adolescent thought. It is characterized by the imaginary audience, in which the adolescent is always "on stage." Another characteristic is the personal fable, in which the adolescent believes that nobody can understand what he or she is going through; a third characteristic is excessive hypocrisy; and the fourth characteristic is pseudostupidity, or thinking about issues by using oversimplified logic.

3. Distinguish between the theories of moral development proposed by Kohlberg and Gilligan.

Kohlberg views moral development as progressing in three stages. In the first stage, called the premoral level, moral judgments are made for rewards and to avoid punishment. In the second level, called the conventional level, moral decisions are based on rules. In the third level, called the principled level, decisions are based on one's principles of morality. Kohlberg's theory has been criticized for emphasizing a male perspective and largely ignoring a female perspective on moral development. Gilligan's theory, emphasizing a female perspective, also describes morality as progressing through three stages. The first, morality as individual survival, also emphasizes rewards and punishment. The second perspective, called morality as self-sacrifice, emphasizes sacrificing as one's own needs and meeting the needs of others. In the final stage, morality as equality, the person views his or her needs as being equal to those of others.

Answers to Review At A Glance

1.	development	20.	biologically	39.	physical
2.	developmental	21.	cognitive	40.	senses
3.	nature	22.	moral	41.	sensorimotor
4.	nurture	23.	premoral	42.	actively
5.	maturation	24.	conventional	43.	object permanence
6.	maturation	25.	principled	44.	telegraphic
7.	imprinting	26.	few	45.	smiling
8.	critical period	27.	girls	46.	anger
9.	social	28.	abstractions	47.	6 to 9
10.	isolation	29.	survival	48.	visual
11.	mother	30.	self-sacrifice	49.	preoperational
12.	abnormal	31.	equality	50.	mental
13.	rejected	32.	crises	51.	egocentric
14.	humans	33.	personality	52.	animism
15.	between	34.	development	53.	transductive
16.	within	35.	neonatal	54.	language
17.	stage	36.	rooting	55.	solitary
18.	qualitatively	37.	12	56.	parallel
19.	quantitatively	38.	infant	57.	cooperative

58.	sex-typed	84.	risky	111.	middle adulthood
59.	concrete operational	85.	early	112.	climacteric
60.	abstract	86.	vision	113.	severe
61.	seriation	87.	smell	114.	expectations
62.	reversibility	88.	facts	115.	integrity
63.	conservation	89.	meanings	116.	despair
64.	decenter	90.	reasoning	117.	men
65.	peers	91.	word	118.	differences
66.	cliques	92.	abstract	119.	stages
67.	puberty	93.	power	120.	psychological
68.	ovulation	94.	achievement	121.	engaged
69.	sperm cells	95.	stages	122.	myths
70.	primary sex characteristics	96.	Erikson	123.	conscientious
71.	menarche	97.	vary	124.	truthful
72.	two	98.	biological	125.	cheerful
73.	secondary sex characteristics	99.	intimacy	126.	authoritarian
		100.	isolation	127.	permissive
74.	adolescent growth spurt	101.	entry	128.	authoritative
75.	formal operational	102.	age 30 transition	129.	authoritative
76.	adolescent egocentrism	103.	early adulthood	130.	parents'
77.	imaginary audience	104.	becoming	131.	children's
78.	personal fable	105.	are	132.	inappropriate
79.	hypocrisy	106.	meaning	133.	overreactivity
80.	pseudostupidity	107.	generativity vs. stagnation	134.	family
81.	peers	108.	midlife transition	135.	individualistic
82.	parents	109.	middle adulthood	136.	day care
83.	moods	110.	transition	137.	emotional turmoil

Multiple Choice Answers

1. The answer is *b*. "Nature" refers to biological factors and "nurture" refers to environmental factors.
2. The answer is *a*. Maturational factors refer to the systematic physical growth of the body, including the nervous system. The experience of the twins suggests that, with potty training, a child isn't ready until he's ready.
3. The answer is *c*. According to Lorenz, imprinting is a special form of learning because it is highly constrained by biological factors. Goslings will imprint on the first noisy, moving object they see, and this generally occurs only during a brief "window" of time, called the critical period.
4. The answer is *c*. The Harlows conducted research with monkeys who were raised in isolation for the first few months of their lives. Later in the monkey's lives, they exhibited gross abnormalities in their behavior.
5. The answer is *d*. Although many psychologists are engaged in trying to describe and understand the normal developmental changes that take place in childhood, it is important to realize that development is highly variable.
6. The answer is *b*. Stage theorists believe that the changes occurring from one stage to the next make children different "in kind" rather than merely "different in amount."
7. The answer is *c*. According to Kohlberg, children at the conventional level are concerned with making moral decisions on the basis of what others, especially parents, will think of them. At the next level, called the principled level, actions come to be based on the ethical principles involved.
8. The answer is *d*. According to Gilligan, in this most advanced stage of morality, the woman views her own needs as equal to those of others.
9. The answer is *a*. Kohlberg has argued that Gilligan's approach overestimates sex differences in moral development.

10. The answer is *c*. According to Erikson, each stage presents a crisis or turning point, the outcome of which will determine future personality development. The challenge of the stage of industry vs. inferiority, which occurs between the ages of 5 and 11, is to meet the demands imposed by school and home; if these demands are not met, the child will come to feel inferior to others.

11. The answer is *c*. Erikson's theory would suggest that feelings of inferiority regarding math skills (and potentially other skills) might be a consequence of this situation. On the other hand, mastering skills leads to a sense that effort leads to success.

12. The answer is *c*. During this period of time, the infant engages in a variety of reflexes, displays well-developed sensory abilities, and exhibits the following emotional states: surprise, happiness, discomfort, distress, and interest.

13. The answer is *a*. Although recent research has underscored the cognitive achievements of infancy, the most dramatic changes of infancy appear to be related to physical growth.

14. The answer is *d*. Transductive reasoning refers to errors in cause-and-effect reasoning which are commonly made by preoperational children. Before proceeding, be sure you can describe object permanence, telegraphic speech, and separation anxiety.

15. The answer is *d*. According to Piaget, another characteristic of the preoperational stage is animism (the belief that inanimate objects are alive). The child is not ready for abstract thought, according to Piaget, until the formal operational stage.

16. The answer is *c*. This sequence seems to parallel cognitive development. That is, children whose thinking is still highly egocentric might be expected to engage in solitary play. As egocentric thinking declines, cooperative play becomes possible.

17. The answer is *b*. These friendship groups occur in middle childhood, a time marked by the intellectual achievements of conservation, reversibility and decentering.

18. The answer is *b*. Reversibility is the concrete operational concept that logical operations can be reversed. Decentering allows the concrete operational child to consider more than one feature of an object at a time. Formal operation is the last stage of Piaget's theory.

19. The answer is *b*. Primary sex characteristics indicate that the adolescent has the ability to reproduce; thus, ovulation and menstruation in females and the production of mature sperm cells in males are considered primary sex characteristics. The more obvious changes, such as development of the breasts and hips in females and the lowering of the voice in males, are considered secondary sex characteristics.

20. The answer is *b*. The formal operational stage is characterized by an ability to use abstract concepts, such as liberty and justice. Pseudostupidity and hypocrisy are characteristics of adolescent egocentrism, discussed in the next question.

21. The answer is *b*. The imaginary audience is characterized by the belief that others are watching the adolescent's every move; hence, any blunder will be noticed by everyone. Adolescent egocentrism is also characterized by excessive hypocrisy and by pseudostupidity, the use of oversimplified logic.

22. The answer is *d*. In spite of these problem areas, current research suggests that a majority of adolescents are relatively happy and well-adjusted.

23. The answer is *b*. Reasoning about everyday problems does not decline before age 75. Slight declines occur in abstract problem solving, divergent thinking, and cognitive skills involving speed.

24. The answer is *d*. Fluid intelligence, introduced in the previous chapter, refers to the ability to learn or invent new strategies to solve a new problem. Short-term memory skills also decline during later adulthood.

25. The answer is *a*. Some traits, such as enjoyment of being with other people, enjoyment of excitement, and the general level of activity are stable throughout adulthood.

26. The answer is *d*. According to Erikson, the older adult who sees meaning in his or her life continues to live a satisfying existence, while the person who sees life as a series of unmet goals may come to experience despair.

27. The answer is *a*. According to Levinson, the entry into middle adulthood generally takes place from ages 45 to 50 and is occasionally marked by career and other dramatic changes such as divorce or geographical moves. For most, however, it is a period of calm and stability.

28. The answer is *d*. Although men produce fewer sperm cells and experience slight changes in the pattern of sexual arousal, the climacteric seems to have few psychological or sexual effects for men.

29. The answer is *c*. Menopause refers to the cessation of menstruation and the capacity to reproduce. According to Masters and Johnson, many women experience no sexual difficulties or loss of sexual interest after menopause.

30. The answer is *a*. Although stage theories have been popular in developmental psychology, in part because they are easy to understand, they have been criticized on gender, cultural and historical grounds.

31. The answer is *b*. An explanation of this finding is that cheerful children were more likely to take risks and to smoke and drink as adults.

32. The answer is *c*. Refusing to accept the stereotypes associated with older adulthood is an important component of "happy aging."

33. The answer is *c*. At first glance the words *authoritarian* and *authoritative* might seem similar, but there are important differences. According to Baumrind, authoritarian parents dole out strict rules and little discussion. Authoritative parents, however, act as authority figures for their children, but encourage their children to voice their opinions as well. Permissive parents provide few rules and rarely punish misbehavior.

34. The answer is *d*. The concept is actually quite logical: The child's behavior influences the style of discipline used by the parents and vice versa.

35. The answer is *d*. Research has not found any differences in these characteristics between day care children and children raised by parents at home.

Answers to True-False Questions

1. F
2. T
3. T
4. F
5. F
6. T
7. F
8. T
9. F
10. T

Chapter 9   Motivation and Emotion

Learning Objectives

1. Distinguish between motivation and emotion. (p. 280)

2. Describe the relationship between primary motives and homeostatic mechanisms. (p. 281)

3. Describe the biological and psychological regulation of hunger. (p. 281)

4. Discuss the biological and psychological regulation of thirst. (p. 284)

5. Identify the need for novel stimulation and distinguish between optimal arousal theory and the Yerkes-Dodson law. (p. 286)

6. Distinguish between affiliation motivation and achievement motivation. (p. 287)

7. Distinguish between intrinsic and extrinsic motivation. (p. 289)

8. Identify the components of Maslow's hierarchy of motives. (p. 291)

9. Describe Watson and Tellegen's emotional map. (p. 294)

10. Describe the cognitive theory of emotion. (p. 295)

11. Discuss the roles of learning and culture in emotions. (p. 298)

12. Distinguish among the following theories of aggression: Freud's instinct theory, the frustration-aggression theory, and the social learning theory. (p. 299)

13. (From the *Application of Psychology* section) Describe the American obsession with being thin and identify methods suggested to successfully lose weight. (p. 303)

Chapter Overview

"Motivation" refers to an internal state that activates behavior and gives direction to our thoughts. Emotions are positive or negative feelings usually accompanied by behavior and physiological arousal that generally occur in response to stimulus situations.

Primary motives are motives for things that are necessary for survival, such as food, water, and warmth. Homeostatic mechanisms in the body help to regulate biological imbalances and stimulate actions to restore the proper balance.

Hunger is a primary motive that is biologically regulated by three centers in the hypothalamus; one is referred to as the feeding system; another is called the satiety system. The third center both increases and decreases appetite by controlling blood sugar levels. Among humans, the cues that help regulate hunger on a daily basis are stomach contractions and blood sugar levels; body fat levels appear to be involved in the long-term regulation of hunger. Psychological factors, such as learning, emotions, and incentives, are also involved in the regulation of food intake.

Thirst is also regulated by the hypothalamus. The cues that help regulate drinking include mouth dryness, loss of water by cells, and reductions in blood volume. Psychological factors such as learning and incentives also help to regulate thirst.

Psychological motives are motives that are related to the individual's happiness and well-being, but not to survival. Among the important psychological motives are 1) seeking novel stimulation; 2) seeking an optimal level of arousal (the Yerkes-Dodson law states that if arousal is too low, performance will be inadequate, but if arousal is too high, it may disrupt performance); 3) the motive for affiliation, the preference to be with others; and 4) achievement motivation, the psychological need for success.

Motivation can also be characterized as either intrinsic, which refers to motives stimulated by the inherent nature of the activity, or extrinsic, those stimulated by external rewards. According to Maslow, motives are organized in a hierarchy, arranged from the most basic to the most personal and advanced.

Emotions are the experiences that give color, meaning, and intensity to our lives. According to Schachter and Singer, the cognitive process involves interpreting stimuli from both the environment and the body. Most psychologists believe that many basic emotions are primarily inborn but that learning plays an important role in emotions.

Aggression is a complex phenomenon, and its origins are the subject of continuing controversy. Freud suggested that all people are born with potent aggressive instincts released through the process of catharsis, while other psychologists believe that aggression is a reaction to the blocking of important motives (the frustration-aggression theory). A third view, held by social learning theorists, explains aggression as learned behavior.

Although many people are dieting to try to lose weight at any given time, there are dangers to dieting. These include the risks of developing anorexia nervosa or bulimia, and the health risks associated with yo-yo dieting. The text recommends eating differently instead of dieting, exercising regularly, and avoiding lapses in a healthy lifestyle.

Key Terms Exercise

For each of the following exercises, match the key terms on the left with the correct definitions on the right. Page references to the text follow the terms so that you may refer to the text for any items you answer incorrectly or do not understand completely. You may check your responses immediately by referring to the answers that follow each exercise.

Primary Motives

_____ 1. motivation (p. 280)
_____ 2. emotion (p. 281)
_____ 3. primary motives (p. 281)
_____ 4. homeostatic mechanism (p. 281)
_____ 5. lateral hypothalamus (p. 282)
_____ 6. ventromedial hypothalamus (p. 282)
_____ 7. paraventricular nucleus (p. 282)
_____ 8. incentives (p. 284)

a. motives for things that are necessary for survival
b. an internal mechanism that regulates bodily functions
c. external cues that activate motivation
d. an internal state that activates behavior and gives it direction
e. positive and negative feelings that are accompanied by physiological arousal
f. a part of the hypothalamus involved in inhibiting eating; the satiety center
g. a part of the hypothalamus that regulates blood sugar
h. a part of the hypothalamus involved in feeling hungry; the feeding center

ANSWERS
1. d   5. h
2. e   6. f
3. a   7. g
4. b   8. c

Psychological Motives (I)

_____ 1. psychological motives (p. 286)
_____ 2. novel stimulation (p. 286)
_____ 3. optimal level of arousal (p. 287)
_____ 4. Yerkes-Dodson law (p. 287)
_____ 5. motive for affiliation (p. 287)
_____ 6. acievement motivation (p. 288)

a. new or changed experience
b. effective performance is more likely if the level of arousal is suitable for the activity
c. individuals are motivated to achieve an optimal level of arousal by increasing or decreasing their stimulation
d. motives related to happiness and well-being, but not to survival
e. the psychological need for success in competitive situations
f. the general preference to be with other people

ANSWERS
1. d   4. b
2. a   5. f
3. c   6. e

Psychological Motives (II)/Theories of Emotion and Aggression

_____ 1. intrinsic motivation (p. 289)
_____ 2. extrinsic motivation (p. 290)
_____ 3. Maslow's hierarchy of motives (p. 291)
_____ 4. self-actualization (p. 291)
_____ 5. Freud's instinct theory (p. 300)
_____ 6. frustration-aggression theory (p. 300)

a. the inner drive of humans to use their potential to the fullest
b. motives stimulated by external rewards
c. the view that humans have inborn aggressive instincts that must be released in some way
d. motives stimulated by the inherent nature of the activity
e. the view that human motives are organized from the most basic (biological) to the most advanced (self-actualization)
f. the theory that aggression is a natural reaction to the frustration of important motives

ANSWERS
1. d   4. a
2. b   5. c
3. e   6. f

Review At A Glance

(Answers to this section may be found on page 166)

Definitions of Motivation and Emotion

Motivation refers to an ____(1)____ state that activates and gives direction to our thoughts. The positive or negative feelings in response to stimulus situations are called ____(2)____. Emotions are accompanied by ____(3)____ arousal. Motivation and emotion are closely linked in the following ways: 1) both motivation and emotion ____(4)____ behavior; 2) motives are often accompanied by emotions; and 3) emotions often have motivational properties of their own. Human motives for things that are necessary for survival are called ____(5)____ motives. The essential life elements in the body are regulated by an internal mechanism called the ____(6)____ mechanism.

The biological control center for hunger is the ____(7)____. Hunger is regulated in the hypothalamus by three systems: the one that initiates eating when food is needed, called the ____(8)____ system is located in the ____(9)____ hypothalamus. A second system, which signals the body to stop eating, is called the ____(10)____ system and is located in the ____(11)____ hypothalamus. Destruction of the ventromedial hypothalamus leads to a condition called ____(12)____. The paraventricular nucleus, also located in the hypothalamus, regulates appetite by controlling blood ____(13)____ levels. Two cues regulate hunger on a daily basis: ____(14)____ contractions and ____(15)____ sugar levels. The liver and the ____(16)____ send messages to the hypothalamus to help regulate eating. The islets of ____(17)____ secrete two hormones that help regulate hunger. A feeling of hunger is produced when ____(18)____ is secreted into the bloodstream; conversely, a person no longer feels hungry when ____(19)____ is injected into the bloodstream. Long-term maintenance of body weight is regulated by the hypothalamus as it monitors ____(20)____ levels. When leptin is detected by the hypothalamus, it reacts in three different ways: the ventromedial satiety center sends a message to ___(21)___ eating, the paraventricular nucleus regulates the blood ___(22)___ level, and the ventromedial hypothalamus activates the ___(23)___ nervous system. Scientists have hypothesized that each of us has a different ___(24)_____ for body fat. It appears to be difficult to raise or lower body weight above or below the (25)_____.

Psychological factors, such as learning and ___(26)___, also regulate food intake. People trying to limit their food intake may have trouble with external cues (such as the sight of a dessert) that activate motives; these are referred to as ___(27)___. Laboratory research with animals has shown that incentives can push weight above the natural ___(28) _____.

The hypothalamus also contains two centers that control drinking, the ___(29)___ system and the ___(30)_____ system. The hypothalamus uses three main cues in regulating drinking: mouth ___(31)___, cell ___(32) levels, and total ___(33)_____.

Psychological Motives

Motives that are not directly related to biological survival are called ___(34)___ motives.

Most people are easily bored if there is little stimulation; we have an apparently inborn motive to seek ___(35)_____. Too much stimulation or too little stimulation makes us feel uncomfortable; individuals strive for an ___(36)___ level of arousal. To achieve an effective performance, the level of arousal must be suitable for the activity, according to the ___(37)___-_____ law.

Another psychological motive is the preference to be with other people, called the motive for ___(38)___. Some psychologists believe that this motivation is an ___(39)___ need, while others believe it is a ___(40)___ motive. Researchers have found that ___(41)___ and painful experiences increase our motive to affiliate.

The psychological motive to succeed is called ___(42)_____. According to research by Elliott and Church, key elements in achievement motivation among college students include establishing ___(43)___ goals, performance-___(44)___ goals, and performance-___(45)___ goals. In research conducted in a college course, these different types of achievement motivation were associated with different ___(46)___ at the end of the course. A factor that can lead people to achieve below their potential is fear of ___(47)___.

When people are motivated by the inherent nature of the activity or its natural consequences, the situation is referred to as ___(48)___ motivation. Motivation which is external to an activity is called ___(49)___ motivation. Although low frequency behaviors can be increased with extrinsic motivation, adding incentives to an activity that is already intrinsically motivated may ___(50)___ from the intrinsic motivation. Research suggests that ___(51)___ factors are important in understanding motivation.

Abraham Maslow's theory states that motives are arranged in a ___(52)___. If lower needs are not met, then ___(53)___ motives will generally not operate. According to Maslow, individuals are motivated to realize their full potential, a process he called ___(54)___-_____. Some research suggests that high levels of motivation to achieve financial success are ___(55)___ correlated with levels of self-actualization. Research also suggests that the ___(56)___ we want to achieve success are almost as important as the way we ___(57)___ success.

Emotions

According to Watson and Tellegen, most human emotions can be thought of as combinations of ___(58)___ and ___(59)___ emotions. This view suggests that fear and ___(60)___ are variations of the same emotion

The dominant theory of emotion emphasizes the ___(61)___ interpretation of events. Cognitive theorists hold that cognitive interpretation of emotions involves interpreting stimuli from both the ___(62)___ and the ___(63)___.

According to Schachter and Singer's model of emotion, the autonomic arousal that accompanies all emotions is similar; our ___(64)___ of the arousal is important.

Cultural learning influences the ___(65)___ of emotions. Culture also has a great deal to do with the ___(66)___ of situations that create emotional reactions.

Aggression: Emotional and Motivational Aspects

Sigmund Freud believed that aggression is the result of potent aggressive ___(67)___. Freud believed that aggressive energy must be released in some way. This process is called ___(68)___.

The belief that aggression is a natural reaction to the frustration (blocking) of important motives is called the ___(69)___- ___ theory. Recent research suggests a link between high temperatures and ___(70)___ crime. By contrast, social learning theorists believe that people act aggressively in reaction to frustration only if they have ___(71)___ to do so.

Application of Psychology: Should You Lose Weight? If So, How?

Our society generally values ___(72)___. More people think they are overweight than is actually the case. At any one time, 24 percent of men and ___(73)___ percent of women are on a diet. People in our society are ___(74)___ against persons who are overweight. Two dangerous eating disorders, particularly for women, are ___(75)___ ___ and ___(76)___. When dieters establish a pattern of gaining and then losing weight, this is referred to as ___(77)___- ___ dieting. In the Framingham health study, repeated yo-yo dieting was associated with increased ___(78)___ ___. Among the suggestions from the text are: don't "diet"—eat ___(79)___, emphasize ___(80)___, and don't let yourself lapse.

Concept Check

Fill in the missing components of the following concept box. The correct answers are located in the "Answers" section at the end of the chapter.

Psychological Motives

Type of motivation	Explanation
incentives	
	motivation to seek new or changed experiences
optimal arousal	
	best performance occurs when the level of arousal is suitable for the activity
motive for affiliation	
	psychological need for success
	motivation stimulated by the inherent nature of an activity or by its natural consequence
extrinsic motivation	motivation stimulated by external rewards

Extending the Chapter: Psychology, Societal Issues, and Human Diversity

These questions may be assigned to you. Whether or not they are assigned, they are designed to be challenging questions to encourage you to think independently about the material in the chapter. Many of the questions have no right or wrong answers.

I. From the *Applications of Psychology* section

1. What do you feel can be done to modify our culture's current obsession with being thin?

2. Based on the information provided in the text, what advice would you give to somebody trying to lose weight?

II. Psychology, Societal Issues, and Human Diversity

1. Discuss the steps our society can take to reduce the amount and intensity of aggressive behavior from its members (road rage, assault, homicide and so on).

2. In what ways are affiliation and achievement motivation different in other cultures?

3. (From the *Human Diversity* section of the text) Describe the challenges faced by first-generation college students.

Practice Quiz

The practice quiz consists of three sections: 1) Short answer questions, 2) Multiple choice questions, and 3) True-False questions. At the end of the chapter you will find suggested answers to the short answer questions, answers and explanation for the multiple choice questions, and answers to the true-false questions.

Short Answer Questions

1. Describe the role played by the hypothalamus in regulating hunger.

_____

_____

2. List and discuss the cues used by the hypothalamus in regulating thirst.

_____

_____

3. Contrast the following three views of aggression: Freud's instinct theory, frustration-aggression theory, and social learning theory.

_____

_____

Multiple Choice Questions

1. An internal state or condition that activates and gives direction to our thoughts is called
   a. motivation.
   b. emotion.
   c. aggression.
   d. all of the above.
   LO 1

2. Each of the following is a component of the definition of emotion *except*
   a. positive or negative feelings.
   b. reaction to stimuli.
   c. primary motives.
   d. physiological arousal.
   LO 1

3. Homeostatic mechanisms are involved in
   a. drinking.
   b. eating.
   c. maintaining body temperature.
   d. all of the above.
   LO 2

4. Each of the following is a primary motive *except*
   a. hunger.
   b. thirst.
   c. avoidance of pain.
   d. desire to be competent.
   LO 2

5. Hyperphagic rats are the result of
   a. surgically destroyed satiety centers in the hypothalamus.
   b. surgically destroyed feeding centers in the hypothalamus.
   c. artificially raised blood sugar levels.
   d. blood fat levels that have been lowered.
   LO 3

6. Each of the following is a cue that helps the hypothalamus regulate eating *except*
   a. stomach contractions.
   b. blood sugar levels.
   c. red blood cell levels.
   d. body fat levels.
   LO 3

7. Which of the following controls the level of blood sugar?
   a. lateral hypothalamus
   b. ventromedial hypothalamus
   c. paraventricular nucleus
   d. angiotensin
   LO 3

8. According to the text, which of the following is a psychological factor in hunger?
   a. incentives
   b. learning
   c. anxiety
   d. all of the above
   LO 3

9. Each of the following is a cue in regulating drinking *except*
   a. mouth dryness.
   b. cell fluid levels.
   c. blood sugar levels.
   d. total blood volume.
   LO 4

10. What happens when cell fluid levels in the body decrease?
    a. Sodium salts draw water out of cells.
    b. The hypothalamus signals the pituitary gland to secrete ADH.
    c. The hypothalamus signals the cerebral cortex to initiate a search for liquids.
    d. All of the above.
    LO 4

11. An effective performance is more likely if the level of arousal is suitable for the activity, according to the
    a. optimal level of arousal.
    b. performance-arousal model.
    c. Yerkes-Dodson law.
    d. James-Lange theory of motivation.
    LO 5

12. The general preference among humans to be with others is called the
a. affiliation motive.
b. need for achievement.
c. need for self-actualization.
d. group motive.
LO 6

13. Research conducted on the motive for affiliation suggests when participants are anxious, their need to affiliate with others
a. increases.
b. decreases.
c. virtually disappears.
d. is not changed.
LO 6

14. If a young businesswoman is concerned about the impact of having a great career and how the career might affect later romantic relationships, she could be typified as having
a. high extrinsic motivation.
b. fear of failure.
c. low need for achievement.
d. a fear of success.
LO 6

15. High levels of fear of success were correlated with high
a. extrinsic motivation.
b. fear of failure.
c. self-esteem.
d. self-actualization.
LO 6

16. People who donate anonymously to charity are probably motivated by
a. intrinsic motivation.
b. extrinsic motivation.
c. biological motivation.
d. affective habituation.
LO 7

17. If an individual is already intrinsically motivated to perform an activity, adding an extrinsic reward will probably
a. sharply increase the intrinsic motivation.
b. increase both the intrinsic and extrinsic motivation.
c. decrease the intrinsic motivation.
d. none of the above
LO 7

18. In Maslow's hierarchy of needs, which needs must be met before all other needs?
a. self-actualization
b. safety
c. self-esteem
d. biological
LO 8

19. According to Maslow, the highest motive people can experience is
a. biological.
b. intellectual.
c. self-esteem.
d. self-actualization.
LO 8

20. According to Watson and Tellegen's emotional map, all human emotions can be thought of as different combinations of what?
a. love and hate
b. happiness and sadness
c. positive and negative emotions
d. arousal and experience
LO 9

21. Which of the following theories emphasizes the interpretation both of incoming stimuli and bodily stimuli in explaining emotions?
a. cognitive theory of emotion
b. frustration-aggression theory
c. social learning theory
d. Freud's theory
LO 10

22. Which of the following processes may influence the role of learning in our emotions?
a. modeling
b. reinforcement
c. classical conditioning
d. all of the above
LO 11

23. By studying different cultures, psychologists have concluded that learning influences
a. the development of basic emotions.
b. do not affect the interpretation of emotions.
c. have had no effect on how emotions are displayed.
d. the expression of emotions.
LO 11

24. Which of the following is true regarding the roles of learning and culture on emotions?
    a. Learning and culture play minimal roles, since all emotions are genetic.
    b. Cultural learning influences the expression of emotions.
    c. Learning affects our emotional reactions to various stimuli.
    d. *b* and *c* above.
       LO 11

25. Which explanation of aggression involves the process of catharsis?
    a. Freud's instinct theory
    b. the frustration-aggression hypothesis
    c. social learning theory
    d. none of the above
       LO 12

26. According to the frustration-aggression hypothesis, aggression is a natural reaction to
    a. frustration.
    b. pain.
    c. heat.
    d. all of the above.
       LO 12

27. Which of the following correctly summarizes the positions taken on televised violence?
    a. Both the social learning and Freudian positions favor televised aggression as an outlet for people.
    b. Neither the social learning nor the Freudian positions view televised aggression favorably.
    c. The social learning theorists opposed televised aggression, whereas the Freudians view it as catharsis.
    d. The social learning theorists favor televised aggression while the Freudians oppose it.
       LO 12

28. According to the text, yo-yo dieting is
    a. a reasonable way to lose a lot of weight quickly.
    b. effective because it moves the body's metabolism up and down.
    c. self-defeating and leads to a slowed metabolism.
    d. linked to anorexia nervosa.
       LO 13

29. According to the text, regular exercise is advantageous when dieting because it
    a. can burn calories.
    b. helps the metabolism to fall while you are dieting.
    c. helps keep the metabolism from falling.
    d. *a* and *c* above.
       LO 13

30. To control your weight, the text recommends each of the following *except*
    a. emphasize exercise.
    b. eat differently.
    c. Diet.
    d. don't give up when you lapse.
       LO 13

True-False Questions

_____1. Food, water, and warmth are examples of primary motives.

_____2. Blood protein levels are an important cue in the regulation of hunger.

_____3. Total blood volume is important in regulating thirst.

_____4. According to the optimal arousal theory, after we adjust to high levels of stimulation, we actively seek more stimulation.

_____5. The enjoyment a person gets from keeping a personal journal is an example of extrinsic motivation.

_____6. According to Maslow, most of us will become fully self-actualized during adulthood.

_____7. According to Izard, the most important feedback in the experience of emotions comes from the facial muscles.

_____8. Although the cognitive theory of emotions makes logical sense, there is little research to support this view.

_____9 According to Schachter and Singer, the autonomic arousal that accompanies all emotions is similar.

_____10. Freud's ideas about catharsis encourage the release of instinctual aggressive energy.

ANSWER SECTION

Concept Check

Psychological Motives

Type of motivation	Explanation
incentives	external cues that activate motivation
novel stimulation	motivation to seek new or changed experiences
optimal arousal	motivation caused by too much or too little stimulation
Yerkes-Dodson law	best performance occurs when the level of arousal is suitable for the activity
motive for affiliation	motivation to be with others and to have personal relationships
achievement motivation	psychological need for success
intrinsic motivation	motivation stimulated by the inherent nature of an activity or by its natural consequence
extrinsic motivation	motivation stimulated by external rewards

Answers Review At A Glance

1. internal
2. emotions
3. physiological
4. activate
5. primary
6. homeostatic
7. hypothalamus
8. feeding
9. lateral
10. satiety
11. ventromedial
12. hyperphagia
13. sugar
14. stomach
15. blood
16. duodenum
17. Langerhans
18. insulin
19. glucagon
20. body fat
21. inhibit
22. sugar
23. sympathetic
24. set point
25. set point
26. emotions
27. incentives
28. set point
29. drink
30. stop drinking
31. dryness
32. fluid
33. blood volume
34. psychological
35. novel stimulation
36. optimal
37. Yerkes-Dodson
38. affiliation
39. inborn
40. learned
41. fear
42. achievement motivation
43. mastery
44. approach
45. avoidance
46. outcomes
47. success
48. intrinsic
49. extrinsic
50. detract
51. sociocultural
52. hierarchy
53. higher
54. self-actualization
55. negatively
56. reasons
57. define
58. positive
59. negative
60. anger
61. cognitive
62. environment
63. body
64. cognitive interpretation
65. expression
66. interpretation
67. instincts
68. catharsis
69. frustration-aggression
70. violent
71. learned
72. thinness
73. 40
74. prejudiced
75. anorexia nervosa
76. bulimia
77. yo-yo
78. heart disease
79. differently
80. exercise

Sample Answers to Short Answer Questions

1. **Describe the role played by the hypothalamus in regulating hunger.**

   The hypothalamus contains three areas that help to regulate hunger. The lateral hypothalamus initiates eating; it is referred to as the feeding system. The ventromedial hypothalamus signals the cessation of eating when sufficient food has been consumed; it is referred to as the satiety system. The third area is called the paraventricular nucleus. This area helps to control appetite by controlling the level of sugar in the blood. The hypothalamus relies on three basic cues to help it in the regulation of hunger; these are stomach contractions, blood sugar levels, and body fat levels.

2. **List and discuss the cues used by the hypothalamus in regulating thirst.**

   The hypothalamus uses three main cues in the regulation of thirst. The first and most obvious is mouth dryness. A second cue is a decrease in cell fluid levels. When cell fluid levels drop, the fluids begin to dehydrate the cells of the body. The third cue is a decrease in total blood volume. The kidneys react to this drop by signaling the hypothalamus.

3. Contrast the following three views of aggression: Freud's instinct theory, frustration-aggression theory, and social learning theory.

According to Freud's theory, aggressive energy is instinctual and must be released in some way. The goal of society is to find socially acceptable way to provide these cathartic experiences. Frustration-aggression theory states that aggression is a natural reaction to frustration. Therefore, in order to minimize aggression, society should seek to minimize frustration for its members. According to social learning theory, people are aggressive because they have learned to be aggressive. Modeling and positive reinforcement are two ways in which people become conditioned to use aggression. Social learning theorists argue that watching violent television or playing violent video games does not reduce aggression (as Freud's approach might suggest); instead, these activities actually increase aggression.

Multiple Choice Answers

1. The answer is *a*. Emotions are positive or negative feelings in reaction to stimuli. Motivation and emotion are closely linked concepts; motives are often accompanied by emotions, and emotions typically have motivational properties of their own.
2. The answer is *c*. Primary motives refer to motives for things that are necessary for our survival, such as food and water. Each of the other choices is part of the definition of emotion.
3. The answer is *d*. Homeostatic mechanisms refer to internal mechanisms that help to regulate many bodily functions. Among the functions that are regulated are eating, drinking, and maintaining body temperature.
4. The answer is *d*. Primary motives refer to biological needs; these needs must be met or else the organism will die. The desire to be competent is an important psychological need, but not a primary motive.
5. The answer is *a*. Although the rats don't eat more often daily, they eat much longer—the signal to stop eating apparently has been destroyed.
6. The answer is *c*. Stomach contractions and blood sugar levels help to regulate hunger on a daily basis; blood fat levels help to regulate hunger on a long-term basis.
7. The answer is *c*. This center both increases and decreases appetite by controlling the level of blood sugar.
8. The answer is *d*. Incentives are external cues that activate motivation. In the case of hunger, the smell or sight of a favorite food can start those neurons firing in your hypothalamus. Learning and emotions are other psychological factors that impact on hunger.
9. The answer is *c*. In the same manner that the hypothalamus regulates eating with a feeding system and a satiety system, it likewise regulates drinking with "drink" and "stop drinking" systems.
10. The answers is *d*. A complex process, initiated largely by the cells of the hypothalamus, is set into motion when cell fluid levels decrease.
11. The answer is *c*. The Yerkes-Dodson law suggests that if arousal is too low (in other words, if you're not "psyched up" enough), performance will be inadequate, but if arousal is too high, performance may become disrupted.
12. The answer is *a*. Explanations of the motive for affiliation once again raise the nature-nurture issue. Some psychologists believe that the need for affiliation is inborn, while others suggest that motive is learned.
13. The answer is *a*. In Schachter's research, subjects who were frightened about their well-being preferred to wait in a room with others.
14. The answer is *d*. Fear of success can motivate people to achieve below their potential.
15. The answer is *c*. Kumari's research was conducted on women.
16. The answer is *a*. Presumably, people who donate anonymously to a charity are motivated by the desire to do a "good thing," but do not seek the recognition or attention that often comes with such donations. Therefore, their behavior seems to be an example of intrinsic motivation.
17. The answer is *c*. The basic idea is that if somebody already enjoys something (intrinsic motivation), extrinsic rewards could weaken this motivation.
18. The answer is *d*. According to Maslow, if these basic needs are not met, other needs are not important.

19. The answer is *d*. According to Maslow's theory, our motives are organized in a hierarchy. The "higher" human motives, however, cannot operate until the more basic, lower needs, such as hunger, thirst, and safety, have been met. At the highest level, according to Maslow, we are "dreaming our impossible dream" and realizing our full potential.

20. The answer is *c*. An implication of Watson and Tellegen's theory is that human emotions can be thought of as combinations of positive and negative emotions.

21. The answer is *a*. The cognitive theory emphasizes the cognitive interpretation of stimuli as the major influence in emotions.

22. The answer is *d*. Although most psychologists who study emotions would agree that basic human emotions are inborn, the study of individuals in different cultures, in different families, and under different circumstances also underscores the importance of learning in many of our emotions.

23. The answer is *d*. Evidence suggests that learning influences both the expression of emotions and the way we interpret situations.

24. The answer is *d*. Although basic emotions are inborn, culture and learning affect the expression of emotions and our reactions to various stimuli.

25. The answer is *a*. According to Freud, aggression is instinctual, and aggressive energy must be released. Catharsis refers to the process of releasing instinctual energy. Freud believed that societies should find nonviolent ways for its members to release this energy.

26. The answer is *d*. Whereas Freud viewed aggression as an inborn part of human nature, frustration-aggression advocates view aggression as a natural reaction to the blocking of important motives.

27. The answer is *c*. The position of the social learning theorists is that people will behave aggressively only if they have learned to do so. Televised aggression, therefore, will increase violence. The Freudian position, on the other hand, suggests that watching televised aggression and experiencing violence vicariously lead to a good cathartic release.

28. The answer is *c*. Yo-yo dieting is not only self-defeating; it was found to be associated with increased heart disease.

29. The answer is *d*. The body tends to try to compensate for dieting by lowering the metabolic rate. Exercise, however, helps to keep the metabolic rate from falling while dieting.

30. The answer is *c*. According to the text, when we lose weight by "dieting" we almost always regain the weight after we go off the diet.

Answers to True-False Questions

1. T	6. F
2. F	7. T
3. T	8. F
4. F	9. T
5. F	10. T

Chapter 10 Gender and Sexuality

Learning Objectives

1. Distinguish among the definitions of sex, gender, and sexual orientation. (p. 308)

2. Distinguish between gender identity and gender role. (p. 308)

3. Describe the results of research regarding gender similarities and gender differences. (p. 309)

4. Describe the results of research regarding gender differences in the brain. (p. 314)

5. Distinguish between the evolutionary and the social-role theories of gender differences. (p. 316)

6. (From the *Application of Psychology* section) Distinguish between a heterosexual and homosexual orientation and describe the results of the University of Chicago survey regarding sexual practices. (p. 321)

7. (From the *Application of Psychology* section) Compare the theories of Money and Bem regarding the origins of sexual orientation. (p. 322)

Chapter Overview

Although a person's sex is defined by their male and female genitals, a person's gender is the psychological experience of one's sex. The subjective experience of being a male or female is referred to as gender identity. Gender identity develops early in childhood. A person who has both feminine and masculine traits is referred to as androgynous.

Although cognitive differences exist between men and women in some areas, the differences tend to be small and there are far more gender similarities than differences. Researchers have found greater differences regarding emotional and social behavior. Gender differences have also been found in the brain. For example, males have slightly larger cerebral cortex, and amygdala regions, whereas females have a larger corpus callosum and hippocampus. Two theories that have been advanced to explain gender differences are the evolutionary theory and the social-role theory

The issues surrounding sexual orientation have been the subject of much research and controversy. Theories on the origins of sexual orientation emphasize social learning and predisposing biological factors.

Key Terms Exercise

For each of the following exercises, match the key terms on the left with the correct definitions on the right. Page references to the text follow the terms so that you may refer to the text for any items you answer incorrectly or do not understand completely. You may check your response immediately by referring to the answers that follow each exercise.

Sex, Gender, and Sexual Orientation

_____ 1. sex (p. 308)
_____ 2. gender (p. 308)
_____ 3. gender identity (p. 308)
_____ 4. gender role (p. 308)
_____ 5. sexual orientation (p. 308)
_____ 6. androgynous (p. 308)
_____ 7. evolutionary theory of gender differences (p. 316)
_____ 8. social-role theory of gender differences (p. 318)

a. a person who has both typical masculine and feminine characteristics

b. the psychological experience of being a female or male

c. gender differences are based on genes that resulted from different evolutionary pressures on women and men

d. the distinction between men and women based on biological characteristics

e. the behaviors consistent with being male or female in a given culture

f. one's view of oneself as male or female

g. the preference for romantic and sexual partners of the same or different sex

h. opportunities and restrictions in women's and men's different social roles create psychological gender differences

ANSWERS

1. d	5. g
2. b	6. a
3. f	7. c
4. e	8. h

Review At A Glance
(Answers to this section may be found on page 177)

Gender

Although a person's sex is defined by their male or female genitals, a person's __(1)__ is the psychological experience of one's sex. The subjective experience of being a male or female is __(2)__ _____. The behaviors that communicate the degree to which we are feminine or masculine refer to a person's __(3)__ _____. The behaviors in which we engage for sexual pleasure, as well as the related feelings and beliefs, are referred to as __(4)__. The tendency to prefer romantic and sexual partners of the same or different sex is __(5)__ _____.

Gender __(6)__ develops early in infancy. Recent views of gender roles have conceived them as being on a __(7)__, with people displaying varying degrees of both masculinity and femininity. A person who has both female and male characteristics is referred to as __(8)__. Androgynous people are more likely to adapt well to a variety of situations because of their greater __(9)__.

Regarding gender differences in physical strength and skills, men on the average have greater __(10)__ - _____ strength, and can throw objects farther and with greater __(11)__ than women. Generally, women and men are more similar in __(12)__ ability than they are different. On average, women perform better in a range of __(13)__ skills, verbal and __(14)__ memory, perceptual speed and __(15)__ motor skills, whereas men perform better in mathematics, __(16)__, and social studies. Although most of these average differences are small, men on average score considerably higher on tests of __(17)__ and mechanical reasoning. With regard to mathematical ability, the average gender difference is small, although scores at the highest end of the scale are more common for __(18)__. The greater success of men in scientific and technological fields may be explained in part by __(19)__ against women. Although women, on the average, receive higher grades in __(20)__ courses at all levels, they attribute their success in math courses to hard work, whereas men tend to attribute their success to __(21)__ ability.

Most gender differences in social and emotional functioning tend to be greater than the differences in __(22)__ performance. Women tend to be __(23)__, friendly and helpful, whereas men tend to be __(24)__, dominant, and assertive. Women are more likely to be anxious, depressed, and have slightly low __(25)__ - _____, whereas men are more likely to engage in __(26)__ aggression and risky behavior, and are more likely to commit most kinds of __(27)__.

Regarding mating and sexual behavior, men tend to prefer a mate who is younger and physically attractive and has good __(28)__ skills. Women tend to prefer mates who are __(29)__, have good character, and high __(30)__ potential, Many studies indicate that men are far more willing to engage in __(31)__ sex.

Origins of Gender Differences

According to brain imaging studies, the cortex of men is about 10 percent larger than those of women; the difference is due to a greater volume of myelinated __(32)__. As adults, the relative size of the right cerebral hemisphere is larger in __(33)__. The __(34)__ _____ reaches a larger size in the adult female. Research on brain activity of males and females during a rhyming activity showed that men tended to use language areas only in the __(35)__ cerebral hemisphere, whereas females tend to use language areas in __(36)__ cerebral hemispheres. This difference is consistent with the superior __(37)__ skills of women.

As children grow older, the __(38)__ increases more rapidly in males, whereas the __(39)__ increases more rapidly in female children. The amygdala is associated with the expression of __(40)__; the hippocampus plays a role in everyday __(41)__ and in the inhibition of previously __(42)__ behavior. Structural differences are also found in the __(43)__. Biological differences in the brain may be the __(44)__ of gender differences, but they may be the result of gender differences as well.

A theory emphasizing genes that resulted from differing evolutionary pressures on ancestral men and women is called the __(45)__ theory of gender differences. According to this theory, gender differences have resulted from: 1) pressures associated with __(46)__, 2) selection of dominance and __(47)__, 3) pressure created by child __(48)__, 4) pressures created by differences in parental __(49)__, and 5) pressures in mate __(50)__. Among the criticisms of this approach are that it is dehumanizing, a self-serving attempt by males to __(51)__ their behavior, and it implies a genetic lock into gender differences. Evolutionary theory can't be tested __(52)__.

A theory that the opportunities and restrictions inherent in different social roles creates psychological gender differences is called the __(53)__-_____ theory of gender differences. According to this view, __(54)__ differences created the initial gender-based division of labor in the past, but gender roles are maintained today by the way we are __(55)__. In support of this theory, research by Steele suggests that expectations of gender differences can create gender differences in __(56)__ performance. Some cross-cultural research on __(57)__ _____ supports social-role theory.

Application of Psychology: Sexual Orientation

People who are attracted to members of the other sex are termed __(58)__, while those who are attracted to the same sex are __(59)__. People who are attracted both to members of the same sex and to members of the other sex are called __(60)__. In a 1994 survey conducted by the University of Chicago, 2.8 percent of males and 1.4 percent of females identified themselves as homosexual or __(61)__. Gays and lesbians tend to live in __(62)__ cities.

Persecution and discrimination against gays and lesbians is widespread and often reaches extreme forms of __(63)__. Acts of aggression perpetrated against gays and lesbians are called __(64)__ _____.

According to Money, social learning plays a role in the development of homosexuality, along with predisposing biological factors such as __(65)__ and prenatal __(66)__. According to Bem, predisposing factors interact with atypical ___(67)___ - _____ behavior in the development of homosexuality. Bem's theory is ___(68)___ and doesn't explain the fact that many gays and lesbians did not show atypical sex-typed behavior as children.

Concept Check

Fill in the missing components of the following concept boxes. The correct answers are located in the "Answers" section at the end of the chapter.

Gender Differences and Sexual Orientation

Name of theory/theorist	Explanation
evolutionary theory of gender differences	
	opportunities and restrictions in social roles create psychological gender differences
John Money	
Daryl Bem	

Extending the Chapter: Psychology, Societal Issues, and Human Diversity

These questions may be assigned to you. Whether or not they are assigned, they are designed to be challenging questions to encourage you to think independently about the material in the chapter. Many of the questions have no right or wrong answers.

I.   From the *Applications of Psychology* section

1.   If sexual orientation is determined, at least in part, by biological factors, what impact would this have on society's views about homosexuality and heterosexuality?

II.   Psychology, Societal Issues, and Human Diversity

1.   Discuss the reasons for the continuing existence of widespread gender stereotypes, even among educated college students.

2.   In the United States and elsewhere, gender relationships have increasingly been subject to public policy regulation. For example, laws exist to safeguard individuals against sexual discrimination and sexual harassment. To what extent should gender relations be regulated by public policy?

Practice Quiz

The practice quiz consists of three sections: 1) Short answer questions, 2) Multiple choice questions, and 3) True-False questions. At the end of the chapter you will find suggested answers to the short answer questions, answers and explanation for the multiple choice questions, and answers to the true-false questions.

Short Answer Questions

1. Contrast the social-role and evolutionary theories of gender differences.

   _____

   _____

2. Contrast the views of Money and Bem on the origins of sexual orientation.

   _____

   _____

Multiple Choice Questions

1. Which of the following is most directly related to the gender to whom a person is attracted romantically and sexually?
    a. sex
    b. gender
    c. gender role
    d. sexual orientation
        LO 1

2. The behaviors consistent with being male or female in a given culture defines
    a. gender.
    b. gender identity.
    c. gender role.
    d. sex.
        LO 2

3. The view of oneself as being male or female is
    a. gender.
    b. gender identity.
    c. gender role.
    d. sex.
        LO 2

4. On the average, women score higher than men on tests of
    a. language skills.
    b. math.
    c. science.
    d. aggression.
        LO 3

5. When presented with a rhyming task, males showed increased activity only in the left hemisphere, whereas females showed increased activity
   a. only in the right hemisphere.
   b. in both the left and right hemispheres.
   c. only in the corpus callosum.
   d. in the cerebellum.
   LO 4

6. Research suggests men's brains have a relatively larger
   a. cortex.
   b. corpus callosum.
   c. hippocampus.
   d. hindbrain.
   LO 4

7. Gender differences are maintained by the socialization process, according to which theory of gender differences?
   a. social-role theory
   b. evolutionary theory
   c. Darwin's theory
   d. gender identity theory
   LO 5

8. Which of the following theories is most likely to emphasize Darwin's theory of selection?
   a. social-role theory
   b. psychoanalytic theory
   c. evolutionary theory
   d. social learning theory
   LO 5

9. According to the 1994 University of Chicago survey, individuals with a homosexual orientation are
   a. more common than other studies have found.
   b. less common than other studies have found.
   c. more likely to be found living in small towns.
   d. likely to exhibit a narrow range of gender. roles
   LO 6

10. Which of the following best reflects the view of researchers regarding admitting homosexual men and women into the military?
    a. Homosexuals should be admitted, but they should be in separate units.
    b. Homosexuals should not be admitted because the morale of the military would suffer.
    c. Homosexuals should be admitted, and programs should be initiated to reduce prejudice and stereotyping.
    d. The present policy of not directly addressing the issue has worked for centuries and should continue.
    LO 7

11. According to Money, individuals develop a homosexual orientation as a result of
    a. social learning.
    b. biological factors.
    c. learned gender roles.
    d. *a* and *b* above.
    LO 8

12. One explanation of homosexuality in Daryl Bem's theory is that children with atypical sex-typed behavior find children of the same sex to be
    a. upsetting and later emotionally arousing.
    b. attractive even before puberty.
    c. easier to be with and more understanding.
    d. more valued than the opposite sex.
    LO 8

True-False Questions

_____1. Gender identity is the psychological experience of being a male or a female.

_____2. Gender differences in cognitive performance tend to be greater than differences in social and emotional functioning.

_____3. Researchers have found the corpus callosum tends to be larger in the adult male than in the adult female.

_____4. The brain area called the amygdala is larger in males than in females.

_____5. Research results have conclusively supported the social-role theory of gender differences.

_____6. According to John Money, biological factors are an insignificant factor in the development of homosexuality.

ANSWER SECTION

Concept Checks

Gender Differences and Sexual Orientation

Name of theory/theorist	Explanation
evolutionary theory of gender differences	gender differences are based on genes that resulted from different evolutionary pressures on women and men
social-role theory of gender differences	opportunities and restrictions in social roles create psychological gender differences
John Money	social learning plays a role in the development of homosexuality, in combination with predisposing biological factors
Daryl Bem	predisposing factors lead some children to exhibit behavior more typical of the other sex and to prefer playing with children of the other sex

Answers to Review At A Glance

1. gender
2. gender identity
3. gender role
4. sexuality
5. sexual orientation
6. identity
7. continuum
8. androgynous
9. flexibility
10. upper-body
11. accuracy
12. cognitive
13. language
14. spatial
15. fine
16. science
17. spatial
18. men
19. prejudice
20. math
21. intellectual
22. cognitive
23. nurturing

24. competitive
25. self-esteem
26. physical
27. crimes
28. housekeeping
29. older
30. earning
31. casual
32. axons
33. males
34. corpus callosum
35. left
36. both
37. language
38. amygdala
39. hippocampus
40. aggression
41. memory
42. punished
43. hypothalamus
44. cause
45. evolutionary
46. hunting

47. aggression
48. care
49. investment
50. selection
51. justify
52. directly
53. social-role
54. biological
55. socialized
56. cognitive
57. selection
58. heterosexual
59. homosexual
60. bisexual
61. bisexual
62. larger
63. violence
64. gay-bashing
65. genetics
66. hormones
67. sex-typed
68. speculative

Sample Answers for Short Answer Questions

1. **Contrast the social-role and evolutionary theories of gender differences.**

   According to the social-role theory, gender differences are explained by each society's division of labor, and by the different social roles society creates for men and women. These gender-based social roles eventually become internalized. The evolutionary theory views gender differences as based on genetic factors. According to this view, differing evolutionary pressures on women and men favored some genetic characteristics and caused other characteristics to disappear.

2. **Contrast the views of Money and Bem on the origins of sexual orientation.**

   According to Money, social learning and predisposing biological factors are involved in developing a homosexual orientation. According to Bem, predisposing factors lead some children to play more often with the other sex and to exhibit behavior more typical of the other sex.

Multiple Choice Answers

1. The answer is *d*. Sexual orientation is defined by those with whom we have a sexual or romantic relationship.
2. The answer is *c*. Gender identity is one's view of oneself as being male or female, and gender is the psychological experience of being male or female.
3. The answer is *b*. Gender roles consist of those behaviors consistent with being a male or female in a given culture.
4. The answer is *a*. Keep in mind, however, that the differences between women's and men's averages scores usually are small and are characterized by considerable overlap.
5. The answer is *b*. Researchers have also found the corpus callosum of females and the hippocampus to be larger in females, whereas the amygdala is larger in men.
6. The answer is *a*. This difference is due to a greater volume of "white matter," the myelinated axons, in the cortex. No gender differences have been found in the "gray matter," the cell bodies of neurons.
7. The answer is *a*. According to this theory, gender differences are the result of different opportunities, challenges, experiences, and restrictions that social roles create for women and men.
8. The answer is *c*. Evolutionary theory states that gender differences are based on genes that resulted from different evolutionary pressures on ancestral men and women. This theory relies upon Darwin's ideas regarding natural selection.
9. The answer is *b*. This survey found lower levels than the Kinsey surveys many years ago. The study found that people with a homosexual orientation tend to live in larger urban areas.
10. The answer is *c*. Researchers suggest that when people with prejudices work together, the prejudice diminishes dramatically.
11. The answer is *d*. According to Money, biological factors predispose some people towards homosexuality. Research studies on twins, on prenatal development, and on the hypothalamus are consistent with Money's hypothesis.
12. The answer is *a*. According to Bem this occurs as "the exotic becomes erotic."

Answers to True-False Questions

1. F   4. T

2. F   5. F

3. F   6. F

Chapter 11   Personality Theories and Assessment

Learning Objectives

1.   Define the term personality. (p. 328)

2.   Distinguish among Allport's cardinal, central, secondary, and common traits. (p. 328)

3.   List and describe the "big five" personality traits. (p. 329)

4.   Distinguish among Freud's concepts of conscious mind, the preconscious mind, and the unconscious mind as part of his psychoanalytic theory. (p. 331)

5.   Distinguish among the id, ego, and superego in Freud's psychoanalytic theory. (p. 332)

6.   Distinguish among the processes Freud referred to as displacement, sublimation, and identification. (p. 334)

7.   Explain Jung's theory of the mind; distinguish between extroversion and introversion and between personal unconscious and the collective unconscious. (p. 335)

8.   Distinguish between the theories of Alfred Adler and Karen Horney. (p. 335)

9.   Discuss Bandura's social learning theory, including the roles of cognition in personality development. (p. 337)

10.   Discuss the alternative explanations to trait theories called situationism and interactionism. (p. 339)

11. Identify the basic concepts of humanistic theory, including inner-directedness and subjectivity. (p. 341)

12. Distinguish between the "self" and the "ideal self" and understand the importance of congruence and conditions of worth in Rogers' personality theory. (p. 342)

13. Compare and contrast humanistic, psychoanalytic, and social learning theories of personality and discuss the relationship between personality and culture. (p. 343)

14. Understand how interviews and observational methods are used to assess personality. (p. 348)

15. Understand how projective tests are used and distinguish between the TAT and the Rorschach Inkblot Test. (p. 348)

16. Discuss the use of objective tests such as the MMPI-2. (p. 348)

17. Discuss the usefulness and accuracy of personality tests. (p. 349)

18. (From the *Application of Psychology* section) Describe the role of situational influences in everyday life. (p. 351)

Chapter Overview

Personality is the sum total of the typical ways of acting, thinking, and feeling that make each person unique. Some psychologists believe that personality can be described in terms of traits. Traits are relatively enduring and consistent ways of behaving. There is now consensus that five traits are useful in describing personality; these are neuroticism, extroversion, openness, agreeableness, and conscientiousness. One influential theory of personality, psychoanalytic theory, was developed in the late nineteenth century by Sigmund Freud. Freud's theory distinguished three levels of conscious awareness—the conscious mind, the preconscious mind, and the unconscious mind. According to Freud, the mind is composed of the following three parts: 1) the id, which operates on the pleasure principle and seeks to obtain immediate pleasure and to avoid pain; 2) the ego, which operates on the reality principle and seeks safe and realistic ways of satisfying the id; and 3) the superego, which opposes the id by imposing moral restrictions and striving for perfection. Freud suggested that when the ego cannot find ways to satisfy the id, it seeks a substitute. The process of substituting a more acceptable goal is called displacement; the displacement of a socially desirable goal is termed sublimation. Another process that allows individuals to operate in society without friction is called identification; we tend to model our actions after individuals who are successful in gaining satisfactions from life.

Alfred Adler and Carl Jung were two associates of Freud. They both developed influential personality theories of their own. Jung differed with Freud over his emphasis on sexual motivation. Jung believed that the unconscious mind contains positive and even spiritual motives. He also felt that we each possess both a personal unconscious and a collective unconscious. Adler felt that the primary struggle in personality development was the effort to overcome feelings of inferiority in social relationships and to develop feelings of superiority. Karen Horney was another influential revisionist of Freudian psychoanalysis. She felt that anxious insecurity, which stems from inadequate childrearing experiences, is the source of all personality conflicts.

Other personality theorists, the social learning theorists, emphasize classical conditioning, operant conditioning, and modeling in the development of personality. Albert Bandura, a prominent social learning theorist, believes that social learning is determined by the actions of behavior on the environment, and vice versa. Bandura also believes that behavior is self-regulated by our internalized cognitive standards for self-reward and limited by our perception of our own self-efficacy. Some psychologists believe that situations determine behavior; this is known as situationism. Social learning theorists have suggested a compromise termed interactionism, which states that behavior is influenced by a combination of personality traits and the situation.

Members of a third group of personality theorists, humanistic theorists, believe that humans possess an inner-directedness that pushes them to grow. To the humanist, reality is subjective. The concept of "self" is central to the personality theory of Carl Rogers and other humanists. Our self-concept is our subjective perception of who we are and what we are like. Rogers distinguishes between the self (the person I think I am) and the ideal self (the person I wish I were). Problems result when there are major discrepancies between the self and the ideal self, or when a person's self-concept is not congruent with the way he or she actually acts, thinks, and feels. There is growing awareness that personality can best understood only in the context of an individual's culture.

Personality assessment is the use of psychological methods to learn about a person's personality. The most widely used method is the interview. Personality is also assessed by observing the person's behavior in a natural or simulated situation. Rating scales are used to help make observational methods more objective. The second most widely used method of personality assessment is the projective test, which psychoanalysts believe reveals the motives and conflicts of the unconscious mind. Objective personality tests, such as the MMPI-2, consist of questions that measure different aspects of personality. Objective personality tests are generally better at assessing personality than projective techniques, but all personality tests are only partly accurate.

Key Terms Exercise

For each of the following exercises, match the key terms on the left with the correct definitions on the right. Page references to the text follow the terms so that you may refer to the text for any items you answer incorrectly or do not understand completely. You may check your responses immediately by referring to the answers that follow each exercise.

Personality/Psychoanalytic Theory (I)

_____ 1. personality (p. 328)
_____ 2. traits (p. 328)
_____ 3. psychoanalytic theory (p. 331)
_____ 4. unconscious mind (p. 332)
_____ 5. repression (p. 332)
_____ 6. id (p. 333)
_____ 7. pleasure principle (p. 333)

a. the theory of personality developed by Sigmund Freud
b. the sum total of ways of acting, thinking, and feeling that make each person unique
c. the part of the mind of which we are never directly aware
d. pushing unpleasant information into unconsciousness
e. the attempt of the id to seek immediate pleasure
f. the inborn part of the unconscious mind
g. enduring patterns of behavior that are consistent across situations

ANSWERS
1. b   5. d
2. g   6. f
3. a   7. e
4. c

Psychoanalytic Theory (II)

_____ 1. primary process thinking (p. 333)
_____ 2. ego (p. 333)
_____ 3. reality principle (p. 333)
_____ 4. superego (p. 334)
_____ 5. ego ideal (p. 334)
_____ 6. displacement (p. 334)
_____ 7. sublimation (p. 334)
_____ 8. identification (p. 334)
_____ 9. feelings of inferiority (p. 335)

a. the part of the mind that enforces strict moral restrictions
b. formation by the id of wish-fulfilling mental images
c. substitution of an acceptable goal for an unacceptable goal of the id
d. the ego's attempt to find realistic ways to meet the needs of the id
e. the standard of perfect conduct of the superego
f. the part of the mind that uses the reality principle to satisfy the id
g. according to Adler, the feelings that result from children being less powerful than adults
h. the process of modeling one's actions after others
i. substitution of a highly desirable goal for one that is harmful

ANSWERS
1. b.   6. c
2. f   7. i
3. d   8. h
4. a   9. g
5. e

Social Learning Theory

_____ 1. social learning theory (p. 337)
_____ 2. reciprocal determination (p. 338)
_____ 3. self-efficacy (p. 338)
_____ 4. self-regulation (p. 339)
_____ 5. situationism (p. 339)
_____ 6. person X situation interactionism (p. 339)

a.   the perception of being capable of achieving one's goals
b.   the view that the individual and the social learning environment continually influence each other
c.   the view that behavior is influenced by characteristics of both the person and the situation
d.   the theory that our personalities are formed through learning from others
e.   the process of cognitively reinforcing and punishing ourselves, depending on our personal standards
f.   the view that behavior is consistent only if situations remain consistent

ANSWERS
1. d   4. e
2. b   5. f
3. a   6. c

Humanistic Theory

_____ 1. humanistic theory (p. 341)
_____ 2. inner-directedness (p. 341)
_____ 3. subjective reality (p. 341)
_____ 4. self-concept (p. 342)
_____ 5. symbolization (p. 342)
_____ 6. conditions of worth (p. 342)
_____ 7. projective test (p. 348)

a.   an internal force that leads people to grow and improve
b.   the third force in psychology
c.   our subjective perceptions of who we are
d.   representation of experience, thought, or feelings in mental symbols
e.   a test that uses ambiguous stimuli to reveal the client's personality
f.   standards that are used by others or ourselves in judging our worth
g.   each individual's unique perception of reality

ANSWERS
1. b   5. d
2. a   6. f
3. g   7. e
4. c

Who Am I?

Match the psychologists on the left with their contributions to the field of psychology on the right. Page references to the text follow the names of the psychologists so that you may refer to the text for further review of these psychologists and their contributions. You may check your responses immediately by referring to the answers that follow each exercise.

_____ 1. Sigmund Freud (p. 331)
_____ 2. Alfred Adler (p. 335)
_____ 3. Carl Jung (p. 335)
_____ 4. Karen Horney (p. 336)
_____ 5. Albert Bandura (p. 337)
_____ 6. Carl Rogers (p. 341)
_____ 7. Gordon Allport (p. 328)

a. The personal unconscious and the collective unconscious are important to my theory.
b. I developed psychoanalytic theory.
c. I am a cognitive behaviorist and a leader in social learning theory.
d. My theory emphasizes overcoming feelings of inferiority, developing social interest, and achieving goals.
e. The concept of "self" is central to my personality theory.
f. I believe that personality traits are either cardinal, central, or secondary.
g. It was my belief that anxious insecurity is the source of all personality conflicts.

ANSWERS
1. b   5. c
2. d   6. e
3. a   7. f
4. g

Review At A Glance
(Answers to this section may be found on page 193)

Definition of Personality/ Trait Theory: Describing the Consistencies of Personality

Personality is the sum total of all the ways of acting, thinking, and feeling that are ___(1)___ for a person and make that person ___(2)___ from all others.

Psychologists refer to relatively enduring and consistent ways of behaving as ___(3)___. Trait theories of personality are more concerned with ___(4)___ traits than with ___(5)___ their origins.

According to Gordon Allport, the most important traits are those that relate to our ___(6)___. Allport called the traits that dominate a person's life ___(7)___ traits. He felt that few people possess these traits. Allport labeled those traits which influence much of our behavior ___(8)___ traits. The traits that are specific to a situation are ___(9)___ traits. There is considerable agreement among trait theorists that there are ___(10)___ basic personality traits.

Psychoanalytic Theory: Sigmund Freud

While working with patients experiencing conversion disorders, Freud became convinced that all such cases were caused by unexpressed ___(11)___ motives.

Freud believed that conscious awareness exists on three levels. The portion of the mind of which an individual is presently aware is the ___(12)___ mind. Memories that are not presently conscious but that can be easily brought into consciousness are found in the ___(13)___ mind. The storehouse for primitive instinctual motives and repressed memories and emotions is the ___(14)___ mind.

Freud also divided the mind in a different, but related, way. He viewed the mind as being composed of the ___(15)___, the ___(16)___, and the ___(17)___. At birth, the mind has only one part, the ___(18)___. The id is composed of two sets of instincts, the ___(19)___ instincts, which Freud termed ___(20)___, and the ___(21)___ instinct. The two most important motives of the life instinct are ___(22)___ and ___(23)___ motives. According to Freud, the id functions entirely at the ___(24)___ level. The id operates according to the ___(25)___ principle and attempts to satisfy its needs by using wish-fulfilling mental images, a process Freud called ___(26)___ thinking. As we grow, we develop a second part of the mind, called the ___(27)___. The ego helps us to deal with the world through the ___(28)___ principle. The ego can be thought of as the ___(29)___ of the personality.

The only part of the mind containing a sense of morality is the ___(30)___. The superego is created mainly by ___(31)___. Parental punishment creates the moral inhibitions called ___(32)___, while parental rewards establish a standard of conduct called the ___(33)___.

Sometimes the ego must settle for a substitute for the goals of the id. This process is called ___(34)___. A form of displacement in which a socially desirable goal is substituted for a socially harmful goal is called ___(35)___. The process of thinking, acting, and feeling like individuals who are successful in gaining satisfactions from life is called ___(36)___.

Carl Jung believed that people have a pair of opposite personality traits—a desire to be open and friendly, called ___(37)___, and a desire to be shy and focus attention on ourselves, called ___(38)___. He also felt that the unconscious contained two elements: motives that have been repressed because they are threatening, called the ___(39)___ unconscious, and an unconscious mind with which all humans are born, called the ___(40)___ unconscious.

According to Alfred Adler, the task of personality development is to overcome feelings of ___(41)___. Later in his career, Adler felt that all humans are born with ___(42)___, which involves establishing relationships with others.

Another influential revisionist of Freudian psychoanalysis is Karen Horney. She believed that anxious ___(43)___, which stems from inadequate ___(44)___ experiences, is the source of all personality conflicts.

Social Learning Theory: Albert Bandura

According to social learning theorists, personality is ___(45)___ from other members of society. Albert Bandura is a leading social learning theorist. Although he is a behaviorist, he emphasizes the importance of ___(46)___ in personality and believes that people play an ___(47)___ role in determining their actions. Bandura has observed that the individual and the social learning environment continually influence each other; that is, they are ___(48)___. According to Bandura, the perception of being able to achieve one's goals is called ___(49)___-___. Bandura believes that we cognitively reinforce or punish ourselves, depending on whether or not our behavior has met our personal standards; this process is called ___(50)___-___.

     Some psychologists believe that behavior is determined by the situations people find themselves in rather than by the traits inside the person; this approach is called ___(51)___. A compromise, called ___(52)___ ___ ___, suggests that behavior is influenced both by the characteristics of the person as well as by the situation. According to Mischel and Shoda, the only way to fully describe personality is by using ___(53)___ statements. Two important factors in understanding interactionism are: 1) evidence exists that people select situations that are consistent with their ___(54)___ ___; and 2) according to Bem, some people are influenced more than others by ___(55)___.

Humanistic Theory

Humanistic psychology is often referred to as the ___(56)___ ___. Humanists believe that all people possess an internal force that leads them to grow and improve. This force is called ___(57)___-___. To the humanist, reality is ___(58)___.

     Our selective perception of who we are is called our ___(59)___-___. Carl Rogers distinguishes between the person one thinks he is, called the ___(60)___, and the person one wishes to be, called the ___(61)___ ___. Discrepancies between the self and the ideal self can be ___(62)___. An obscure view of ourselves may arise when our self-concept is not ___(63)___ with the way we actually are. According to Rogers, when a person denies feelings that are incongruent with her self-concept, she fails to ___(64)___ her experience. The process of denying awareness to certain feelings begins when parents ___(65)___ some behaviors but ___(66)___ others. This creates standards which Rogers calls ___(67)___ ___ ___. We often deny these feelings that are ___(68)___ with our internalized conditions of worth.

     Humanistic psychology, psychoanalysis, and social learning theory all differ in their views of the basic ___(69)___ of human beings and society. Recently, there are signs that the major theories have begun to grow more ___(70)___. Recently, investigators have questioned whether the five-factor model and other trait approaches are applicable in ___(71)___ cultures.

Personality Assessment: Taking a Measure of the Person

Psychologists use personality assessment techniques to develop a picture of their client's personality in a relatively brief amount of time. The most universally used method of personality assessment is the ___(72)___. Although widely used, interviews have limitations; they are inherently ___(73)___, and they are ___(74)___ situations. An alternative to the interview is to watch the person's behavior in a natural or simulated situation; this is called the ___(75)___ method. In an attempt to make observational methods more objective, a variety of ___(76)___ _____ have been developed.

A personality test that uses ambiguous stimuli to reveal the contents of the client's unconscious mind is the ___(77)___ test. The individual is asked to make up a story about ambiguous pictures in the ___(78)___ _____ _____ (TAT); symmetrical inkblots are used in the ___(79)___ _____ _____.

An example of an objective personality test is the ___(80)___ _____ _____ _____ (MMPI-2).

Research with projective tests indicates they are generally not successful in predicting behavior. Although objective personality tests fare somewhat better, ___(81)___ is recommended in interpreting the results of personality tests.

Application of Psychology: Situational Influences on Personality in Everyday Life

Considerable research supports the importance of ___(82)___ in determining human behavior.

Concept Check

Fill in the missing components of the following concept box. The correct answers are located in the "Answers" section at the end of the chapter.

Major Theories of Personality

Theorist	Approach	Basic Components of Theory
Freud	Psychoanalytic	Emphasis on id, ego, superego; importance of displacement and identification; and five stages of personality development: oral, anal, phallic, latency, and genital
Jung	Psychoanalytic	Emphasis on extroversion/introversion traits, personal unconscious, and collective unconscious
Adler	Psychoanalytic	Effort to overcome feelings of inferiority is primary emphasis
Horney	Psychoanalytic	Anxious insecurity is the source of all conflicts
Bandura	Social learning	Personality is learned but reciprocally determined. Emphasizes the role of cognition in personality development
Carl Rogers	Humanistic	Importance is placed on self, self-concept, and ideal self
Allport	Trait theory	Cardinal, central and secondary traits

Extending the Chapter: Psychology, Societal Issues, and Human Diversity

These questions may be assigned to you. Whether or not they are assigned, they are designed to be challenging questions to encourage you to think independently about the material in the chapter. Many of the questions have no right or wrong answers.

I.   From the *Applications of Psychology* section

1.   What are the implications of the power of situational influences in life?

2.   In the debate over traits vs. situationism, which side do you favor? Explain your answer.

II. Psychology, Societal Issues, and Human Diversity

1. Describe the challenges faced by psychologists as they integrate sociocultural factors into a general theory of personality.

2. If you were applying for a job and could choose to be evaluated by only one type of personality assessment, which would you choose? Why?

3. Some people seem to be more prone to be involved in automobile accidents. If psychologists could devise a measure of personality to predict those at greater risk for an accident, should this measure be required of all drivers? Should those people whose score indicates they are at higher risk for accidents be denied licenses? Explain your answer.

4. What steps should be taken to safeguard the results of personality tests in industrial, educational, and clinical settings? What implications do the use of computers have for the storage and transmission of these data?

Practice Quiz

The practice quiz consists of three sections: 1) Short Answer questions, 2) Multiple choice questions, and 3) True-False questions. At the end of the chapter you will find suggested answers to the short answer questions, answers and explanation for the multiple choice questions, and answers to the true-false questions.

Short Answer Questions

1. List and describe the three parts of the mind as theorized by Freud.

_____

_____

2. Distinguish between Bandura's concepts of self-efficacy and self-regulation.

_____

_____

3. List and describe three different approaches to the assessment of personality.

_____

_____

Multiple Choice Questions

1. Which of the following helps define the term *personality?*
   a. characteristics that are typical for a person
   b. characteristics that make a person unique
   c. acting, thinking, and feeling
   d. all of the above
   LO 1

2. Allport calls the traits that influence and organize much of our behavior
   a. cardinal traits.
   b. central traits.
   c. secondary traits.
   d. source traits.
   LO 2

3. Each of the following is considered to be one of the "big five" personality traits *except*
   a. neuroticism.
   b. extraversion.
   c. conscientiousness.
   d. friendliness.
   LO 3

4. According to Freud, primitive instinctual motives and repressed memories are stored in the
   a. conscious mind.
   b. preconscious mind.
   c. unconscious mind.
   d. superego.
   LO 4

5. According to Freud, information that you are not currently aware of that can be easily recalled into awareness resides in which part of the mind?
   a. preconscious
   b. conscious
   c. unconscious
   d. subconscious
   LO 4

6. The executive of the personality, which operates according to the reality principle, is the
   a. id.
   b. ego.
   c. superego.
   d. none of the above.
   LO 5

7. According to Freud, which part of the mind is dominated by the pleasure principle?
   a. the id
   b. the ego
   c. superego
   d. the superid
   LO 5

8. According to Freud, which part of the mind corresponds roughly to conscience?
   a. the id
   b. the ego
   c. the superego
   d. the superid
   LO 5

9. All of the following are examples of sublimation *except*
   a. competing in contact sports.
   b. robbing a bank.
   c. painting nude portraits.
   d. competing in business.
   LO 6

10. To prevent itself from being overwhelmed by excessive demands from the id and superego, the ego relies on
    a. the Oedipus complex.
    b. defense mechanisms.
    c. the reality principle.
    d. the pleasure principle.
    LO 6

11. According to Jung, the unconscious mind with which all humans are born is called the
    a. preconscious.
    b. personal conscious.
    c. collective unconscious.
    d. none of the above.
    LO 7

12. Most people intuitively understand that incest is wrong, even though they are not told this directly. Jung would explain that the incest taboo is part of the
    a. innate id.
    b. collective unconscious.
    c. collective superego.
    d. Electra complex.
    LO 7

13. According to Adler, to develop a healthy personality it is necessary to learn to express
    a. the social interest.
    b. the selfish interest.
    c. the superego.
    d. sexual and aggressive motives.
    LO 8

14. According to Karen Horney
    a. Anxious insecurity is the source of all conflicts.
    b. Self-actualization is a basic human motive.
    c. Conflict is the inevitable result of the inborn motives of the id.
    d. We each possess both a personal unconscious and a collective unconscious.
    LO 8

15. To the social learning theorist, each of the following processes is important in the development of personality *except*
    a. classical conditioning.
    b. operant conditioning.
    c. modeling.
    d. feelings of inferiority.
    LO 9

16. According to Bandura, self-efficacy and self-regulation emphasize the importance of what determinant of behavior?
    a. learning
    b. traits
    c. situations
    d. cognitions
    LO 9

17. The mutual interaction between a person's behavior and his or her social learning environment is called
    a. reciprocal determination.
    b. self-efficacy.
    c. self-regulation.
    d. efficient regulation.
    LO 9

18. The view that behavior is influenced by characteristics of both the person and the situation is called
    a. situationism.
    b. interactionism.
    c. the trait approach.
    d. a and b above.
    LO 10

19. The humanistic view states that
    a. humans possess an inner-directedness.
    b. humans possess an objective view of reality.
    c. people should not frustrate themselves by. continually trying to change and improve.
    d. personality is dominated by an active. unconscious
    LO 11

20. Rogers believes that differences between the self and the ideal self
    a. are uncomfortable.
    b. lead to incongruence.
    c. lead to unsymbolized feelings.
    d. all of the above.
    LO 12

21. Which approach to psychology is referred to as the "third force"?
    a. psychoanalysis
    b. social learning theory
    c. humanistic theory
    d. trait theory
    LO 13

22. Humanistic psychologists believe that people are born _____, whereas social learning theorists believe that people are born _____.
    a. good, selfish
    b. selfish, good
    c. neutral, good
    d. good, neutral
    LO 13

23. Which of the following is a problem with the use of interviews as a method of personality assessment?
    a. They are subjective.
    b. They are artificial situations.
    c. They may bring out atypical behavior.
    d. all of the above
    LO 14

24. Which of the following is an example of a projective personality test?
    a. Thematic Apperception Test (TAT)
    b. Minnesota Multiphasic Personality Inventory (MMPI-2)
    c. Rorschach inkblot test
    d. a and c above
    LO 15

25. Which of the following characterizes the MMPI-2?
    a. It consists of multiple-choice and fill-in questions.
    b. It is designed to reveal unconscious conflicts.
    c. It allows for objective interpretation of the results.
    d. The items are divided into 25 different "scales."
    LO 16

26. Which objective personality test can be used to assess depression?
    a. MMPI-2
    b. TAT
    c. interview
    d. observation
    LO 16

27. Which of the following statements is correct?
    a. Projective tests are generally good predictors of behavior.
    b. Psychologists generally agree about the usefulness of personality tests.
    c. Objective personality tests are often more effective than projective tests in distinguishing among groups with different traits.
    d. Projective tests are generally more effective than objective tests in distinguishing among groups with different traits.
    LO 17

28. According to the text, most personality researchers agree that personality is influenced strongly by
    a. traits.
    b. situations.
    c. situations and personal characteristics.
    d. human altruism.
    LO 18

True-False Questions

_____1. Trait theories are useful because they help to explain differences in personality.

_____2. One of the "big five" personality traits is extroversion.

_____3. According to Freud, the superego operates according to the pleasure principle.

_____4 Freud believed that all of the cultural and economic achievements of society were the result of sublimation.

_____5. According to Jung, all humans are born with the collective unconscious.

_____6. Bandura believes that cognition plays a very small role in the development of our personality.

_____7. Humanistic theory emphasizes inner-directedness and subjective reality.

_____8. According to the text, researchers agree that the five-factor model of personality applies equally well to all cultures.

_____9. Objective tests can provide valuable information about an individual's unconscious activity.

_____10. Projective tests are highly successful in predicting behavior.

ANSWER SECTION

Concept Check

Major Theories of Personality

Theorist	Approach	Basic Components of Theory
Freud	Psychoanalytic	Emphasis on id, ego, superego; importance of displacement and identification; and five stages of personality development: oral, anal, phallic, latency, and genital
Jung	Psychoanalytic	Emphasis on extroversion/introversion traits, personal unconscious, and collective unconscious
Adler	Psychoanalytic	Effort to overcome feelings of inferiority is primary emphasis
Horney	Psychoanalytic	Anxious insecurity is the source of all conflicts.
Bandura	Social learning	Personality is learned but reciprocally determined. Emphasizes the role of cognition in personality development
Carl Rogers	Humanistic	Importance is placed on self, self-concept, and ideal self
Allport	Trait theory	Cardinal, central and secondary traits

Answers to Review At A Glance

1. typical
2. different
3. traits
4. describing
5. explaining
6. values
7. cardinal
8. central
9. secondary
10. five
11. sexual
12. conscious
13. preconscious
14. unconscious
15. id
16. ego

17. superego
18. id
19. life
20. libido
21. death
22. sexual
23. aggressive
24. unconscious
25. pleasure
26. primary process
27. ego
28. reality
29. executive
30. superego
31. parents
32. conscience

33. ego ideal
34. displacement
35. sublimation
36. identification
37. extroversion
38. introversion
39. personal
40. collective
41. inferiority
42. social interest
43. insecurity
44. childrearing
45. learned
46. cognition
47. active
48. reciprocally determined

49. self-efficacy	61. ideal self	74. artificial
50. self-regulation	62. uncomfortable	75. observational
51. situationism	63. congruent	76. rating scales
52. person × situation interactionism	64. symbolize	77. projective
53. if...then	65. praise	78. Thematic Apperception Test
54. personal characteristics	66. punish	79. Rorschach Inkblot Test
55. situations	67. conditions of worth	80. Minnesota Multiphasic Personality Inventory
56. third force	68. inconsistent	81. caution
57. inner-directedness	69. nature	82. situation
58. subjective	70. similar	
59. self-concept	71. non-Western	
60. self	72. interview	
	73. subjective	

Sample Answers for Short Answer Questions

1.   List and describe the three parts of the mind as theorized by Freud.

According to Freud's theory of personality, the mind is composed of three parts. The id, according to Freud, is the inborn part of the mind. It engages in primary process thinking to satisfy its needs. The id is selfish and it is dominated by the pleasure principle. The id wants to obtain immediate pleasure and to avoid pain regardless of the effect it has on others. The second part of the mind, the ego, is referred to as the executive of the personality. It operates on the reality principle. It holds the id in check until it finds a safe way to satisfy the demands of the id. The third part of the mind is the superego. The superego enforces moral restrictions as taught by parents and others. The superego opposes the desires of the id.

2.   Distinguish between Bandura's concepts of self-efficacy and self-regulation.

According to Bandura, our learned cognitions are the prime determinant of our behavior. When people perceive they are doing what is necessary to achieve their goals (both behaviorally and emotionally) they are demonstrating self-efficacy. We have all learned personal standards of behavior. When we cognitively reward or punish ourselves on the basis of these personal standards, then we are engaging in self-regulation.

3.   List and describe three different approaches to the assessment of personality.

One widely used method of assessing personality is the interview. This is a highly subjective method, and the person being interviewed may react to this situation with atypical behavior. Another method involves the use of projective tests, such as the Rorschach and the TAT. These tests present ambiguous stimuli in an effort to reveal the client's unconscious mind. A third method uses objective personality tests, such as the MMPI-2. Although there are no "right" answers, the test is an objective test. Answers are compared with the answers of others with known personality characteristics who have taken the test.

Multiple Choice Answers

1. The answer is *d*. Although it might appear contradictory on the surface, the definition focuses on characteristics that are typical for the person, yet make the individual different from others.

2. The answer is *b*. According to Allport, cardinal traits are those that dominate a person's life. Relatively few people possess cardinal traits. Secondary traits are those that are more specific but less important in an overall view of a person's personality.

3. The answer is *d*. A considerable degree of consensus exists among trait theorists that there are five basic personality traits.

4. The answer is *c*. According to Freud, the conscious mind contains our present awareness, but is actually just the "tip of the iceberg" of our mind. The preconscious mind, just below the surface, contains memories of which we are not currently conscious, but can easily be brought into our consciousness. The unconscious mind contains information that is not easily brought into consciousness.

5. The answer is *a*. The preconscious mind is the vast storehouse of easily accessible memories. The conscious mind is the portion of the mind of which we are presently aware. The unconscious mind is the storehouse of primitive instinctual motives and repressed memories.

6. The answer is *b*. According to Freud, the id is composed primarily of life instincts and death instincts. Life instincts consist largely of sexual and aggressive urges. The ego attempts to find realistic ways of satisfying the id's urges. The superego, the moral part of the mind, strives to attain a goal of perfection.

7. The answer is *a*. According to Freud, the id is the selfish beast of the mind, seeking immediate gratification and the avoidance of pain at any cost.

8. The answer is *c*. The superego develops as restrictions are placed on the actions of the id and ego, and parental punishment helps to establish the conscience.

9. The answer is *b*. Sublimation is a form of displacement in which a socially desirable goal is substituted for a socially harmful goal.

10. The answer is *b*. An example of such a defense mechanism is displacement, the process of substituting a more acceptable goal.

11. The answer is *c*. According to Jung, the personal unconscious contains threatening motives, conflicts, and information that have been repressed, while the collective unconscious is the unconscious mind with which all humans are born.

12. The answer is *b*. According to Jung, the collective unconscious is the unconscious mind with which all humans are born.

13. The answer is *a*. According to Adler, the social interest is an inborn motive to establish loving, helpful relationships with other people.

14. The answer is *a*. According to Horney, if parents are indifferent, harsh, or overprotective, the child will lose confidence in parental love and become anxiously insecure.

15. The answer is *d*. Social learning theorists hold that our personalities are formed primarily through interactions with other members of society. Thus, basic learning concepts, such as classical and operant conditioning and modeling, are the important forces in shaping personality.

16. The answer is *d*. According to Bandura, important determinants of personality are the cognitions both about ourselves and our relationships with others.

17. The answer is *a*. According to Bandura, reciprocal determination implies that we play an active role in our own lives.

18. The answer is *b*. As a counterpoint to the trait approach offered by Allport and Cattell, situationism suggests that behavior is consistent only as long as situations (especially those regarding other people) remain consistent. Interactionism represents a compromise between the trait and situationism approaches.

19. The answer is *a*. Humanistic psychology, sometimes called the third force in psychology (the first two are psychoanalysis and behaviorism), suggests that humans have freedom to make choices. Inner-directedness is an internal force that pushes people to grow and to improve.

20. The answer is *d*. According to Rogers, the self is the person you believe yourself to be, whereas the ideal self is the person you wish to be. Although Rogers' theory suggests that slight differences between the self and ideal self are not a cause for concern, major discrepancies can lead to difficulties.

21. The answer is *c*. Humanistic theory burst on the psychological scene in the 1950s, - relatively late in psychology's history, after psychoanalysis and behaviorism were already established forces.

22 The answer is *d*. Humanistic psychologists believe that the inner-directedness with which we are born is basically a positive force. Social learning theorists, however, judge our slate to be clean (neutral) at birth; we can learn to be good or bad.

23. The answer is *d*. The interview is the most universally used, yet one of the most limited, methods for obtaining information about personality.

24. The answer is *d*. Projective personality tests use ambiguous stimuli in an effort to get the client to project his or her unconscious mind. The TAT asks the client to make up a story about ambiguous pictures. The Rorschach presents the client with a series of symmetrical inkblots.

25. The answer is *c*. The MMPI-2 is an objective test—no effort is made by the test to consider what the respondent meant by each answer. Items on the test are presented as true–false questions and are divided into 10 scales, each measuring a different aspect of personality.

26. The answer is *a*. The only objective test listed among the choices is the MMPI-2.

27. The answer is *c*. Research suggests that projective tests are generally not successful in predicting behavior. The results suggest caution in the interpretation of personality tests.

28. The answer is *c*. The research cited in the *Application of Psychology* section strongly supports the influence of person × situational factors in determining personality.

Answers to True-False Questions

1. F   6. F

2. T   7. T

3. F   8. F

4. T   9. F

5. T   10. F

Chapter 12   Stress and Health

Learning Objectives

1. Define stress and list the sources of stress. (p. 358)

2. Distinguish among the differing types of conflict. (p. 358)

3. Discuss the relationship between life events and stress. (p. 360)

4. Discuss our reactions to stress, and list and describe the stages of Selye's general adaptation syndrome; describe both healthy and unhealthy aspects of the general adaptation syndrome. (p. 362)

5. List and describe factors that influence reactions to stress. (p. 367)

6. Describe cognitive factors in stress reactions and identify the characteristics of the Type A personality. (p. 369)

7. List and describe three effective methods of coping with stress. (p. 371)

8. List and describe three ineffective methods of coping with stress. (p. 372)

9. Distinguish among Freud's major defense mechanisms. (p. 373)

10. Describe how progressive relaxation training is used to prevent health problems. (p. 375)

11. Discuss the ways in which improved eating habits and aerobic exercise affect one's health. (p. 376)

12.   (From the *Application of Psychology* section) Understand the role health psychology can play in the prevention and management of AIDS. (p. 379)

Chapter Overview

Health psychology is a relatively new field in psychology; health psychologists attempt to prevent health problems by helping individuals cope with stress and by helping to promote healthy lifestyles. Stress is any event that strains or exceeds an individual's capacity to cope. Among the major sources of stress in our lives are frustration, the inability to satisfy a motive, and conflict, the result of two or more incompatible motives. Four types of conflict are: 1) approach-approach conflict, 2) avoidance-avoidance conflict, 3) approach-avoidance conflict, and 4) multiple approach-avoidance conflict. Pressure, an additional source of stress, arises from the threat of negative events. Another source of stress comes from the positive and the negative changes that occur in our lives. Reactions to stress are very similar whether the stress is physical or psychological. Selye has identified a consistent pattern of bodily responses to stress called the general adaptation syndrome. This syndrome consists of three stages: the alarm stage, the resistance stage, and the exhaustion stage. Stress affects our emotions, our immune system, our motivations, and our cognition.

Events are generally less stressful when we have had some prior experience with them, when they are predictable, when we have some control over them, and when we receive social support. The characteristics of individuals also affect their reactions to stress. Cognitive factors are important in our reaction to stress.

Much research has been conducted on the Type A personality and its link to heart disease. Hostility seems to be the dangerous component of Type A behavior.

Our efforts to cope with stress can be either effective or ineffective. Effective methods of coping with stress include removing the source of stress, cognitive coping, and managing our reactions to stress. Ineffective coping strategies include withdrawal, aggression, and the use of defense mechanisms.

A major goal of health psychology is to prevent health problems. Relaxation training is one technique used to achieve this goal. Health psychologists also seek to reduce health risks by helping individuals exercise properly and eat a healthy diet.

Some health psychologists seek to treat health problems. Psychologists have become involved with the AIDS epidemic through efforts to understand and control behavioral aspects of the transmission of AIDS and through efforts to slow the progress of the disease in those who are infected.

Key Terms Exercise

For each of the following exercises, match the key terms on the left with the correct definitions on the right. Page references to the text follow the terms so that you may refer to the text for any items you answer incorrectly or do not understand completely. You may check your responses immediately by referring to the answers that follow each exercise.

Stress: Challenges to Coping (I)

_____ 1. health psychology (p. 358)
_____ 2. stress (p. 358)
_____ 3. frustration (p. 358)
_____ 4. conflict (p. 358)

a. any event that strains or exceeds an individual's ability to cope
b. occurs when two or more motives cannot be satisfied because they interfere with each other
c. the field within psychology that seeks to promote healthy life-styles
d. occurs when we are unable to satisfy a motive

ANSWERS
1. c   3. d
2. a   4. b

Stress: Challenges to Coping (II)

_____ 1. approach-approach conflict (p. 358)
_____ 2. avoidance-avoidance conflict (p. 358)
_____ 3. approach-avoidance conflict (p. 358)
_____ 4. multiple approach-avoidance conflict (p. 360)
_____ 5. pressure (p. 360)
_____ 6. life events (p. 360)
_____ 7. general adaptation syndrome (GAS) (p. 362)

a. the individual must choose between two negative outcomes
b. the changes in our lives that require readjustment and coping
c. the individual must choose between several alternatives that each contain both positive and negative consequences
d. conflict in which achieving a positive goal will produce a negative outcome as well
e. the individual must choose between two positive goals
f. a pattern of responses used by the body to ward off stress
g. the stress that arises from the threat of negative events

ANSWERS
1. e   5. g
2. a   6. b
3. d   7. f
4. c

Factors that Influence Reactions to Stress/Coping with Stress/Changing Health-Related Behavior Patterns/Prevention and Treatment of AIDS

_____ 1. social support (p. 367)
_____ 2. person variables (p. 368)
_____ 3. Type A personality (p. 369)
_____ 4. coping (p. 371)
_____ 5. defense mechanisms (p. 373)
_____ 6. progressive relaxation training (p. 375)

a. differences between people that help to explain our different reactions to stress

b. having somebody to whom one can talk, as well as receive advice and reassurance

c. a personality characterized by intense competitiveness, hostility, and a sense of time urgency

d. a method of learning to deeply relax the muscles of the body

e. according to Freud, the ego's effort to discharge tension

f. efforts to deal with the source of stress or to control reactions to stress

ANSWERS

1. b	4. f
2. a	5. e
3. c	6. d

Review At A Glance

(Answers to this section may be found on page 210)

Stress: Challenges to Coping

The field that has emerged within psychology that seeks to promote healthy life-styles is called ___(1)___ _____.

Any event that strains or exceeds an individual's capacity to cope is called ___(2)___. One major source of stress occurs when we are not able to satisfy a motive; this is called ___(3)___. Another source of stress occurs when two motives cannot be satisfied because they interfere with one another; this is referred to as ___(4)___. There are four major types of conflict: 1) when the individual must choose between two positive goals of approximately equal value, this is a(n) ___(5)___-_____ conflict; (2) when we must choose between two or more negative outcomes, this is referred to as a(n) ___(6)___-_____ conflict; (3) when obtaining a positive goal necessitates a negative outcome, this is called a(n) ___(7)___-_____ conflict; (4) when an individual must choose between alternatives that contain both positive and negative consequences, this is termed a(n) ___(8)___ _____-_____ conflict.

A third source of stress arises from the threat of negative events; this is called ___(9)___. Another type of stress comes from changes in our lives, both positive and negative; these are referred to as ___(10)___ _____. Negative life events such as the death of a family member, ___(11)___ disasters, witnessing violence, or being an assault victim are all important sources of ___(12)___. Lazarus has found that daily ___(13)___ of life can be sources of stress. Even ___(14)___ life events, such as marriage and job promotions can be sources of stress.

Recent findings about stress suggest: 1) stress produces both ___(15)___ and ___(16)___ reactions; and 2) our reactions to stress are very similar whether the stress is ___(17)___ or ___(18)___.

Hans Selye has identified a pattern of bodily responses to stress called the ___(19)___ _____ _____. This syndrome consists of three stages: 1) the body begins to mobilize its resources in the ___(20)___ _____ stage, sometimes referred to as the ___(21)___-or-_____ reaction; 2) the body's resources are fully mobilized in the ___(22)___ stage; and (3) the individual's resources are depleted and resistance to stress is lowered in the ___(23)___ stage. Although the GAS is helpful in dealing with emergencies and disease, prolonged stress can lead to dangerous changes in the ___(24)___ system. Although stress can harm the functioning of the immune system, in some cases ___(25)___ _____ can restore immune system functioning.

The psychological reactions to stress include changes in emotions, ___(26)___, and cognitions.

Factors that Influence Reactions to Stress

Stress reactions are generally less severe when the individual has had some ___(27)___ _____ with the stress. Also, events are generally less stressful when they are ___(28)___, when we perceive that we have some degree of ___(29)___ over the stress, and when we have ___(30)___ _____ from friends and family members. One of the important benefits of social support appears to be having someone in whom to ___(31)___. Personal characteristics, referred to as person ___(32)___, are also important in determining our responses to stress.

Emotional factors and personality factors confirm the importance of viewing stress in terms of a ___(33)___ _____ interaction. The person with a Type A personality shows many of the following characteristics: highly ___(34)___ __, works ___(35)___, workaholic, speaks ___(36)___, perfectionistic and ___(37)___, and hostile or ___(38)___. An important Type A characteristic appears to be a particular kind of ___(39)___; individuals who react to frustration with ___(40)___ or ___(41)___ aggression seem to be at slightly higher risk for coronary heart disease. Type A behavior appears to be indirectly linked to heart disease through two major factors: high ___(42)___ _____ and ___(43)___.

Coping with Stress

Effective methods of coping with stress include removing the ___(44)___ of stress, ___(45)___ coping, and managing our ___(46)___ to stress. Psychological counseling involving all three methods has been successful in modifying ___(47)___ _____ behavior. Ineffective coping strategies include ___(48)___, aggression, and the use of ___(49)___ _____. According to Freud, the major defense mechanisms include 1) directing aggressive or sexual feelings toward someone safe, called ___(50)___, 2) converting impulses into sexually approved activities, called ___(51)___; 3) viewing one's own unacceptable desires as the desires of others, termed ___(52)___; 4) unconsciously transforming desires into the opposite desires, called ___(53)___ _____; 5) returning to an infantile pattern of behavior, termed ___(54)___; 6) "explaining away" stressful events, called ___(55)___; 7) keeping stressful, unacceptable desires out of consciousness, called ___(56)___; 8) blocking information that is threatening from conscious awareness, called ___(57)___; and 9) reducing the emotional nature of threatening events to cold logic, called ___(58)___.

Changing Health-Related Behavior Patterns

A major goal of health psychology is to ___(59)___ health problems by helping individuals modify behaviors that create health risks. One example involves teaching individuals to ___(60)___. Individuals are taught to deeply relax their large body muscles in a technique called ___(61)___ _____ training. This technique has been found to be effective in treating ___(62)___, both tension and ___(63)___ headaches, and high blood pressure. Relaxation training has also been shown to reduce the recurrence of genital ___(64)___ infections.

Psychologists have had some success in getting people to eat healthier diets. Although the health benefits of regular exercise are well established, the majority of Americans do not get regular ___(65)___ exercise. Research suggests that the following factors can help individuals adhere to a regular exercise program: social ___(66)___, setting ___(67)___ _____, and avoiding excessively ___(68)___ exercise.

Application of Psychology: The Prevention and Treatment of AIDS

AIDS is caused by the human ____(69)____ _____ virus (HIV). HIV infection leads to the destruction of immune cells called ____(70)____, thus rendering useless the important ____(71)____ of the immune system. AIDS is much more common in some ____(72)____ groups. The HIV virus is spread through ____(73)____ _____. The most common means of transmission is through ____(74)____ _____. Other modes of transmission include ____(75)____ drug use and transmission from an infected mother to her infant during birth. There is virtually no chance of acquiring AIDS if a person is not sexually active or is involved in a ____(76)____ sexual relationship with a partner who is not infected with HIV. A study conducted by Kelly demonstrates the effectiveness of ____(77)____ for individuals engaging in high-risk sexual behaviors. Some research supports the benefits of ____(78)____ exercise on the immune system. Taylor has found benefits for those who actively ____(79)____ the reality of their impending death when they learn of their infection.

Concept Check

Fill in the missing components of the following concept boxes. The correct answers are located in the "Answers" section at the end of the chapter.

Sources of Stress

Name	Description
	inability to satisfy a motive
conflict	
	the threat of negative events
life events	

Stages in Selye's general adaptation syndrome

Stage	Description
alarm reaction	
resistance stage	
exhaustion stage	

Factors that influence reactions to stress

Factor	Description
prior experience	
predictability and control	
social support	
person variables	cognitive factors (sensitizers and repressors), emotional factors, and personality characteristics (Type A personality)

Extending the Chapter: Psychology, Societal Issues, and Human Diversity

These questions may be assigned to you. Whether or not they are assigned, they are designed to be challenging questions to encourage you to think independently about the material in the chapter. Many of the questions have no right or wrong answers.

I.   From the *Application of Psychology* section

1.   Discuss the efforts of psychologists to aid in the prevention of AIDS.

2.   Describe the results of research by psychologists in helping HIV patients to better manage their disease.

II.   Psychology, Societal Issues, and Human Diversity

1.   Do you believe that members of our society experience more stress now than previous generations? Explain your answer.

2.   Has the rapid advancement of technology created new stressors for members of our society? Explain your answer.

3.   Given the fact that certain widely available foods are likely to contribute to heart disease, cancer, and other diseases, should these foods be more closely regulated? If known carcinogens are banned from public consumption, why should artery-clogging hamburgers be allowed? Where should our society draw the line on keeping its members healthy (and who should draw the line)?

4.   (From the *Human Diversity* section) Discuss health psychology challenges that are unique to women.

Practice Quiz

The practice quiz consists of three sections: 1) Short Answer questions, 2) Multiple choice questions, and 3) True-False questions. At the end of the chapter you will find suggested answers to the short answer questions, answers and explanation for the multiple choice questions, and answers to the true-false questions.

Short Answer Questions

1.   List and explain the four major types of conflicts discussed in the text.

_____

_____

2.   Describe both effective and ineffective methods of coping with stress.

_____

_____

3. Discuss the results of research on life events as a source of stress.

_____

_____

Multiple Choice Questions

1. A health psychologist would agree with all of the following *except*
   a. The functioning of the body is linked to psychological factors.
   b. Health psychologists seek to promote healthy life-styles.
   c. Stress is less of a factor in health psychology than it was a few years ago.
   d. Our patterns of behavior have direct impact on our health.
   LO 1

2. Stress has been linked to
   a. heart disease.
   b. strokes.
   c. decreased immunity to infections.
   d. all of the above.
   LO 1

3. A source of stress characterized by the inability to satisfy a motive is called
   a. conflict.
   b. life events.
   c. frustration.
   d. pressure.
   LO 1

4. Conflicts that require choosing "the lesser of two evils" are
   a. approach-approach conflicts.
   b. avoidance-avoidance conflicts.
   c. approach-avoidance conflicts.
   d. double-approach-avoidance conflicts.
   LO 2

5. As Jennifer approaches the end of her senior year in college, she is excited about the prospects of graduating but scared about being "on her own." Jennifer is experiencing
   a. an approach-avoidance conflict.
   b. an approach-approach conflict.
   c. an avoidance-avoidance conflict.
   d. the exhaustion stage of the general adaptation syndrome.
   LO 2

6. In a study by Lazarus, participants recorded major life events, daily hassles, and daily positive events for a year. What was found to be the BEST predictor of both health and psychological well-being?
   a. daily hassles
   b. positive events
   c. major life events
   d. number of conflicts
   LO 3

7. In which stage of the general adaptation syndrome is resistance to stress lowered?
   a. the resistance stage
   b. the exhaustion stage
   c. the alarm stage
   d. the defensive stage
   LO 4

8. In which stage of the GAS are the body's resources fully mobilized and resistant to stress?
   a. alarm reaction
   b. resistance stage
   c. exhaustion stage
   d. any of the above
   LO 4

9. In general, stress events are less stressful when they are
   a. predictable.
   b. unpredictable.
   c. controllable.
   d. a and c.
   LO 5

10. With repeated exposures to stressful situations, a person's general stress level
    a. increases.
    b. disappears.
    c. decreases.
    d. remains constant.
    LO 5

11. Research on sharing negative feelings with others ("getting it off your chest") found that participants
    a. had elevated blood pressure immediately after venting their feelings.
    b. reported feeling better immediately after venting their feelings.
    c. were less ill and visited the health center less often during the following six months.
    d. a and c above.
    LO 5

12. Each of the following is true of social support *except*
    a. Individuals with social support react to stress with less depression and anxiety.
    b. The ability to confide in others is an important benefit of social support.
    c. There is little proven health benefit in sharing negative feelings with others.
    d. Social support can help us when we have to make stressful decisions.
    LO 5

13. Which of the following components of Type A behavior has a strong negative effect on cardiac functioning?
    a. hostile/verbally aggressive
    b. hostile/suspicious
    c. highly competitive
    d. perfectionistic
    LO 6

14. Research on Type A behavior suggests that the link to heart disease may stem from
    a. high blood pressure.
    b. high cholesterol.
    c. poor dietary habits.
    d. a and b above.
    LO 6

15. After being promoted to department head, Bill found the job to be uncomfortable and highly stressful. Ultimately, Bill resigned from the position and returned to his former job, where he reported being much happier. Which method of coping with stress did Bill use?
    a. managing stress reactions, an effective coping method
    b. withdrawal, an ineffective coping method
    c. removing stress, an effective coping method
    d. excessive use of defense mechanisms, an ineffective coping method
    LO 7

16. Each of the following is an effective method of coping with stress *except*
    a. removing stress.
    b. cognitive coping.
    c. defense mechanisms.
    d. managing stress reactions.
    LO 7

17. Jeff used a coping strategy that was ineffective because it distorted reality. What kind of strategy did he use?
    a. cognitive coping
    b. defense mechanism
    c. sensitization
    d. stress removal
    LO 8

18. Each of the following is considered to be an ineffective method of coping with stress *except*
    a. withdrawal.
    b. aggression.
    c. use of defense mechanisms.
    d. cognitive coping.
    LO 8

19. The process of blocking out of consciousness any upsetting thoughts is the defense mechanism called
    a. projection.
    b. reaction formation.
    c. denial.
    d. intellectualization.
       LO 9

20. When Ken called Barbie to ask her for a date, Barbie said, "I'm sorry, but I think I'm busy for the rest of my life!" Ken has decided that he is really relieved because Barbie has lots of faults anyway. Which defense mechanism is he using?
    a. displacement
    b. repression
    c. rationalization
    d. suppression
       LO 9

21. Teaching a person to alternately tense the major muscles and then release that tension is used in
    a. progressive relaxation.
    b. aerobic exercise.
    c. behavioral inhibition.
    d. aversion therapy.
       LO 10

22. Which of the following has been successfully treated with progressive relaxation?
    a. insomnia
    b. tension and migraine headaches
    c. high blood pressure
    d. all of the above
       LO 10

23. According to psychologists, which of the following would be good advice for keeping a commitment to an exercise program?
    a. social support
    b. setting clear personal goals
    c. avoiding excessively strenuous exercise
    d. all of the above
       LO 11

24. Health psychologists can lessen the negative impact of the AIDS epidemic by
    a. helping individuals change their high-risk behaviors.
    b. helping to cure those with the HIV infection by counseling.
    c. helping individuals with HIV to confront the reality of their disease.
    d. a and c above.
       LO 12

True-False Questions

_____1. The first stage of the general adaptation syndrome is called the resistance stage.

_____2. Positive life events are an important source of stress.

_____3. Stress reactions are generally more severe when the individual has prior experience with the stress.

_____4. According to the text, social support is not a significant factor in our reactions to stress.

_____5. Stressful events are generally more stressful when they are predictable.

_____6. The Type A personality dimension that increases one's risk for heart disease involves verbal and/or physical aggression.

_____7. According to the text, using defense mechanisms is an ineffective way to cope with stress.

_____8. Throwing temper tantrums or giving a friend the "silent treatment" are examples of the defense mechanism called reaction formation.

_____9. Progressive relaxation training focuses primarily on the small muscle groups of the body.

_____10. HIV attacks lymphocytes and T-4 Helper cells.

ANSWER SECTION

Concept Check

Sources of Stress

Name	Description
frustration	inability to satisfy a motive
conflict	occurs when two motives cannot be satisfied because they interfere with each other
pressure	the threat of negative events
life events	negative life events, small daily hassles, and even positive life events

Stages in Selye's general adaptation syndrome

Stage	Description
alarm reaction	the body mobilizes its stored resources; sympathetic arousal occurs as the "fight or flight" reaction occurs
resistance stage	the body's resources are fully mobilized, and resistance to stress is high; any additional stress might overwhelm the body
exhaustion stage	individual's resources are exhausted, and resistance to stress is lowered

Factors that influence reactions to stress

Factor	Description
prior experience	stress reactions are generally less severe when the individual has some prior experience with the stress
predictability and control	generally, events are less stressful when they are predictable and when the individual can exert some control over the stress
social support	the effects of stress are lessened when the individual has good quality social support
person variables	cognitive factors (sensitizers and repressors), emotional factors, and personality characteristics (Type A personality)

Answers to Review At A Glance

1. health psychology
2. stress
3. frustration
4. conflict
5. approach-approach
6. avoidance-avoidance
7. approach-avoidance
8. multiple approach-avoidance
9. pressure
10. life events
11. natural
12. stress
13. hassles
14. positive
15. psychological
16. physiological
17. physical
18. psychological
19. general adaptation

syndrome
20. alarm reaction
21. fight/flight
22. resistance
23. exhaustion
24. cardiac
25. stress management
26. motivations
27. prior experience
28. predictable
29. control
30. social support
31. confide
32. variables
33. person X situation
34. competitive
35. hurriedly
36. loudly
37. demanding
38. aggressive

39. hostility
40. verbal
41. physical
42. blood pressure
43. cholesterol
44. source
45. cognitive
46. reactions
47. Type A
48. withdrawal
49. defense mechanisms
50. displacement
51. sublimation
52. projection
53. reaction formation
54. regression
55. rationalization
56. repression
57. denial
58. intellectualization

59. prevent	67. personal goals	75. intravenous
60. relax	68. strenuous	76. monogamous
61. progressive relaxation	69. immune deficiency	77. counseling
62. insomnia	70. lymphocytes	78. aerobic
63. migraine	71. B-cells	79. confront
64. herpes	72. sociocultural	
65. aerobic	73. bodily fluids	
66. support	74. sexual intercourse	

Sample Answers For Short Answer Questions

1. **List and explain the four major types of conflicts discussed in the text.**

   In approach-approach conflicts, the person must choose between two positive goals, such as two equally attractive job offers. In avoidance-avoidance conflicts, the individual must choose between two negative outcomes, such as an undesirable job and unemployment. Approach-avoidance conflicts cause stress because the same goal has both attractive and unattractive components. Finally, multiple approach-avoidance conflicts involve several alternatives, each of which contains both positive and negative components.

2. **Describe both effective and ineffective methods of coping with stress.**

   According to the text, effective methods of coping with stress involve removing the source of stress (example: quit a highly stressful job), cognitive coping (change the way you think about the stresses in your life) and managing your reactions to stress (learning to relax). Ineffective methods of coping with stress include withdrawal, aggression, and using defense mechanisms to help discharge tension. While these ineffective methods may provide some comfort in the short run, they can lead to further problems in the long run.

3. **Discuss the results of research on life events as a source of stress.**

   Life events create stress because they represent change and require adjustment and coping. Negative life events, such as the death of a family member or being the victim of an assault, lead to anxiety and depression for extended periods of time beyond the event. The daily hassles of life have also been studied, and have been found to be related to health and psychological well-being. Even positive life events can be stressful under some circumstances.

Multiple Choice Answers

1. The answer is *c*. According to the text, stress is "perhaps the key factor that must be understood if psychology is to improve our health and happiness."
2. The answer is *d*. Research has implicated stress in a wide variety of diseases and maladies in addition to those listed in the question.
3. The answer is *c*. While frustration refers to the inability to satisfy a motive, conflict refers to a situation in which motives cannot be satisfied because they interfere with one another.
4. The answer is *b*. Situations in which we are faced with having to choose between two or more negative outcomes are called avoidance-avoidance conflicts.
5. The answer is *a*. Approach-approach conflict refers to situations in which the individual must choose between two positive goals; in avoidance-avoidance conflict, the individual must choose between two negative outcomes.
6. The answer is *a*. According to the text, daily hassles may be both a cause and a result of stress.

7. The answer is *b*. According to Selye, the body's resources begin to be mobilized in the stage called the alarm reaction. During the second stage, called the resistance stage, the body's resources are fully mobilized. In the final stage, the exhaustion stage, the individual's resources have become exhausted; thus resistance to stress is lowered.

8. The answer is *b*. The resistance stage, the second in the GAS, fully mobilizes the body's resources but leaves it vulnerable to further stress.

9. The answer is *d*. Stressful events are less stressful both when they are predictable *and* when the individual can exert some control over the stress.

10. The answer is *c*. According to the text, prior exposure to stress may "innoculate" us to that specific stressor.

11. The answer is *d*. Although student participants felt sad and experienced a rise in blood pressure immediately after venting their feelings, the same students reported being ill less in the following six months. The research supports the value of "getting it off your chest."

12. The answer is *c*. The study by Pennebaker and Beall described in the text suggests that there are positive health benefits in sharing negative feelings with others.

13. The answer is *a*. While characteristics of the Type A personality include each of those listed in the question, research suggests that those who express their hostility with verbal or physical aggression are at risk for coronary heart disease.

14. The answer is *d*. One theory advanced to explain this suggests that Type A personalities react physiologically more to stress than do others.

15. The answer is *c*. Three effective methods for coping with stress are removing stress, cognitive coping, and managing stress reactions. When Bill resigned his position, he removed the source of stress.

16. The answer is *c*. The use of defense mechanisms is often an ineffective method for coping with stress.

17. The answer is *b*. According to the text, each of us uses defense mechanisms to some extent. The danger arises when we rely heavily on defense mechanism to cope with stress.

18. The answer is *d*. Cognitive coping, or changing how we think about stress, is considered to be an effective method for coping with stress.

19. The answer is *c*. Denial is commonly seen with individuals who have problems with health, drugs, and relationships.

20. The answer is *c*. Ken has successfully "explained" or justified to himself and others why he is relieved about Barbie. As the text suggests, the use of defense mechanisms, when used in moderation, can be relatively harmless. Problems begin when people rely too heavily on defense mechanisms.

21. The answer is *a*. Relaxation training has been found to be effective in helping to treat health problems from genital herpes to high blood pressure.

22. The answer is *d*. Progressive relaxation training teaches people to deeply relax their large body muscles.

23. The answer is *d*. As is true with changing unhealthy eating habits, many people know about the importance of regular exercise, but adhering to behavioral changes seems to be difficult.

24. The answer is *d*. While psychologists have had limited success thus far in helping people to change their high-risk behavior and in teaching skills to slow the progression of the disease, there is as yet no cure for AIDS.

Answers to True-False Questions

1. F	6. T
2. T	7. F
3. F	8. F
4. F	9. F
5. F	10. T

Chapter 13   Abnormal Behavior

Learning Objectives

1. Define abnormal behavior. (p. 386)

2. Describe the different ways abnormal behavior has been viewed throughout history, including supernatural theories, biological theories, and psychological theories. (p. 386)

3. Define insanity and describe its different legal meanings. (p. 389)

4. Distinguish among specific phobia, social phobia, and agoraphobia. (p. 391)

5. Distinguish between generalized anxiety disorder and panic anxiety disorder. (p. 392)

6. Discuss the causes and effects of post-traumatic stress disorder. (p. 392)

7. Distinguish between obsessions and compulsions. (p. 394)

8. Identify the following somatoform disorders: somatization disorders, conversion disorders, somatoform pain disorders. (p. 394)

9. Distinguish between depersonalization, dissociative amnesia, and dissociative fugue. (p. 395)

10. Define dissociative identity disorder and discuss the controversies surrounding its diagnosis. (p. 396)

11. Identify the characteristics of mood disorders including major depression and bipolar affective disorder. (p. 398)

12. Discuss the importance of cognitive factors in depression and describe bipolar affective disorder. (p. 399)

13. Identify the three types of problems that characterize schizophrenia. (p. 402)

14. Distinguish among the following types of schizophrenia: paranoid schizophrenia, disorganized schizophrenia, and catatonic schizophrenia. (p. 402)

15. Identify the characteristics of the personality disorders, including schizoid personality disorder and antisocial personality disorder. (p. 403)

16. (From the *Application of Psychology* section) Discuss the civil liberty and psychological implications of homelessness and physician-assisted suicide. (p. 407)

Chapter Overview

Abnormal behavior includes actions, thoughts, and feelings that are harmful to the person and/or to others. Historically, the causes of abnormal behavior have been explained by supernatural theories, biological theories, and psychological theories. Contemporary psychologists view abnormal behavior as a natural phenomenon with both biological and psychological causes. The term *insanity* is a legal term with several different meanings.

Anxiety disorders, characterized by excessive anxiety, include the following: 1) phobias, which are intense and unrealistic fears; 2) general anxiety disorders, which are characterized by free-floating anxiety; 3) panic anxiety disorders, which involve attacks of intense anxiety; 4) post-traumatic stress disorders, a reaction to the stress of war, assault, or other trauma; and 5) obsessive-compulsive disorders, characterized by persistent, anxiety-provoking thoughts and by urges to repeatedly engage in a behavior.

Somatoform disorders are conditions in which the individual experiences symptoms of health problems that are psychological rather than physical in origin. One type of somatoform disorder is referred to as somatization disorder. This disorder involves multiple minor symptoms of illness that indirectly create a high risk of medical complications. Another type of somatoform disorder is the conversion disorder. This involves serious specific somatic symptoms without any physical cause; somatoform pain disorders involve pain without any physical cause.

In the various types of dissociative disorders, there is a change in memory, perception, or identity. For example, dissociative amnesia and dissociative fugue are characterized by memory loss that has psychological rather than physical causes. Individuals experiencing depersonalization feel that they or their surroundings have become distorted or unreal. Individuals who exhibit dissociative identity disorder (multiple personality) appear to possess more than one personality in the same body. The recent increase in the diagnosis of dissociative identity disorder has stirred controversy.

Affective disorders are disturbances of mood. The individual experiencing major depression is deeply unhappy and lethargic. In the condition known as bipolar affective disorder, periods of mania alternate irregularly with periods of severe depression.

Schizophrenia involves three major areas of abnormality: delusions and hallucinations, disorganized thinking emotions and behavior, and reduced enjoyment and interests. The major types of schizophrenia include 1) paranoid schizophrenia, in which the individual holds false beliefs or delusions—usually of grandeur and persecution—that seriously distort reality; 2) disorganized schizophrenia, which is characterized by extreme withdrawal from normal human contact, fragmented delusions and hallucinations, and a shallow "silliness" of emotion; and 3) catatonic schizophrenia, which is marked by stupors during which the individual may remain in the same posture for long periods of time. Psychologists believe that schizophrenia may have biological causes such as deterioration of the cortex and abnormal prenatal development. Psychologists also view stress as a trigger for the disorder in those who are genetically predisposed to schizophrenia.

Personality disorders are thought to result from personalities that developed improperly during childhood rather than from breakdowns under stress. Schizoid personality disorders are characterized by a loss of interest in proper dress and social contact, a lack of emotion, and an inability to hold regular jobs. The antisocial personality frequently violates social rules and laws, is often violent, takes advantage of others, and feels little guilt about it.

Two important societal issues that have important implications for psychology are homelessness and physician-assisted suicide.

Key Terms Exercise

For each of the following exercises, match the key terms on the left with the correct definitions on the right. Page references to the text follow the terms so that you may refer to the text for any items you answer incorrectly or do not understand completely. You may check your responses immediately by referring to the answers that follow each exercise.

Anxiety Disorders

_____ 1. anxiety disorders (p. 391)
_____ 2. specific phobia (p. 391)
_____ 3. social phobia (p. 391)
_____ 4. agoraphobia (p. 391)
_____ 5. generalized anxiety disorder (p. 392)
_____ 6. panic anxiety disorder (p. 392)
_____ 7. obsessive-compulsive disorders (p. 394)

a. a phobic fear of leaving home or other familiar places
b. disorders involving anxiety-provoking thoughts and irresistible urges
c. an uneasy sense of general tension and apprehension that is almost always present
d. psychological disorders that involve excessive levels of nervousness, tension, worry, and anxiety
e. an intense, irrational fear of one relatively specific thing
f. an anxiety pattern in which long periods of calm are broken by an attack of anxiety
g. a phobic fear of social interactions

ANSWERS
1. d   5. c
2. e   6. f
3. g   7. b
4. a

Somatoform Disorders/Dissociative Disorders

_____ 1. somatoform disorders (p. 394)
_____ 2. somatization disorders (p. 394)
_____ 3. conversion disorders (p. 394)
_____ 4. somatoform pain disorders (p. 395)
_____ 5. dissociative disorders (p. 395)

a. intense and chronic symptoms of somatic illness that have no physical cause
b. disorders in which the individual experiences symptoms of physical health problems that have psychological causes
c. somatoform disorders characterized by serious somatic symptoms, such as blindness and deafness
d. somatoform disorders characterized by a specific and chronic pain
e. conditions involving sudden cognitive changes, such as changes in memory, perception, or identity

ANSWERS
1. b   4. d
2. a   5. e
3. c

_____ 1. mood disorders (p. 398)
_____ 2. major depression (p. 398)
_____ 3. bipolar affective disorder (p. 400)
_____ 4. schizophrenia (p. 402)
_____ 5. paranoid schizophrenia (p. 402)
_____ 6. disorganized schizophrenia (p. 403)
_____ 7. catatonic schizophrenia (p. 403)
_____ 8. personality disorders (p. 403)
_____ 9. schizoid personality disorder (p. 403)
_____ 10. antisocial personality disorder (p. 404)

a. a psychological disorder involving cognitive and emotional disturbance and reduced interests

b. an affective disorder characterized by episodes of deep unhappiness, loss of interest in life, and other symptoms

c. psychological disorders involving depression and/or abnormal elation

d. a condition characterized by periods of mania alternating with periods of severe depression

e. a type of schizophrenia characterized by shallow "silliness," extreme social withdrawal, fragmented delusions and hallucinations

f. a type of schizophrenia in which the individual spends long periods of time in an inactive, statue-like state

g. a type of schizophrenia characterized by false beliefs or delusions that seriously distort reality

h. a personality disorder characterized by smooth social skills and a lack of guilt about violating social rules and laws

i. psychological disorders believed to result from personalities that develop improperly in childhood

j. a personality disorder characterized by blunted emotions, little interest in social relationships, and social withdrawal

ANSWERS

1. c.   6. e
2. b   7 f
3. d   8. i.
4. a   9. j
5. g   10. h

Review At A Glance
(Answers to this section may be found on page 225)

Abnormal Behavior

Actions, thoughts, and feelings that are harmful to the person or to others are called ___(1)___ behaviors. Approximately ___(2)___ percent of the people in the United States are considered seriously abnormal. This definition is ___(3)___ because 1) it is difficult to decide whether an individual's problems are ___(4)___ enough to be harmful, and 2) it is difficult to define what is ___(5)___.

The oldest writings about behavior indicate that abnormal behavior was believed to be caused by ___(6)___ _____. In medieval Europe, abnormal behavior was treated by ___(7)___. Hippocrates believed that abnormal behavior resulted from an imbalance of the body's ___(8)___. Although inaccurate, Hippocrates' theory influenced other scientists to search for ___(9)___ causes of abnormal behavior.

In the 1800s, Krafft-Ebing's discovery of the relationship between paresis and syphilis contributed to the formation of the medical specialty of ___(10)___. Krafft-Ebing's discovery led to expectations that other forms of abnormal behavior also had ___(11)___ causes.

Pythagoras, an ancient Greek, believed that abnormal behavior was caused by ___(12)___ factors. Although others throughout history have also advocated psychological factors, this approach did not become widely accepted until

(13)____ theory was published. The contemporary view is that both ___(14)___ and ___(15)___ factors are involved in many psychological disorders.

The term ___(16)___ is a legal term. The term *insane* has three different legal meanings: 1) as a ___(17)___ defense in some states, not guilty by reason of insanity; 2) in hearings regarding ___(18)___ to stand trial; and 3) in hearings to determine involuntary ___(19)___ to mental institutions.

Anxiety Disorders

Ten to fifteen million Americans experience the disruptive levels of anxiety called ___(20)___ _____. An anxiety disorder characterized by intense, irrational fear is called a ___(21)___. The least disruptive phobias are called ___(22)___ phobias. A phobic fear of social interactions is called a ___(23)___ phobia. The most damaging of all the phobias involves a phobic fear of leaving familiar places; this is termed ___(24)___.

While phobias are linked to specific situations, free-floating anxiety is experienced by individuals with ___(25)___ anxiety disorder. People who experience this anxiety feel uncomfortable because of its almost ___(26)___ presence.

An anxiety in which periods of calm are broken by an anxiety attack is called ___(27)___ _____ disorder. Many individuals experience an occasional ___(28)___ attack. While uncomfortable, they should not be a serious concern unless they are ___(29)___ or severe.

Reactions that many soldiers experience to the stress of combat are called ___(30)___ (PTSD). For women, the leading causes of PTSD are physical ___(31)___, rape and sexual molestation, and witnessing ___(32)___. The percent of victims who develop PTSD depends in part on the type of ___(33)___. About ___(34)___ of those who experience the sudden loss of a loved one develop PTSD, whereas 75 percent of women who are ___(35)___ victims experience PTSD. Researchers found more mental health problems among rape victims than among victims of ___(36)___ assault and other crimes.

Obsessive-compulsive disorders are two separate problems that often occur together. Anxiety-provoking thoughts that will not go away are called ___(37)___, while irresistible urges to engage in irrational behaviors are termed___(38)___.

Disorders in which the individual experiences the symptoms of physical health problems that have psychological causes are called ___(39)___ disorders. Intensely and chronically uncomfortable conditions that involve many symptoms of bodily illness are called ___(40)___ disorders. Dramatic somatoform disorders which involve serious symptoms, such as functional blindness and paralysis are___(41)___ disorders. Some individuals with conversion disorders are not upset by their condition; this characteristic is known as ___(42)___ _____. Conversion disorders usually begin during periods of acute stress and generally provide some kind of ___(43)___ to the individual. Somatoform pain disorders are characterized by pain that has no ___(44)___ cause.

Dissociative Disorders

Conditions in which there are sudden cognitive changes, such as changes in memory or perception, are called ___(45)___ disorders. A type of dissociative disorder in which the individual feels that his or her body has become distorted or unreal, or that the surroundings have become unreal, is called ___(46)___. Experiences of depersonalization are common in ___(47)___ adults. A dissociative disorder in which there is a memory loss that is psychologically caused is called ___(48)___. A state of amnesia that is so complete the individual cannot remember his or her previous life is a ___(49)___. The fugue episode may also involve a period of "wandering." Individuals who shift abruptly from one "personality" to another are exhibiting dissociative ___(50)___ disorder (formerly called multiple personality). Some psychologists believe dissociative identity disorder is the result of childhood ___(51)___; other psychologists believe it is the result of social learning. According to the social learning theorists, the multiple personalities are taught to suggestible patients by their ___(52)___.

Mood Disorders

The two primary types of mood disorders are ___(53)___ and ___(54)___. Extreme unhappiness and loss of interest in life are symptoms of ___(55)___. In most cases, the individual experiences symptoms for a period of time and returns to normal; major depression is an ___(56)___ disorder. This disorder affects about 10 million Americans. Most cases of depression are mild; severe cases may require ___(57)___.

Aaron Beck and others emphasize the importance of ___(58)___ in emotional problems. According to Beck, ___(59)___ views of oneself are a critical component of depression. Beliefs that trouble many depressed people are ___(60)___ demands. Research by Lewinsohn has found that, under some circumstances, people who are depressed engage in ___(61)___ cognitive distortions than those who are not depressed.

Individuals who have periods of mania that alternate irregularly with periods of severe depression are experiencing ___(62)___ disorder. The portion of this experience characterized by euphoria and unrealistic optimism is called ___(63)___.

Schizophrenia

Schizophrenia involves the following three characteristics: 1) delusions and ___(64)___, 2) ___(65)___ thinking, emotions and behavior, and 3) reduced enjoyment and ___(66)___. According to the DSM-IV, there are three subtypes of schizophrenia: 1) ___(67)___ schizophrenia, characterized by false beliefs, delusions of grandeur, delusions of persecution, and hallucinations; 2) ___(68)___ schizophrenia, characterized by extreme withdrawal from normal human contact and a shallow "silliness" of emotion; and 3) ___(69)___ schizophrenia, an inactive, statue-like state, frequently broken by periods of agitation. A fourth category called ___(70)___ schizophrenia classifies those who don't fit the other categories.

Personality Disorders

Although schizophrenia and other disorders are breakdowns in relatively normal personalities, the results of improperly developed personalities are called ___(71)___. All personality disorders share these characteristics: 1) they begin ___(72)___ in life; 2) they are ___(73)___ to the person or to others; and 3) they are very ___(74)___ to treat. One example, ___(75)___ personality disorder, is characterized by extreme social withdrawal and a loss of interest in social conventions. Another personality disorder, in which the individual has smooth social skills but violates social rules and takes advantage of others without feeling guilty, is called ___(76)___ personality disorder. The primary harmfulness of this disorder is in the damage done to ___(77)___.

Other personality disorders, as listed in the DSM-IV, are 1) characterized by few friendships and strange ideas, called the ___(78)___ personality disorder; 2) suspiciousness, irritability, and coldness, called ___(79)___ personality disorder; 3) self-centered and manipulating by exaggerating feelings, called the ___(80)___ personality disorder; 4) unrealistic sense of self-importance, requiring constant attention and praise, called the ___(81)___ personality disorder; 5) impulsive and unpredictable with unstable relationships, called the ___(82)___ personality disorder; 6) extremely shy and withdrawn and low self-esteem, called the ___(83)___ personality disorder; 7) passive dependence on others for support and low self-esteem, called the ___(84)___ personality disorder; and 8) perfectionistic, dominating, and excessively devoted to work, called the ___(85)___-___ personality disorder.

Application of Psychology: Abnormal Psychology and Civil Liberties

Research has found a high rate of serious psychological disorders among ___(86)___ people. Psychologists are divided on the issue of whether psychological treatment for homeless people with psychological disorders should be ___(87)___ or ___(88)___. Another issue with strong implications for civil liberties is ___(89)___-___ suicide.

Concept Check

Fill in the missing components of the following concept box. The correct answers are located in the "Answers" section at the end of the chapter.

Major Disorders

Category	Description	Examples
anxiety disorders		
somatoform disorders		somatization, conversion disorder, and pain disorder
dissociative disorders		
	individual has disturbances of positive or negative moods	
schizophrenia		
	beginning early in life, these individuals are disturbing to themselves or others and are difficult to treat	

Extending the Chapter: Psychology, Societal Issues, and Human Diversity

These questions may be assigned to you. Whether or not they are assigned, they are designed to be challenging questions to encourage you to think independently about the material in the chapter. Many of the questions have no right or wrong answers.

I.   From the *Applications of Psychology* section

1.   What civil liberty questions are raised by homelessness and physician-assisted suicide?

2.   What is your opinion of the right of individuals to be homeless and to refuse psychological treatment? Explain your answer.

3.   What role should psychology play in physician-assisted suicide?

II. Psychology, Societal Issues, and Human Diversity

1. A friend who knows you're taking a psychology class says to you, "I think Jason is schizophrenic or something. Sometimes when I see him he's friendly and warm, but other times he's mean and nasty." How would you respond to your friend?

2. In some cultures, a person who is able to communicate with a deceased ancestor is considered to have good fortune. Compare this to definitions of hallucinations and delusions in the text, and discuss the implications for diagnosis and treatment.

3. To what extent does our society view individuals as being responsible for their mental states? Provide evidence for your answer.

4. (From the *Human Diversity* section of the text) Discuss the roles played by ethnicity, race, age, and gender in psychological diagnoses.

Practice Quiz

The practice quiz consists of three sections: 1) Short answer questions, 2) Multiple choice questions, and 3) True-False questions. At the end of the chapter you will find suggested answers to the short answer questions, answers and explanation for the multiple choice questions, and answers to the true-false questions.

Short Answer Questions

1. List and describe the historical views of abnormal behavior.

_____

_____

2. Describe the different legal meanings of the term "insanity."

_____

_____

3. List and describe the various types of anxiety disorders.

_____

_____

Multiple Choice Questions

1. In what ways are subjective judgments used to define abnormal behavior?
   a. deciding whether problems are severe enough to be harmful
   b. deciding what is harmful
   c. deciding if a pattern is unusual
   d. *a* and *b* above
   LO 1

2. Throughout history the prevailing view of the cause of abnormal behavior was
   a. evil spirits.
   b. biological theories.
   c. psychological theories.
   d. sociocultural theories.
   LO 2

3. Treatment for the disorder known as paresis was important in advancing the _____ theory of abnormal behavior.
   a. supernatural
   b biological
   c. psychological
   d. interpersonal
   LO 2

4. Each of the following is an application of the term insanity *except*
   a. not guilty by reason of insanity.
   b. insanity due to genetic inheritance.
   c. incompetent to stand trial.
   d. involuntary commitment.
   LO 3

5. Maria feels extremely uncomfortable walking outside her home, even to check the mail or to pick up the morning newspaper. A psychologist might suggest she is experiencing
   a. agoraphobia.
   b. social phobia.
   c. obsessive-compulsive disorder.
   d. simple phobia.
   LO 4

6. Anxieties that occur due to irrational fears, usually of a specific event or object, are called
   a. compulsions.
   b. obsessions.
   c. conversions.
   d. phobias.
   LO 4

7. A usually mild, but relentless type of free-floating anxiety is experienced by those with
   a. panic anxiety disorder.
   b. phobic disorder.
   c. generalized anxiety disorder.
   d. agoraphobia.
   LO 5

8. A disorder in which long periods of calm are broken by sharp, intense periods of anxiety is called
   a. phobic disorder.
   b. simple anxiety.
   c. panic anxiety disorder.
   d. generalized anxiety disorder.
   LO 5

9. Post-traumatic stress disorder has been linked to
   a. war veterans.
   b. rape victims.
   c. concentration camp survivors.
   d. all of the above.
   LO 6

10. Post-traumatic stress disorder falls under the classification of _____ disorders.
    a. somatoform
    b. dissociative
    c. anxiety
    d. mood
    LO 6

11. Obsessions refer to
    a. thoughts.
    b. behaviors.
    c. psychotic behavior.
    d. insane behavior.
    LO 7

12. Each of the following is a compulsion *except*
    a. repeatedly washing one's hands.
    b. checking and rechecking the locks on doors.
    c. touching a spot on one's shoulder over and over.
    d. uncontrollable thoughts about somebody.
    LO 7

13. Individuals whose symptoms include chronic aches and pains without physical cause are experiencing
    a. dissociative disorder.
    b. somatization disorder.
    c. conversion disorder.
    d. fugue disorder.
    LO 8

14. Each of the following is a type of somatoform disorder *except*
    a. somatization disorder.
    b. somatoform pain disorder.
    c. conversion disorder.
    d. obsessive-compulsive disorder.
    LO 8

15. "La belle indifference" is experienced by those experiencing
    a. depersonalization.
    b. somatization disorder.
    c. conversion disorder.
    d. somatoform pain disorder.
    LO 8

16. Individuals who suffer pain that has no physical cause are experiencing
    a. conversion disorder.
    b. somatoform pain disorder.
    c. obsessive pain disorder.
    d. agoraphobia.
    LO 8

17. Which of the following dissociative disorders involves an inability to remember one's previous life and involves "wandering"?
    a. dissociative amnesia
    b. dissociative fugue
    c. depersonalization
    d. dissociative identity disorder
    LO 9

18. The sensation of leaving one's body may occur to the individual who is experiencing
    a. depersonalization.
    b. psychogenic amnesia.
    c. psychogenic fugue.
    d. conversion disorder.
    LO 9

19. The movie *The Three Faces of Eve* focused on a type of disorder categorized as
    a. depersonalization.
    b. neurotic disorder.
    c. somatization disorder.
    d. dissociative identity disorder.
    LO 10

20. According to the social learning view of dissociative identity disorders, multiple personalities are commonly taught to patients by
    a. parents and relatives.
    b. movies and video games.
    c. psychotherapists.
    d. the media.
    LO 10

21. Cindy, age 47, has begun experiencing deep unhappiness, frequent lethargy, and sleep problems. A psychologist might consider that she is experiencing
    a. bipolar affective disorder.
    b. dissociative amnesia.
    c. major depression.
    d. schizophrenia.
    LO 11

22. Which affective disorder involves periods of mania that alternate with periods of depression?
    a. bipolar affective disorder
    b. major depression
    c. schizophrenia
    d. somatization disorder
    LO 11

23. Which of the following has been identified as a cognitive factor in depression?
    a. perfectionistic beliefs
    b. repressive coping
    c. obsessive behavior
    d. a and b above
    LO 12

24. All of the following are characteristics of schizophrenia *except*
    a. delusions.
    b. blunted affect.
    c. disorganized thinking.
    d. alternating between two or more personalities.
    LO 13

25. Delusions of grandeur, delusions of persecution, and hallucinations characterize
    a. paranoid schizophrenia.
    b. disorganized schizophrenia.
    c. catatonic schizophrenia.
    d. undifferentiated schizophrenia.
       LO 14

26. A type of schizophrenia characterized by long periods in an inactive, statue-like state is called
    a. paranoid schizophrenia.
    b. disorganized schizophrenia.
    c. catatonic schizophrenia.
    d. undifferentiated schizophrenia.
       LO 14

27. Which personality disorder is characterized by an unrealistic sense of self-importance and preoccupation with fantasies about future success?
    a. schizotypal
    b. histrionic
    c. narcissistic
    d. borderline
       LO 15

28. Which of the following characterizes the antisocial personality disorder?
    a. smooth social skills
    b. little interest in social contact
    c. lack of guilt about violating social customs
    d. *a* and *c* above
       LO 15

29. Studies of homeless people in large cities support the idea that the homeless
    a. for the most part are just individuals who are down on their luck.
    b. have high rates of chronic mental disorders.
    c. have high rates of substance abuse disorders.
    d. b and c above.
       LO 16

30. High rates of which of the following disorders have been reported among homeless adolescents?
    a. social phobia
    b. schizophrenia
    c. PTSD
    d. dissociative fugue
       LO 16

True-False Questions

_____1. Advocates of the continuity hypothesis favor the use of terms like insanity and mental illness.

_____2. The term insanity is a legal term.

_____3. Specific phobias are the most disruptive of the phobias.

_____4. In obsessive-compulsive disorder, the *obsessions* refer to anxiety-provoking thoughts.

_____5. La belle indifference is a characteristic of major depression.

_____6. Depersonalization is an extremely rare experience.

_____7. According to Beck, perfectionistic beliefs are an important factor in depression.

_____8. In bipolar affective disorder, periods of mania alternate with periods of depression.

_____9. Schizophrenia involves hallucinations, but rarely involves delusions.

_____10. Personality disorders usually begin in early adulthood.

ANSWER SECTION

Concept Check

Major Disorders

Category	Description	Examples
anxiety disorders	the person suffering from anxiety is nervous, tense, and worried	phobias, generalized and panic anxiety disorders, PTSD, and obsessive-compulsive
somatoform disorders	the individual experiences physical health problems that have psychological rather than physical causes.	somatization, conversion disorder, and pain disorder
dissociative disorders	those suffering from a dissociative disorder may have sudden alterations in cognition, characterized by a change in memory, perception, or identity.	dissociative amnesia and fugue, depersonalization, and dissociative identity disorder
mood disorders	individual has disturbances of positive or negative moods	major depression, bipolar disorder
schizophrenia	persons with schizophrenia experience delusions and hallucinations, disorganized thoughts, emotions and behavior, and reduced enjoyment and interests	paranoid, disorganized, and catatonic
personality disorders	beginning early in life, these individuals are disturbing to themselves or others and are difficult to treat	schizoid, antisocial, schizotypal, paranoid, histrionic, narcissistic

Answers to Review At A Glance

1. abnormal
2. 15
3. subjective
4. severe
5. harmful
6. evil spirits
7. exorcism
8. humors
9. natural
10. psychiatry
11. biological
12. psychological
13. Freud's
14. biological
15. psychological
16. insanity
17. legal
18. competence
19. commitment
20. anxiety disorders
21. phobia
22. specific
23. social
24. agoraphobia
25. generalized
26. continual
27. panic anxiety
28. anxiety
29. frequent
30. post-traumatic stress

disorder
31. assault
32. violence
33. stress
34. 15
35. rape
36. aggravated
37. obsessions
38. compulsions
39. somatoform
40. somatization
41. conversion
42. la belle indifference
43. benefit
44. physical

45. dissociative	60. perfectionistic	75. schizoid
46. depersonalization	61. fewer	76. antisocial
47. young	62. bipolar affective	77. others
48. dissociative amnesia	63. mania	78. schizotypal
49. dissociative fugue	64. hallucinations	79. paranoid
50. identity	65. disorganized	80. histrionic
51. abuse	66. interests	81. narcissistic
52. psychotherapists	67. paranoid	82. borderline
53. depression	68. disorganized	83. avoidant
54. mania	69. catatonic	84. dependent
55. major depression	70. undifferentiated	85. obsessive-compulsive
56. episodic	71. personality disorders	86. homeless
57. hospitalization	72. early	87. mandatory
58. cognition	73. disturbing	88. voluntary
59. negative	74. difficult	89. physician-assisted

Sample Answers for Short Answer Questions

1. **List and describe the historical views of abnormal behavior.**

   Ancient writings indicate that the earliest beliefs of abnormal behavior considered them to be caused by various evil spirits. Treatment generally involved prayer, although, at various times, it also included exorcism and the murder of those thought to be "witches." This belief persisted until shortly before the American Revolution. A second approach, proposed by Hippocrates, was that biological disorders caused abnormal behavior. The work of Krafft-Ebing on paresis confirmed the influence of biological factors on mental disorders. The ancient Greek Pythagoras held that psychological factors, including stress, were involved in abnormal behavior. Today, it is widely accepted that both biological and psychological factors are involved in psychological disorders.

2. **Describe the different legal meanings of the term "insanity."**

   The term "insanity" is actually a legal term. Its definition depends upon the context in which it is used. One application is "not guilty by reason of insanity," which means an individual is not legally responsible for a crime if found insane. A second application involves whether a person is competent to stand trial, that is, whether an individual can aid in his own defense. A third application pertains to involuntary commitment to a mental institution.

3. **List and describe the various types of anxiety disorders.**

   One type of anxiety disorder is the category of phobias. These are intense and irrational fears. Three types of phobias are specific phobias, social phobias and agoraphobia. Another type of anxiety disorder is generalized anxiety disorder, characterized by free-floating anxiety. Panic anxiety disorder involves sharp and intense anxiety attacks. Post-traumatic stress disorder involves anxiety and irritability, upsetting memories, dreams, and flashbacks in response to extremely stressful experiences. Obsessive-compulsive disorders involve anxiety-provoking thoughts called obsessions, and irresistible urges to engage in certain behaviors, referred to as compulsions.

Multiple Choice Answers

1. The answer is *d*. The inherent subjectivity of judgments is a continual problem for psychologists who study abnormal behavior.
2. The answer is *a*. Consider an important implication of this question—the treatment and "cures" for those exhibiting abnormal behavior has been strongly influenced by the perceived causes of the abnormal behavior.
3. The answer is *b*. This now rare psychological disturbance was found to be an advanced stage of syphilis.
4. The answer is *b*. Remember that the term insanity is a legal rather than a psychological term.
5. The answer is *a*. Agoraphobia is an intense fear of leaving one's home or other familiar places.
6. The answer is *d*. Specific phobias, social phobias and agoraphobia are all examples of phobias.
7. The answer is *c*. While a person experiencing generalized anxiety disorder has a continual, gnawing sense of uneasiness, the person with panic anxiety disorder usually has periods of calm that are broken by an explosive attack of anxiety.
8. The answer is *c*. While generalized anxiety disorder is characterized by free-floating anxiety that almost always seems to be present, panic anxiety disorder is characterized by a sharp and intense anxiety, although it is not continually present.
9. The answer is *d*. The upsetting recollections, combined with feelings of guilt, disgust, and terrible dreams are all, unfortunately, components of PTSD.
10. The answer is *c*. PTSD is caused by extremely stressful experiences in which the person later experiences anxiety and irritability.
11. The answer is *a*. Whereas obsessions refer to thoughts, compulsions refer to behaviors.
12. The answer is *d*. Compulsions are irresistible urges to engage in behaviors, while obsessions refer to seemingly unstoppable thoughts. They usually go together to form obsessive-compulsive behavior.
13. The answer is *b*. The category of somatoform disorders contains somatization disorder, conversion disorder, and somatoform pain disorder.
14. The answer is *d*. Obsessive-compulsive disorder is an anxiety disorder.
15. The answer is *c*. "The beautiful indifference" refers to the fact that, although individuals with conversion disorder appear to be suffering serious symptoms, such as paralysis or blindness, they often are not upset with their condition.
16. The answer is *b*. Somatoform pain often occurs to the person who is experiencing high levels of stress, and the condition may be beneficial to the individual in some way.
17. The answer is *b*. While dissociative amnesia involves a loss of memory, a dissociative fugue involves such a complete loss of memory that the individual cannot remember his or her identity or previous life. Often, during the fugue episode, the individual will take on a new personality.
18. The answer is *a*. During a depersonalization episode, the individual feels that he or she has become distorted or unreal in some way. The experience of leaving one's body is also a common experience in depersonalization.
19. The answer is *d*. *The Three Faces of Eve* was about dissociative identity disorder. Recall that the category of dissociative disorders consists of amnesia, fugue, depersonalization, and dissociative identity disorder. The common feature is that all involve a change in memory, perception, or identity.
20. The answer is *c*. According to this view, highly suggestible patients are influenced by their psychotherapist's subtle and not-so-subtle interpretations.
21. The answer is *d*. To answer this question correctly, you need to know that major depression is a type of mood disorder.
22. The answer is *a*. Bipolar affective disorder, formerly known as manic-depressive behavior, is a type of mood disorder. Although the manic period can be enjoyable to the person in the short run, it can have disastrous consequences. When mania is recurrent, it alternates with severe depression.
23. The answer is *d*. In addition to the cognitive factors described in the question, research suggests that having a positive opinion of oneself makes depression less likely following stressful life events.
24. The answer is *d*. One of the biggest misconceptions in the field of abnormal psychology continues to be the notion that schizophrenics have a "split" personality.

25. The answer is *a*. Disorganized schizophrenia is also marked by hallucinations and delusions, but the cognitive processes of the individual are extremely disorganized. Disorganized schizophrenia is also characterized by a shallow, silly affect. The catatonic schizophrenic spends long periods of time in a statue-like state often described as "waxy flexibility."

26. The answer is *c*. Catatonic schizophrenics exhibit a "waxy flexibility" while in this stuporous condition..

27. The answer is *c*. The schizotypal is characterized by few friendships and strange ideas; the histrionic is self-centered and uses exaggerated expression of emotions; the borderline is impulsive, unpredictable and has an almost constant need to be with others.

28. The answer is *d*. In fact, many individuals with antisocial personality disorder have disarmingly well-developed social skills.

29. The answer is *d*. Research conducted on the homeless living in New York and in Los Angeles has revealed that a majority of these people have mental and/or substance abuse disorders.

30. The answer is *b*. High rates of alcohol and/or drug dependence are also reported among homeless people.

Answers to True-False Questions

1. F	6. F
2. T	7. T
3. F	8. T
4. T	9. F
5. F	10. F

Chapter 14 Therapies

Learning Objectives

1. Define psychotherapy and describe the ways it is used to help people. (p. 414)

2. Identify the ethical standards for psychotherapy. (p. 414)

3. Discuss the characteristics of psychoanalysis and identify the techniques of psychoanalytic psychotherapy. (p. 415)

4. Identify interpersonal psychotherapy and describe its applications. (p. 418)

5. Describe the goals of client-centered psychotherapy. (p. 420)

6. Describe the use of systematic desensitization in reducing fears and describe social skills training. (p. 423)

7. Describe the goals of cognitive therapy and identify the maladaptive cognitions that, according to Beck, contribute to depression. (p. 427)

8. Discuss the use of medical therapies and distinguish among drug therapy, electroconvulsive therapy, and psychosurgery. (p. 431)

9. (From the *Application of Psychology* section) Identify the guidelines for selecting a psychotherapist. (p. 435)

10. (From the *Application of Psychology* section) Identify ethnic and gender issues in seeking psychotherapy. (p. 435)

Chapter Overview

Psychotherapy is form of therapy in which a trained professional uses methods based on psychological theories to help a person with psychological problems. One form of psychotherapy, founded by Sigmund Freud, is called psychoanalysis. Psychoanalysis tries to help the patient bring unconscious conflict into consciousness. The following techniques are used in psychoanalysis: 1) free association, which is used to relax the censorship of the ego; 2) dream interpretation, in which the symbols of the manifest content of dreams are interpreted to reveal their latent content; 3) resistance, which refers to any form of patient opposition to psychoanalysis; 4) transference, which refers to the development of a relatively intense relationship between patient and therapist during therapy; and 5) catharsis, the release of emotional energy related to unconscious conflicts. A new form of psychotherapy derived from the psychoanalytic tradition is called interpersonal therapy. This type of therapy is used to treat depression by emphasizing the accurate identification of feelings, constructive communication, and improving social relationships.

Humanistic psychotherapists attempt to help the client seek more complete self-awareness to allow the client's inner-directed potential for growth to be realized. One type of humanistic psychotherapy is client-centered therapy. The goal of the client-centered therapist is to create an atmosphere that encourages clients to explore their unsymbolized feelings.

Another approach to psychotherapy is called behavior therapy. Behavior therapists help their clients to unlearn abnormal behavior and learn adaptive ways of thinking, feeling, and acting. A technique used by behavior therapists to reduce fears is called systematic desensitization.

Cognitive therapy assumes that faulty cognitions are the cause of abnormal behavior.

Medical therapies are designed to correct a physical condition that is believed to be the cause of a psychological disorder. Medical therapies include drug therapy, electroconvulsive therapy, and psychosurgery.

Professional mental health services are widely available. Many colleges and universities have student counseling or mental health centers. Referrals and board certification are guides in helping to select a professional. Important ethnic and gender inequalities exist in receiving psychological services in the United States.

Key Terms Exercise

For each of the following exercises, match the key terms on the left with the correct definitions on the right. Page references to the text follow the terms so that you may refer to the text for any items you answer incorrectly or do not understand completely. You may check your responses immediately by referring to the answers that follow each exercise.

Psychoanalysis

_____ 1. psychotherapy (p. 414)
_____ 2. psychoanalysis (p. 415)
_____ 3. free association (p. 416)
_____ 4. dream interpretation (p. 416)
_____ 5. resistance (p. 416)
_____ 6. transference (p. 417)
_____ 7. catharsis (p. 417)
_____ 8. interpersonal psychotherapy (p. 418)

a.   occurs when a patient in psychoanalysis reacts to a therapist in ways that resemble the patient's reaction to other significant adults

b.   the method of psychotherapy developed by Sigmund Freud

c.   the use of a variety of psychological methods to help a patient with psychological problems

d.   the release of emotional energy related to unconscious conflicts

e.   focuses on the accurate identification and communication of feelings and the improvement of current social relationships

f.   a Freudian method that attempts to reveal the latent content of dreams

g.   a Freudian method that encourages the patient to talk about whatever comes to mind

h.   patient opposition to psychoanalysis

ANSWERS

1. c	5. h
2. b	6. a
3. g	7. d
4. f	8. e

Humanistic Psychotherapy/ Behavior Therapy/ Medical Therapies

_____ 1. client-centered psychotherapy (p. 421)
_____ 2. reflection (p. 421)
_____ 3. behavior therapy (p. 423)
_____ 4. systematic desensitization (p. 423)
_____ 5. social skills training (p. 424)
_____ 6. cognitive therapy (p. 427)
_____ 7. drug therapy (p. 431)
_____ 8. electroconvulsive therapy (p. 432)
_____ 9. psychosurgery (p. 433)

a. psychotherapy based on social learning theory
b. a humanistic therapy that tries to create a safe environment for clients so they can discover feelings of which they are unaware
c. a technique in which the therapist reflects clients' emotions in order to help clients clarify their feelings
d. a behavior therapy method that teaches the client to overcome phobias by relaxing in response to increasingly threatening stimuli
e. a medical therapy that involves operating on the brain to alleviate some mental disorders
f. an approach that teaches individuals new cognitions to eliminate abnormal behavior
g. a medical therapy that induces controlled convulsive seizures to alleviate some mental disorders
h. a medical therapy that uses drugs to treat abnormal behavior
i. the use of behavioral techniques to improve social skills

ANSWERS
1. b   6. f
2. c   7. h
3. a   8. g
4. d   9. e
5. i

Review At A Glance
(Answers to this section may be found on page 240)

Psychoanalysis

A trained professional uses psychological methods to help a person with psychological problems in the process called ___(1)___. The following ethical guidelines must be followed by psychotherapists: 1) the goals of treatment must be considered with the ___(2)___; 2) the choices for alternative treatments should be carefully considered; 3) the therapist must treat only the problems that he or she is ___(3)___ to treat; 4) the ___(4)___ of the treatment must be evaluated in some way; 5) the rules and laws regarding ___(5)___ must be fully explained to the client; 6) the therapist must not ___(6)___ the client in sexual or other ways; 7) the therapist must treat clients with dignity and respect differences among people.

Psychoanalysts feel that abnormal behavior is the result of ___(7)___ conflicts among the id, ego, and superego. According to Freud, problems can be solved only when unconscious conflicts are brought into ___(8)___. This can occur only when the ego's guard is temporarily ___(9)___. The job of the psychoanalyst is to 1) relax the censorship of the ___(10)___ and 2) ___(11)___ the revelations of the unconscious mind.

Freud's primary tool of therapy was to encourage the individual to talk about whatever comes to mind, a technique called ___(12)_____. The "glimpse of the unconscious" revealed during free association must be ___(13)___ to the patient by the psychoanalyst. Freud believed that another "window" to the unconscious was provided by ___(14)___ _____. Psychoanalysts believe that the manifest content of dreams symbolically masks the true or ___(15)___ of dreams.

Freud also placed significance on any patient opposition to psychoanalysis, a process he called ___(16)___. Intense relationships often develop between therapist and patient. The patient often reacts to the therapist in ways that resemble how he or she would react to other authority figures. Freud called this process ___(17)___. Releasing emotional energy related to unconscious conflicts is called ___(18)___.

A new form psychotherapy, derived from the psychoanalytic tradition, is called ___(19)___ psychotherapy. Interpersonal psychotherapy emphasizes the accurate identification of ___(20)___, constructive ___(21)___, and improving social ___(22)___. Studies have found interpersonal therapy to be effective in treating ___(23)___.

Humanistic Psychotherapy
Humanists view full self-awareness as necessary for the complete realization of our inner-directed potential; according to humanists, therapy is "growth in ___(24)___." The therapy approach associated with Carl Rogers is called ___(25)___-_____ psychotherapy. According to Rogers, growth in awareness comes when the client feels safe enough to explore ___(26)___ _____. Rogers believes that the therapist must be ___(27)___, able to accept their clients ___(28)___, and able to share their client's emotions, a process called ___(29)___. The closest thing to a technique in client-centered therapy is the process of ___(30)___. Client-centered therapists strictly avoid giving ___(31)___ to clients.

Behavior Therapy
The approach to psychotherapy based on social learning theory is called ___(32)___ therapy. This approach views abnormal behavior as ___(33)___ behavior. The therapist, who plays the role of a teacher, helps the client to unlearn abnormal behavior and to learn more ___(34)___ ways to behave.
Several behavior therapy methods are used to treat phobias. One technique, developed by Joseph Wolpe, is called ___(35)___ _____. In this technique, the client is taught to relax using ___(36)___ _____ _____. During the next part of the procedure, called ___(37)___ _____, the therapist and client rank all aspects of the phobic stimulus, from least feared to most feared. The client is directed to ___(38)___ the weakest phobic stimulus, until it no longer causes fear. Then the client progresses to the next stimulus, and so on. When the graded exposure is conducted in real-life settings, it is called ___(39)___ graded exposure. This procedure can also be accomplished using computer-generated ___(40)___ _____ techniques.

A major emphasis of behavior therapy is on the teaching of new skills using methods derived from ___(41)___ _____. For example, people who have difficulties interacting with other people might benefit from ___(42)___

_____ training. One technique, in which the therapist and client act as if they are people in problematic situations, is called ___(43)_____. Using this technique, the therapist might take the role of the client and ___(44)___ appropriate behavior. The therapist also provides ___(45)_____ for the client by praising the adaptive aspects of the client's behavior.

Cognitive Therapy

A new approach to therapy teaches individuals new cognition—beliefs, expectations, and ways of thinking—to eliminate abnormal behavior. This approach is called ___(46)___ therapy. Cognitive therapists believe that behavior therapists can be more effective if they teach both more adaptive ___(47)___ and ___(48)___.

According to the cognitive therapy program developed by Aaron Beck, depression is caused by the following erroneous patterns of thinking: 1) basing one's thoughts on a detail taken out of context, called ___(49)_____; 2) reaching a general conclusion based on a few bits of evidence, called ___(50)___; 3) reaching a conclusion based on little or no logical evidence, called ___(51)_____; 4) blowing statements out of proportion or minimizing their importance, called ___(52)___/_____; 5) reasoning that external events are directly related to one's behavior, called ___(53)___; and 6) thinking in all-or-nothing terms, called ___(54)___ thinking. Cognitive therapy has been shown to be effective in treating a variety of ___(55)___ disorders, as well as the eating disorder called ___(56)___, and major ___(57)___.

Other Approaches and Models of Therapy

When a physical condition is believed to cause a psychological disorder, ___(58)_____ are used. The most widely used medical therapy is ___(59)___ therapy, which uses chemicals to treat abnormal behavior. A drug that has been successfully used in the treatment of schizophrenia is ___(60)___. Psychiatric medications influence ___(61)___ in the brain. Psychiatric medications often have ___(62)_____.

The use of electrical current to induce controlled convulsive seizures that help alleviate some mental disorders is called ___(63)_____ (ECT). Although side effects such as ___(64)___ loss and ___(65)___ are relatively common, studies have shown that ECT is effective in treating ___(66)___.

The most controversial approach to medical therapy, operating on the brain to alleviate some mental disorders, is called ___(67)___. The most common type of psychosurgery, the ___(68)_____, cuts the neural fibers that connect the frontal region of the cerebral cortex with the hypothalamus. The procedure is performed ___(69)___ today, and its use is still hotly debated. A more precise type of psychosurgery, occasionally performed on individuals with severe obsessive-compulsive disorder, is called a ___(70)___.

Application of Psychology: What to Do if You Think You Need Help

The following are important considerations in deciding whether to use professional mental health services. An important issue concerns the ___(71)___ surrounding seeking professional help. A second consideration is where to get help. Many colleges and universities have a student counseling or mental health center. Services are also provided by professionals in ___(72)___ practice. Referrals and board ___(73)___ are guides in helping to select a professional. Research has also focused on identifying the most effective therapy for ___(74)___ disorders. There are important ___(75)___ and ___(76)___ inequities in terms of receiving psychological services in the United States.

Concept Check

Fill in the missing components of the following concept box. The correct answers are located in the "Answers" section at the end of the chapter.

Approaches to Therapy

Psychologists	Type of Therapy	Techniques
Freud	psychoanalysis	
Sullivan		accurate identification of feelings and improving social relationships
Rogers	humanistic (client-centered)	
Wolpe	systematic desensitization	
Ellis and Beck	cognitive therapy	

Extending the Chapter: Psychology, Societal Issues, and Human Diversity

These questions may be assigned to you. Whether or not they are assigned, they are designed to be challenging questions to encourage you to think independently about the material in the chapter. Many of the questions have no right or wrong answers.

I.   From the *Applications of Psychology* section

1.   If a friend asked you for advice on getting help from a mental health professional, what steps you advise him to take?

II.   Psychology, Societal Issues, and Human Diversity

1.   A client goes to a psychotherapist seeking help for an incapacitating phobia toward almost all members of the opposite sex. Describe what the therapeutic approach might be like if the therapist is a:
    a. psychoanalyst
    b. interpersonal psychotherapist
    c. behavior therapist
    d. cognitive therapist

2.   Although the use of psychosurgery has declined, advocates might argue that, through the continued use of these procedures and the evaluation of results, psychosurgery will become more and more successful. Although the early psychosurgery cases were not completely successful, the same could be said for the first organ transplants and other types of surgery. How would you respond to these comments?

3.   In addition to fees and therapy techniques, what other information should therapists be required to disclose to clients at the start of a therapist-client relationship?

4.   Which of the techniques discussed in this chapter make the most sense to you? Which make the least sense? Which raise ethical concerns? Explain your answer.

Practice Quiz

The practice quiz consists of three sections: 1) Short answer questions, 2) Multiple choice questions, and 3) True-False questions. At the end of the chapter you will find suggested answers to the short answer questions, answers and explanation for the multiple choice questions, and answers to the true-false questions.

Short Answer Questions

1.   Describe similarities and differences between psychoanalysis and humanistic psychotherapy.

_____

_____

2. Describe the process of systematic desensitization.

_____

_____

3. List and describe "maladaptive cognitions" that, according to cognitive therapists, contribute to depression.

_____

_____

Multiple Choice Questions

1. Each of the following is part of the definition of psychotherapy *except*
   a. trained professional.
   b. psychological methods.
   c. medical treatment methods.
   d. based on psychological theory.
   LO 1

2. Which type of psychotherapy views the process of helping others as a form of teaching?
   a. humanistic therapy.
   b. behavior therapy.
   c. psychoanalytic therapy.
   d. client-centered therapy.
   LO 1

3. According to the Association for Advancement of Behavior Therapy, each of the following is an ethical consideration in the use of psychotherapy *except*
   a. the goals of treatment.
   b. the fees (splitting the fees when necessary).
   c. the choice of treatment methods.
   d. client confidentiality.
   LO 2

4. Which of the following is a situation where it is appropriate for a therapist to breach confidentiality?
   a. spouse inquiry
   b. court order
   c. insurance company order
   d. relative asks a question
   LO 2

5. Ann's psychoanalytic therapist asks her to lie on a couch and talk about whatever comes to mind. The technique being used by her therapist is
   a. catharsis.
   b. resistance.
   c. free association.
   d. transference.
   LO 3

6. According to Freud, when the patient reacts to the therapist in ways that resemble how he or she would react to other authority figures, the process is called
   a. resistance.
   b. catharsis.
   c. free association.
   d. transference.
   LO 3

7. In psychoanalysis, the release of emotional energy related to unconscious conflicts is called
   a. resistance.
   b. catharsis.
   c. free association.
   d. transference.
   LO 3

8. A contemporary neo-Freudian form of psychotherapy that ignores unconscious motivation is called
   a. social skills training.
   b. systematic desensitization.
   c. interpersonal psychotherapy.
   d. assertiveness training.
   LO 4

9. Research suggests interpersonal psychotherapy is effective in treating
   a. schizophrenia.
   b. bipolar disorder.
   c. phobias.
   d. depression.
   LO 4

10. According to Rogers, the ability of the therapist to share the client's emotions is an important process called
    a. reflection.
    b. empathy.
    c. catharsis.
    d. transference.
    LO 5

11. The role of the client-centered therapist is to
    a. interpret the client's unconscious conflicts.
    b. create a safe atmosphere for clients to express feelings.
    c. confront and challenge the client and point out inconsistencies.
    d. help the client unlearn abnormal ways of behaving.
    LO 5

12. Which of the following techniques is a client-centered therapist most likely to use?
    a. analysis
    b. giving advice
    c. reflection
    d. aversive conditioning
    LO 5

13. Systematic desensitization is used to treat
    a. schizophrenia.
    b. phobias.
    c. bipolar disorder.
    d. Depression.
    LO 6

14. Training in progressive relaxation and constructing a hierarchy of phobic stimuli and are important steps in
    a. client-centered psychotherapy.
    b. systematic desensitization.
    c. reflection.
    d. a and b above.
    LO 6

15. Behavior therapy teaches skills based on methods derived from
    a. classical conditioning.
    b. operant conditioning.
    c. information-processing theory.
    d. a and b above.
    LO 6

16. After Mike got to college, the first two people he called to ask for a date forcefully told him "No!" Mike has concluded he will never have a date. Beck would say Mike is engaging in
    a. selective abstraction.
    b. personalization.
    c. overgeneralization.
    d. none of the above.
    LO 7

17. With which disorders has cognitive therapy been shown to be effective?
    a. anxiety disorders
    b. bulimia
    c. major depression
    d. all of the above
    LO 7

18. Persuading clients to abandon their erroneous ways of thinking is a goal of
    a. aversive conditioning.
    b. cognitive therapy.
    c. systematic desensitization.
    d. social skills training.
    LO 7

19. The drug Thorazine has been helpful to many individuals suffering from
    a. depression.
    b. schizophrenia.
    c. obsessive-compulsive disorder.
    d. agoraphobia.
    LO 8

20. Electroconvulsive therapy is believed by most psychiatrists to be useful for patients who are
    a. severely schizophrenic.
    b. epileptic.
    c. bipolar.
    d. suicidally depressed.
    LO 8

21. A side effect of electroconvulsive therapy is
    a. memory loss.
    b. increased depression.
    c. increased tendency to have seizures.
    d. a and c above.
    LO 8

22. Board-certified psychologists
    a. are more competent than those who are not.
    b. are eclectic psychiatrists.
    c. are the only ones who accept health insurance.
    d. have met national standards for competency.
    LO 9

23. Which of the following would be good advice for someone considering a therapist?
    a. Eclectic therapists are best because they can provide the widest variety of services.
    b. Student counseling centers are usually staffed by students and recent graduates who don't have much experience.
    c. Anybody can call themselves a "psychologist."
    d. Referrals can be a good guide in choosing a psychologist.
    LO 9

24. Research suggests inequities in receiving psychotherapy based on one's
    a. gender.
    b. ethnicity.
    c. race.
    d. all of the above
    LO 10

True-False Questions

_____1. An intelligent and caring friend who helps others with their emotional problems is engaging in psychotherapy.

_____2. Free association is an important tool in Freudian psychoanalysis.

_____3. Interpersonal psychotherapy has been shown to be effective in treating depression.

_____4. Reflection is an important process in behavior therapy.

_____5. Behavior therapists assume abnormal behavior is learned.

_____6. Systematic desensitization is a behavior therapy technique used to treat phobias.

_____7. According to Aaron Beck, the most effective therapy for depression is electroconvulsive therapy.

_____8. The drug Prozac produces its effects by influencing the neurotransmitter called serotonin.

_____9. Cingulotomies are performed to help relieve patients of phobic behavior.

_____10. Researchers have found one's ethnic background to be an insignificant factor in seeking and receiving psychotherapy.

ANSWER SECTION

Answers to Review At A Glance

1. psychotherapy
2. client
3. qualified
4. effectiveness
5. confidentiality
6. exploit
7. unconscious
8. consciousness
9. relaxed
10. ego
11. interpret
12. free association
13. interpreted
14. dream interpretation
15. latent
16. resistance
17. transference
18. catharsis
19. interpersonal
20. feelings
21. communication
22. relationships
23. depression
24. awareness
25. client-centered
26. hidden emotions

27. warm
28. unconditionally
29. empathy
30. reflection
31. advice
32. behavior
33. learned
34. adaptive
35. systematic desensitization
36. progressive relaxation training
37. graded exposure
38. imagine
39. in vivo
40. virtual reality
41. operant conditioning
42. social skills
43. role playing
44. model
45. positive reinforcement
46. cognitive
47. behaviors
48. cognitions
49. selective abstraction
50. overgeneralization
51. arbitrary inference

52. magnification/minimization
53. personalization
54. absolutistic
55. anxiety
56. bulimia
57. depression
58. medical therapies
59. drug
60. Thorazine
61. neurotransmitter
62. side effects
63. electroconvulsive therapy
64. memory
65. confusion
66. depression
67. psychosurgery
68. prefrontal lobotomy
69. infrequently
70. cingulotomy
71. stigma
72. private
73. certification
74. specific
75. ethnic
76. gender

Concept Check

Approaches to Therapy

Psychologists	Type of Therapy	Techniques
Freud	psychoanalysis	free association, catharsis, and interpretation of dreams, resistance, and transference
Sullivan	interpersonal psychology	accurate identification of feelings and improving social relationships
Rogers	humanistic (client-centered)	focus is on ability of clients to help themselves; the therapist tries to create an emotionally safe atmosphere; the therapist must show warmth, unconditional acceptance, and empathy
Wolpe	systematic desensitization	a fear reduction method that involves relaxation and graded exposure to condition a new response to the phobic stimulus
Ellis and Beck	cognitive therapy	faulty cognitions are seen as the cause of abnormal behavior; examples of erroneous patterns of thinking include selective abstraction, overgeneralization, arbitrary inference, magnification/minimization, personalization, and absolutistic thinking

Sample Answers for Short Answer Questions

1. **Describe similarities and differences between psychoanalysis and humanistic psychotherapy.**

    Both approaches focus on bringing into consciousness feelings of which the individual is unaware. However, whereas Freudians focus on the inborn unconscious, Rogers approach suggests we deny awareness to information and feelings that differ from our concepts of self and ideal self. The methods used by humanistic psychotherapists also differ widely from those used by psychoanalysts. Whereas psychoanalysis uses techniques such as free association, resistance, transference, and so on, client centered psychotherapists emphasize reflection.

2. **Describe the process of systematic desensitization.**

    This approach involves two steps: progressive relaxation training, a method of deeply relaxing the body, and graded exposure, in which the client is exposed to progressively more fearful situations, while learning to master anxiety at each step.

3. List and describe "maladaptive cognitions" that, according to cognitive therapists, contribute to depression.

Aaron Beck has suggested the following erroneous thinking patterns are involved in depression: selective abstraction - basing one's thinking on a small detail; overgeneralization - reaching a general conclusion based on a few bits of evidence; arbitrary inference, - reaching a conclusion based on little or no logical evidence; magnification/minimization - blowing comments out of proportion or minimizing positive comments made by others; personalization - viewing external events as being directly related to you; and absolutistic thinking - viewing the world in extremes (good or bad), when a more moderate view is more rational.

Multiple Choice Answers

1. The answer is *c*. The definition of psychotherapy technically does not include medical treatment methods such as medication or surgery.
2. The answer is *b*. In behavior therapy, an important assumption is that psychological problems are the result of unfortunate learning experiences. A goal of behavior therapy is to unlearn abnormal ways of behaving.
3. The answer is *b*. The issue of fees for providing psychological services is not addressed in the text. It is, however, of special interest to consumers of psychological services.
4. The answer is *b*. Under some circumstances, the courts can require psychotherapists to reveal confidential information.
5. The answer is *c*. At $100 per hour, why do they call it *free* association? Catharsis refers to the release of pent-up emotional energy. Resistance occurs when patients express opposition to the process of psychoanalysis. In transference, the patient in psychoanalysis comes to regard the therapist in ways that resemble the patient's feelings toward other significant adults.
6. The answer is *d*. Transference should be interpreted by the psychoanalyst to give the patient additional insight into his or her situation.
7. The answer is *b*. Catharsis is not really a technique of psychoanalysis; instead, this brief relief from psychic discomfort is considered a benefit of psychoanalysis.
8. The answer is *c*. Interpersonal therapy also differs from traditional psychoanalysis in that it minimizes discussion of the past and does not involve interpretation of the individual's relationship with the therapist.
9. The answer is *d*. Research suggests this approach is as effective as anti-depressant medication, and with fewer side effects.
10. The answer is *b*. Empathy, genuine warmth, and unconditional positive regard are important in client-centered therapy in creating a safe atmosphere.
11. The answer is *b*. According to client-centered therapists, the emphasis is on the ability of clients to help themselves. The goal of the therapist is to create an atmosphere conducive to this process.
12. The answer is *c*. Client-centered therapists steadfastly avoid giving advice to clients. They believe that clients can solve their own problems once the problems have entered awareness.
13. The answer is *b*. The goal of systematic desensitization is to extinguish phobic responses and substitute relaxation responses.
14. The answer is *b*. Systematic desensitization is a process in which the client learns not to fear a formerly phobic stimuli. The procedure involves learning to relax in the presence of progressively more threatening stimuli.
15. The answer is *d*. The assumption of behavior therapy is that abnormal behavior has been learned. Therapy, then, is largely aimed at learning new behaviors.
16. The answer is *c*. Overgeneralization is the process of reaching a general conclusion based on a few specific bits of evidence.
17. The answer is *d*. In most studies, cognitive therapy was found to be superior to either the traditional psychoanalytic or humanistic approaches.
18. The answer is *b*. The assumption of cognitive therapy is that it is a person's maladaptive beliefs and expectations about situations, rather than the situations themselves, that cause abnormal behavior.

19. The answer is *b*. Thorazine belongs to a class of drugs called the phenothiazines. The introduction of these drugs in the 1950s helped to revolutionize the treatment of schizophrenia.
20. The answer is *d*. Although ECT seems to be effective with suicidally depressed patients, nobody seems to know exactly why.
21. The answer is *a*. Temporary or permanent memory loss and confusion continue to be side effects of ECT.
22. The answer is *d*. According to the text, seeking a professional who is board certified may not guarantee the therapist will be competent, but it helps to reduce the uncertainty in choosing a therapist.
23. The answer is *d*. Eclectic therapists are skilled in a variety of therapeutic techniques. This doesn't necessarily make them "the best." Student counseling centers generally provide high-quality services to students at moderate cost. It is true that in many states virtually anybody can call themselves a counselor or therapist, but only licensed individuals can call themselves "psychologists" or "psychiatrists."
24. The answer is *d*. Research suggests that the quality of treatment and whether or not one is receiving necessary treatment depend to a large extent on one's ethnicity, gender, and race.

Answers to True-False Questions

1. F   6. T

2. T   7. F

3. T   8. T

4. F   9. F

5. T   10. F

Chapter 15   Social Psychology

Learning Objectives

1.   Define social psychology. (p. 440)

2.   Describe how groups can contribute to deindividuation and identify the conditions under which a bystander will get involved. (p. 440)

3.   Distinguish among social loafing, social facilitation, and social impairment. (p. 442)

4.   Discuss the ways in which polarization affects group problem solving. (p. 443)

5.   Define conformity and identify the factors that increase group conformity. (p. 443)

6.   Describe social roles and social norms. (p. 445)

7.   Define obedience and discuss Milgram's research on obedience. (p. 445)

8.   Identify the three components of attitudes. (p. 448)

9.   Identify characteristics of the speaker, the message, and the listener that affect persuasion. (p. 449)

10.   Identify techniques used in persuasion. (p. 452)

11.   Define cognitive dissonance and discuss its impact on behavior and attitude change. (p. 452)

12. Discuss the relationship between prejudice and stereotypes and describe how stereotypes affect our attributions about other people's behavior. (p. 454)

13. Distinguish among the explanations for prejudice and identify some effective techniques for combating prejudice. (p. 455)

14. Describe the factors involved in person perception, including negative information, primacy effects, and emotions. (p. 458)

15. Explain the attribution process and describe the fundamental attribution error. (p. 460)

16. Identify the general factors that influence attraction, including proximity, similar and complementary characteristics, competence, physical attractiveness, mutual liking, and gender differences. (p. 462)

17. Identify the roles played by expectations and equity in maintaining relationships. (p. 465)

18 (From the *Application of Psychology* section) Discuss the implications of the gender discrimination lawsuit filed against Price Waterhouse. (p. 468)

Chapter Overview

Social psychology is the branch of psychology that studies individuals as they interact with others. One topic of interest to social psychologists is the influence that others have on individual behavior. Among the group processes discussed are deindividuation, social loafing, social facilitation, social impairment, and group polarization.

Social psychologists have also studied group phenomena such as our tendency to conform to group pressure, the importance of social roles in our lives, and our tendency to obey authority figures.

Attitudes are beliefs that predispose us to behave in certain ways. Attitudes are learned from direct experience and from others. The persuasiveness of messages is determined by the characteristics of the speaker (credibility, attractiveness, and intent), the message (fear appeals and two-sided arguments), and characteristics of the listeners (intelligence, need for social approval, esteem, and audience size). People are persuaded by such techniques as the "foot-in-the-door" and by "low-balling".

Cognitive dissonance theory has been proposed to explain the process of attitude change. According to Festinger, when behavior and attitudes are inconsistent, attitudes often change to match the behavior rather than the other way around.

Prejudice is a negative attitude based on inaccurate generalizations about a group of people. The inaccurate generalization on which the prejudice is based is called a stereotype. Stereotypes are harmful because they take away our ability to treat each member of a group as an individual and because they lead to faulty attributions.

Friendship and love are powerful social phenomena based on the process of person perception. The process of person perception is complicated by the ways in which we gather and use information about others. Different people will perceive the same individual differently because of differences in interpreting the individual's characteristics. Negative information is generally weighted more than positive information in person perception. First impressions, also known as the primacy effect, generally influence person perception more than information learned about the person at a later date. Prolonged exposure to the person, the passage of time, and knowledge about primacy effects can all reduce the impact of the primacy effect. Person perception is also influenced by the emotional state of the perceiver.

Social behavior is strongly influenced by the attribution process. The fundamental attribution error involves our tendency to underestimate the impact of situations on others while more easily seeing its impact on ourselves. Although many factors ensure that each individual's perception of an individual will be unique, there are some general factors that partly determine to whom we will be attracted: proximity, similar and complementary characteristics, competence, physical attractiveness, and mutual liking. The attribution process is also involved in the perception of others. One aspect of the attribution process is deciding if a person's behavior is caused by the situation (a situational attribution) or by a trait of the person (a dispositional attribution).

Two major factors that determine whether a relationship will last are the differences between what you expect to find in a relationship and what you actually find, and the degree to which the relationship is equitable.

According to Susan Fiske, there are three sources of gender-based job discrimination 1) evaluations of job performance are influenced by gender stereotypes; 2) narrow expectations for behavior created by stereotypes lead to discrimination; and 3) faulty attributions based on gender stereotypes operate in the workplace.

Key Terms Exercise

For each of the following exercises, match the key terms on the left with the correct definitions on the right. Page references to the text follow the terms so that you may refer to the text for any items you answer incorrectly or do not understand completely. You may check your responses immediately by referring to the answers that follow each exercise.

Definition of Social Psychology/Groups and Social Influence

_____ 1. social psychology (p. 440)

_____ 2. deindividuation (p. 440)

_____ 3. diffusion of responsibility (p. 442)

_____ 4. social loafing (p. 442)

_____ 5. social facilitation (p. 442)

a. a process in which group membership leaves one feeling anonymous and unidentifiable

b. the effect of being in a group that reduces an individual's sense of personal responsibility

c. the branch of psychology that studies individuals as they interact with each other

d. the tendency for individuals to work less hard as a member of a group

e. improved performance on individual projects that sometimes occurs as a member of a group

ANSWERS
1. c   4. d
2. a   5. e
3. b

Groups and Social Influence

_____ 1. social impairment (p. 442)
_____ 2. polarization (p. 443)
_____ 3. conformity (p. 443)
_____ 4. obedience (p. 445)

a. yielding to group pressure even when no direct request to comply has been made
b. doing what one is told by people in authority
c. lowered individual performance that occurs while working in the presence of a group
d. the tendency for group discussion to make beliefs and attitudes more extreme

ANSWERS

1. c	3. a
2. d	4. b

Attitudes and Persuasion

_____ 1. attitudes (p. 448)
_____ 2. persuasion (p. 449)
_____ 3. sleeper effects (p. 449)
_____ 4. cognitive dissonance (p. 453)
_____ 5. prejudice (p. 454)
_____ 6. stereotype (p. 454)
_____ 7. attribution theory (p. 454)

a. the process of changing another person's attitudes through arguments and related means
b. beliefs that predispose us to act and feel in certain ways
c. an inaccurate generalization upon which a prejudice is based
d. a negative attitude based on inaccurate generalizations about a group of people
e. the potential for low credibility speakers to gain credibility after a period of time
f. the theory that people tend to look for explanations for their own behavior and that of others
g. the discomfort that results from inconsistencies between attitudes and behavior

ANSWERS

1. b	5. d
2. a	6. c
3. e	7. f
4. g	

Interpersonal Attraction: Friendship and Love

_____ 1. person perception (p. 458)
_____ 2. primacy effect (p. 459)
_____ 3. fundamental attribution error (p. 460)
_____ 4. attribution (p. 460)
_____ 5. situational attribution (p. 460)
_____ 6. dispositional attribution (p. 460)
_____ 7. equity theory (p. 466)

a. the theory that partners will be comfortable in a relationship only when the ratio between their perceived contributions and benefits is equal
b. the process of forming impressions of others
c. the tendency to weigh first impressions heavily in forming opinions about other people
d. the process of attributing behavior to some external cause
e. the process of making judgments about the causes of behavior
f. the process of attributing behavior to an internal motive or trait
g. the tendency to credit our successes to our own talents, but attributing our failures to difficult circumstances

ANSWERS

1. b	5. d
2. c	6. f
3. g	7. a
4. e	

Review At A Glance

(Answers to this section may be found on page 258)

The branch of psychology that studies individuals as they interact with others is called ___(1)___ psychology.

Groups and Social Influence

The group process in which a person feels anonymous and unidentifiable is called ___(2)___. In this state, people are less aware of their own ___(3)___ and less concerned with what others think. According to Latané and Darley, bystanders who are considering helping out in an emergency use a ___(4)___ _____ with several steps. The first step is ___(5)___; the next step is ___(6)___ the situation as an emergency; the bystander must assume ___(7)___ for helping, must know how to help and, finally, must decide to help. ___(8)___ factors affect the second and third stages of the decision process. Groups can create a ___(9)___ of ___(10)___.

When group performance is measured, individuals tend to exert less effort than when individual effort is measured; this phenomenon is called ___(11)___ _____. Working individually in the presence of others sometimes improves performance; this is called ___(12)___ _____. Under some circumstances, working in the presence of others impairs performance; this is termed ___(13)___ _____.

Research suggests that the presence of others improves performance on ___(14)___ tasks and impairs performance on ___(15)___ tasks. A widely cited explanation of this phenomenon is the ___(16)___ level of ___(17)___. We generally offer less ___(18)___ advice when we are alone with the person seeking advice; when groups discuss the same issues, however, they are likely to offer ___(19)___ advice. Group discussion of issues often pushes our opinions toward the extremes, a process called ___(20)___.

Under many circumstances, individuals yield to group pressure, even when no direct request to comply has been made; this is called __(21)__. In a study of conformity conducted by _____(22)_____, participants conformed to the group at least part of the time in __(23)__ percent of the cases. People conform to gain __(24)__, avoid punishment or to gain __(25)__. Sherif's study involving autokinetic effects found that participants not only went along with others' judgments, but actually __(26)__ their own judgments. The following factors affect group conformity: 1) __(27)__ of the group, 2) __(28)__ groups, 3) cultural factors, and 4) gender. The culturally determined guidelines that tell people what is expected of them are called __(29)__ _____. Our behavior is also affected by the spoken and unspoken rules called social __(30)__.

Stanley Milgram has conducted research on __(31)__. Participants believed they were participating in a learning experiment and were asked to administer electric shocks to a "learner" when the learner made a mistake. Milgram found that __(32)__ percent of the participants gave the highest possible shock. Further studies found that the percentage of obedient participants declined 1) when the victim was in the same room, 2) when the __(33)__ of the experimenter was reduced, 3) when the experimenter gave instructions by __(34)__, and 4) when the participant was in the presence of other __(35)__ participants. Although groups can produce negative effects, they can also be __(36)__.

Attitudes and Persuasion

Beliefs that predispose people to act and feel in certain ways are called __(37)__. This definition has three important components: 1) __(38)__, 2) feelings, and 3) __(39)__ to behave. Attitudes are learned from our experiences (they often are __(40)__ conditioned) and from others.

Logic may be one of the least important qualities in determining the __(41)__ of a communication. The qualities of persuasive communication fall into three categories: characteristics of the __(42)__, of the __(43)__, and of the __(44)__. Among the characteristics of the speaker, Aronson and Golden found that the speaker's __(45)__ is important to the persuasiveness of the communication. The key is whether the speaker is a credible source of __(46)__ about the specific argument. Although speakers who are low in credibility are ineffective at first, they often influence opinions after a period of time through __(47)__ _____.

When advertisers use glamorous celebrities to help sell their products, they are using another persuasive characteristic of the speaker- __(48)__. The persuasiveness of attractive speakers is limited to relatively __(49)__ issues.

When the speaker is obviously trying to change an opinion, he or she will be less persuasive. This characteristic is referred to as __(50)__ and helps to explain the use of the "__(51)__ _____" testimonials in television commercials.

One characteristic of the message that influences persuasiveness is an appeal to __(52)__. Listeners will respond favorably to a fear-inducing persuasive communication only if 1) the emotional appeal is __(53)__, 2) the listeners believe the fearful outcome is likely to happen to them, and 3) the message offers a way to __(54)__ the fearful outcome. Another factor that influences persuasiveness relates to presenting different __(55)__ of an argument.

When speaking to an audience that agrees with your position, the message will be more persuasive if you do not present __(56)__ _____ of the argument; however, it's generally better to give both sides of the argument if the audience is initially __(57)__ to your position.

The way in which problems are __(58)__ has a strong influence on how we solve these problems. The following characteristics of listeners help to determine the persuasiveness of an argument. 1) Generally, less __(59)__ people are easier to persuade; however, if the message is complex, more intelligent listeners are easier to persuade. 2) People with a high need for __(60)__ are generally easier to persuade. 3) People with low __(61)__- __ are sometimes easier to persuade. 4) People are easier to persuade when listening to the message in a __(62)__; larger groups are easier to persuade than smaller groups; 5) recent studies have found no gender differences in __(63)__ _. People who agree to a small request are more likely to agree to a second, larger request; this forms the basis for the __(64)__- _____ - _____ -_____ technique. In a related approach, you are initially offered a reasonable deal, and, after accepting it, the deal is changed; this is called the __(65)__- _____ technique.

Sometimes, important differences exist between our attitudes and our __(66)__. When behavior and attitudes are inconsistent, __(67)__ often change to become more consistent with behavior. Cognitive dissonance theory, proposed by Festinger, states that inconsistencies between attitudes and behavior are __(68)__; people will change their attitudes to reduce this discomfort. To demonstrate cognitive dissonance, Festinger asked participants to perform a boring __(69)__ __- _____ task for an hour, and then to tell the next participant that the task was interesting. Half of the participants were paid $20 and half were paid $1. When participants were asked how interesting the task really was, the most positive attitudes were expressed by the group that experienced cognitive dissonance—those that were paid __(70)__. Research suggests cognitive dissonance may explain changes in attitudes toward __(71)__ issues.

A harmful attitude that is based on generalizations about a group of people is called __(72)__. The inaccurate generalization on which the prejudice is based is called a __(73)__. Stereotypes are harmful for three reasons: 1) they take away our ability to treat each member of a group as an individual; 2) they lead to narrow __(74)__ for behavior; and 3) they lead to faulty __(75)__. Attribution theory states that people tend to attribute all behavior to some __(76)__ _. Social psychologists have proposed the following explanations for why prejudice occurs: 1) people compete for scarce resources, according to __(77)__ _____ theory; 2) the world is divided into two groups, __(78)__ versus __(79)__, perpetuated partly because it bolsters the self-esteem of those with a weak __(80)__; and, 3) prejudiced is __(81)__ from others. Among the techniques suggested for combating prejudice are these: 1) __(82)__ prejudice; 2)control __(83)__ responses; and 3) increased __(84)__ among prejudiced groups. In order for increased contact to be effective, several conditions must occur. The groups must be __(85)__ in status, members should view each other as __(86)__ of their respective groups, the tasks should be __(87)__ and the contact should be __(88)__.

Interpersonal Attraction: Friendship and Love

The process of forming impressions of others is called __(89)__ _____. People seem to go through a process of "__(90)__ _____" to help calculate perceptions of others. Other things being equal, a person's __(91)__ qualities are weighted more heavily than the __(92)__ qualities.

The tendency to weigh first impressions heavily in forming opinions of other people is called the __(93)__ _____. The impact of the primacy effect is reduced by (1) prolonged __(94)__ to a person, (2) passage of __(95)__, and (3) __(96)__ of primacy effects.

The emotional state we are in also affects person perception. __(97)__ emotional states lead to greater attraction to others than negative emotions do.

The tendency to underestimate the impact of situations on others, while more easily seeing it in ourselves is called the __(98)__ error. The process of making judgments about what causes people to behave as they do is called __(99)__. When an explanation for behavior is based on an external cause, it is called a __(100)__ attribution; when the explanation is based on an internal motive, it is called a __(101)__ attribution. We tend to attribute the behavior of others to __(102)__ causes. People who live in East Asian collectivistic cultures are less likely to make the __(103)__ error than people who live in individualistic Western cultures.

There are several general determinants of interpersonal attraction. An important factor is __(104)__ or geographical closeness. We are attracted to those people who have __(105)__ values, interests, and attitudes. We are attracted to opposites, however, when those opposite characteristics __(106)__ our own characteristics. It's also more flattering and attractive to be liked by someone who holds __(107)__ views than by someone holding similar views.

With regard to competence, we are more attached to __(108)__ than to incompetent people; however, we are less attracted to those who are seen as being too competent.

Concerning physical attractiveness, people tend to be attracted to physically __(109)__ people. In the early stages of attraction between dates, physical attractiveness seems to be the __(110)__ important factor. In a study in which men thought they were talking to beautiful women, the men talked in a more __(111)__ way. Furthermore, the men apparently induced the women to act in a more __(112)__ way. People tend to choose mates who closely match themselves in __(113)__. Physical beauty is a highly __(114)__ quality. As we get to like people better, we begin to think they are more beautiful. Liking somebody often leads to liking in return; this is the basis for __(115)__.

Recent surveys suggest that both men and women tend to feel that being in love is necessary for marriage. However, women tend to place more emphasis on their romantic partner's __(116)__, character, and education; men place a greater emphasis on __(117)__. People tend to evaluate the same characteristics in others in the different ways.

Two factors are important in maintaining relationships. The first concerns the difference between expectations and __(118)__ in relationships. One common source of unfilled expectations is the shift from passionate love to __(119)__ love. Expectations can fail to match __(120)__ because people change over time. A second factor in maintaining relationships is whether the partners in a relationship feel that the ratio of their perceived contributions and benefits is __(121)__. This is called __(122)__. Although the benefits the two people receive from one another do not have to be equal, the __(123)__ between the benefits and contributions must be equal. Also, the benefits and contributions each person receives are based on their __(124)__. If either member of the relationship perceives the relationship to be inequitable, he or she will either try to restore __(125)__ or leave the relationship.

Application of Psychology: Stereotypes and Discrimination in the Workplace

According to Susan Fiske, there are three sources of gender-based job discrimination: 1) evaluations of job performance are influenced by the ___(126)___ we hold regarding the two genders; 2) the narrow expectations for appropriate behavior encouraged by stereotypes can contribute to workplace ___(127)___; and 3) faulty attributions based on ___(128)___ _____ operate in the workplace. The courts have upheld lawsuits brought against employers who discriminate against employees based on ___(129)___ and on other stereotypes. Some studies suggest prejudicial stereotypes can have ___(130)___ effects in the workplace.

Concept Check

Fill in the missing components of the following concept box. The correct answers are located in the "Answers" section at the end of the chapter.

Classic Social Psychology Research

Psychologist	Social Psychology Area	Research Findings
Asch	conformity	
Milgram	obedience	
Festinger		participants participated in a boring spool-stacking experiment; those who were paid the least expressed the most positive attitudes

Extending the Chapter: Psychology, Societal Issues, and Human Diversity

These questions may be assigned to you. Whether or not they are assigned, they are designed to be challenging questions to encourage you to think independently about the material in the chapter. Many of the questions have no right or wrong answers.

I.   From the *Applications of Psychology* section

1.   Summarize the three sources of gender-based job discrimination presented by Susan Fiske in testimony to the U.S. Supreme Court.

2.   Describe the "paradoxical" effects of prejudicial stereotypes in the workplace.

II.   Psychology, Societal Issues, and Human Diversity

1.   If you were an advertiser, how would you apply the research information on persuasion in order to influence the behavior of consumers?

2.   Describe some ways in which the Internet could potentially affect social relationships.

3.   Had you been a participant in the Milgram or Asch studies, how would you have reacted? If any of these studies were to be repeated today, would participants react differently? Explain your answer.

4.   Will our knowledge of interpersonal attraction ever reach a point at which we can accurately predict which individuals will like or love each other? Why or why not?

5.   In what ways does our society benefit from having members who conform and who are obedient? In what ways are conformity and obedience potentially dangerous to our society?

6.   (From the *Human Diversity* section) What can be done to minimize the stereotypes between able-bodied students and students with physical challenges?

Practice Quiz

The practice quiz consists of three sections: 1) Short answer questions, 2) Multiple choice questions, and 3) True-False questions. At the end of the chapter you will find suggested answers to the short answer questions, answers and explanation for the multiple choice questions, and answers to the true-false questions.

Short Answer Questions

1.   Describe the dynamics that occur when groups engage in problem-solving.

_____

_____

2.   List the characteristics of the speaker that influence the persuasiveness of a communication.

_____

_____

3. Distinguish between situational and dispositional attributions and explain the fundamental attribution error.

_____

_____

Multiple Choice Questions

1. Which of the following topics would be studied by a social psychologist?
   a. attractions to other people
   b. the influence of groups on individual behavior
   c. the formation of stereotypes and prejudices
   d. all of the above
   LO 1

2. The process in which group membership makes a person feel anonymous and unidentifiable is called
   a. deindividuation.
   b. social facilitation.
   c. social impairment.
   d. polarization.
   LO 2

3. Each of the following is part of Latané and Darley's decision tree *except*
   a. noticing that something is out of the ordinary.
   b. interpreting an event as an emergency.
   c. assuming responsibility.
   d. consulting with other bystanders.
   LO 2

4. According to Latané and Darley, the diffusion of responsibility created by groups affects what part of the decision tree?
   a. noticing that something is out of the ordinary
   b. assuming responsibility for helping
   c. interpreting the event as an emergency
   d. deciding whether or not the bystander knows how to help
   LO 2

5. Social impairment is generally more likely to occur on what types of tasks?
   a. easy tasks
   b. well-learned tasks
   c. tasks that involve motor skills
   d. difficult tasks
   LO 3

6. According to Latané and others, how does the effort exerted by individual members of a group compare with the effort exerted by individuals acting alone?
   a. Individuals exert more effort when in a group than when alone.
   b. There are no significant differences.
   c. Individuals exert less effort when in a group than when alone.
   d. Approximately half work harder when in a group and half work harder when alone.
   LO 3

7. Which of the following is more likely to occur with easily accomplished tasks?
   a. social impairment
   b. social facilitation
   c. group polarization
   d. deindividuation
   LO 3

8. In a heated group discussion of politics, Carla is somewhat surprised to hear herself arguing for a more extreme position than she usually does. According to social psychologists, this is due to
   a. polarization.
   b. groupthink.
   c. social loafing.
   d. a and c above.
   e. LO 4

9. Which of the following is a common result of group discussion?
   a. polarization
   b. taking more extreme positions
   c. suggestions involving riskier options
   d. all of the above
   LO 4

10. The study of conformity by Asch found that
    a. most participants refused to conform.
    b. most participants conformed at least part of the time.
    c. participants conformed both privately and outwardly.
    d. b and c above.
       LO 5

11. Many people will sacrifice their own beliefs rather than risk rejection by their peers. This is demonstrated by
    a. Milgram's obedience research.
    b. Festinger's theory of cognitive dissonance.
    c. Asch's research on conformity.
    d. Ellis's theory of maladaptive cognitions.
       LO 5

12. Culturally determined guidelines for determining acceptable and unacceptable behavior in a given situation are called
    a. social norms.
    b. social roles.
    c. social studies.
    d. social facilitation.
       LO 6

13. Milgram's studies demonstrated that people do what they are told when
    a. they are under the grip of polarization.
    b. they are unsure of themselves.
    c. asked by an authority figure.
    d. in stressful situations.
       LO 7

14. In Milgram's research on obedience, which of the following factors decreased participants' willingness to deliver shocks?
    a. when the prestige of the experimenter was reduced
    b. when the experimenter gave instructions by telephone
    c. when the participant was in the presence of other participants who refused to deliver shocks
    e. all of the above

15. Each of the following is a component of the term attitude *except*
    a. beliefs.
    b. facts.
    c. feelings.
    d. dispositions to behave.
       LO 8

16. Sleeper effects refer to the persuasiveness of
    a. speakers who are low in credibility.
    b. speakers who are high in credibility.
    c. intelligent listeners.
    d. emotional appeals.
       LO 9

17. Which of the following approaches can make a fear-inducing communication more powerful?
    a. if the emotional appeal is strong
    b. if the listeners believe the feared outcome is likely to happen to them
    c. if the message offers a way to avoid the fearful outcome
    d. all of the above
       LO 9

18. Each of the following is true regarding characteristics of an audience and persuasiveness of a message *except*
    a. more intelligent audiences are generally easier to persuade.
    b. audiences with a high need for approval are generally easier to persuade.
    c. bigger audiences generally are easier to persuade.
    d. audiences with moderate levels of self-esteem are easier to persuade than people with high self-esteem.
       LO 9

19. Jason is a salesperson who begins his sales presentation with a small, reasonable request. He is using
    a. cognitive dissonance.
    b. low-balling.
    c. the door-in-the-foot technique.
    d. the foot-in-the-door technique.
       LO 10

20. According to Festinger, cognitive dissonance is a phenomenon that
    a. we seek because it makes us comfortable.
    b. we seek to avoid because it makes us uncomfortable.
    c. occurs when attitudes and behavior are consistent with each other.
    d. relies on attribution theory.
       LO 11

21. According to Festinger and others, cognitive dissonance results in
    a. attitudes shifting to become more consistent with behavior.
    b. attitudes shifting to become less consistent with behavior.
    c. behavior shifting to become more consistent with attitudes.
    d. behavior shifting to become less consistent with attitudes.
       LO 11

22. Stereotypes influence our explanations of behavior, according to
    a. cognitive dissonance theory.
    b. attribution theory.
    c. attitudinal modification theory.
    d. dispositional modification theory.
       LO 12

23. Which of the following is a harmful effect of stereotypes?
    a. Stereotypes permit us to treat each member of a group as an individual.
    b. Stereotypes take away our ability to treat each member of a group as an individual.
    c. Stereotypes lead to faulty attributions.
    d. b and c above
       LO 12

24. In a classic study, Sherif and colleagues showed that prejudice can arise between randomly divided students. This study demonstrated the explanation for prejudice called
    a. unrealized conflict.
    b. groupthink.
    c. us versus them.
    d. deindividuation.
       LO 13

25. Increased contact between prejudiced groups is more effective if
    a. the groups are equal in status.
    b. the groups are engaged in cooperative tasks.
    c. the contact is informal.
    d. all of the above.
       LO 13

26. The expression "First impressions are lasting impressions" refers to which person perception variable?
    a. the primacy effect
    b. negative information
    c. individual differences in the evaluation of others
    d. emotional states
       LO 14

27. In the process of person perception, negative information
    a. tends to leave a stronger impression.
    b. tends to leave a weak impression.
    c. is outweighed by positive traits.
    d. is not as long-lasting as positive information.
       LO 14

28. Ron is a salesperson who just made a big sale. He tells another salesperson, "The reason I'm such a successful salesperson is that I'm cheery, friendly, kind, and loyal." Which type of attribution is Ron using?
    a. equitable attribution
    b. dispositional attribution
    c. situational attribution
    d. none of the above
       LO 15

29. Which of the following is a component of the fundamental attribution error?
    a. the tendency to underestimate the impact of situations on others' behavior
    b. the tendency to overestimate the impact of situations on others' behavior
    c. the tendency to attribute our own behavior to situations
    d. a and c above
       LO 15

30. Which of the following expressions best summarizes interpersonal attraction?
    a. "Birds of a feather flock together"
    b. "Opposites attract"
    c. both a and b above
    d. none of the above
       LO 16

31. With regard to romantic attraction, women place more emphasis than men on each of the following factors *except*
    a. intelligence.
    b. character.
    c. physical attractiveness.
    d. education.
    LO 16

32. According to the text, many relationships move predictably from
    a. companionate to passionate.
    b. passionate to companionate.
    c. romantic to passionate.
    d. sublime to ridiculous.
    LO 17

33. Equity theory states that partners will be comfortable in their relationship when the ratio between their perceived contributions and benefits is
    a. balanced.
    b. uneven.
    c. similar.
    d. equal.
    e. LO 17

34. The evidence presented by psychologist Susan Fiske in the Ann Hopkins lawsuit against Price Waterhouse suggested which of the following as a source of gender-based job discrimination?
    a. Job performance is influenced by stereotyped beliefs about the genders.
    b. Narrow expectations for behavior encouraged by gender stereotypes can contribute to workplace discrimination.
    c. Faulty attributions based on gender stereotypes operate in the workplace.
    d. all of the above
    LO 18

True-False Questions

_____1. The feeling of anonymity that can arise from being in a group is called deindividuation.

_____2. Polarization refers to the improved decision making that occurs in groups when compared with individuals.

_____3. Milgram's studies on obedience showed that highly educated participants were far less likely to obey.

_____4. Cognitive dissonance helps to explain shifts in attitude.

_____5. Social psychologists have found that "us versus them" prejudice bolsters the self-esteem of those with weak self-images.

_____6. Social psychologists believe that minimizing contact among members of prejudiced groups can help reduce prejudice.

_____7. Prolonged exposure and the passage of time can help reduce primacy effects.

_____8. According to the fundamental attribution error, we tend to underestimate the importance of situations on the behavior of others.

_____9. Residents of East Asian collectivistic cultures are far more likely to make the fundamental attribution error.

_____10. Relationships tend to shift over time from compassionate to passionate love.

ANSWER SECTION

Concept Check

Classic Social Psychology Research

Psychologist	Social Psychology Area	Research Findings
Asch	conformity	conformity to group pressure was widespread
Milgram	obedience	Milgram found that a majority of participants were willing to obediently shock another participant to the maximum 450-volt level
Festinger	cognitive dissonance	participants participated in a boring spool-stacking experiment; those who were paid the least expressed the most positive attitudes

Answers to Review At A Glance

1. social
2. deindividuation
3. behavior
4. decision tree
5. noticing
6. interpreting
7. responsibility
8. Social
9. diffusion
10. responsibility
11. social loafing
12. social facilitation
13. social impairment
14. easy
15. difficult
16. optimal
17. arousal
18. risky
19. riskier
20. polarization
21. conformity
22. Asch
23. 74
24. rewards
25. information
26. changed

27. size
28. unanimous
29. social roles
30. norms
31. obedience
32. 65
33. prestige
34. telephone
35. disobedient
36. advantageous
37. attitudes
38. beliefs
39. dispositions
40. classically
41. persuasiveness
42. speaker
43. listener
44. message
45. credibility
46. information
47. sleeper effects
48. attractiveness
49. unimportant
50. intent
51. hidden camera
52. fear

53. strong
54. avoid
55. sides
56. both sides
57. unfavorable
58. framed
59. intelligent
60. social approval
61. self-esteem
62. group
63. persuasibility
64. foot-in-the-door
65. low-ball
66. behavior
67. attitudes
68. uncomfortable
69. spool-stacking
70. $1
71. political
72. prejudice
73. stereotype
74. expectations
75. attributions
76. cause
77. realistic conflict
78. us

79. them
80. self-images
81. learned
82. recognize
83. automatic
84. contact
85. equal
86. typical
87. cooperative
88. informal
89. person perception
90. cognitive algebra
91. negative
92. positive
93. primacy effect
94. exposure
95. time
96. knowledge
97. Positive
98. fundamental attribution
99. attribution
100. situational
101. dispositional
102. dispositional
103. fundamental attribution
104. proximity
105. similar
106. complement
107. opposite
108. competent
109. beautiful
110. most
111. sociable
112. likable
113. physical attractiveness
114. subjective
115. mutual liking
116. intelligence
117. physical attractiveness
118. reality
119. companionate
120. reality
121. equal
122. equity theory
123. ratio
124. perceptions
125. equity
126. stereotypes
127. discrimination
128. gender stereotypes
129. gender
130. paradoxical

Sample Answers for Short Answer Questions

1. **Describe the dynamics that occur when groups engage in problem solving.**

   Group problem-solving leads to a variety of phenomena. Social loafing refers to the tendency of group members to work less hard when the performance of the entire group is measured. There are instances when working in the presence of others can improve performance; this is referred to as social facilitation. The presence of others seems to help performance on easy tasks, but can lead to social impairment on difficult tasks. Group discussions can lead to polarization, which refers to making our opinions on issues more extreme. Another group dynamic, more likely to occur in cohesive groups, is called groupthink; groupthink refers to the faulty decision-making that may occur in groups.

2. **List the characteristics of the speaker that influence the persuasiveness of a communication.**

   An important factor in determining the persuasiveness of a communication is the perceived credibility of the speaker. Even low credibility speakers can sometimes be persuasive as the result of sleeper effects. Speakers who are attractive, popular, famous and likable will be more persuasive. Speakers are less persuasive if their intent is to change your opinion, particularly if the speaker stands to gain by persuading you.

3. **Distinguish between situational and dispositional attributions and explain the fundamental attribution error.**

   Situational attributions refer to explanations for a person's behavior based on external causes (the situation), whereas dispositional attributions are explanations for behavior based on personal characteristics of the individual (he's shy, she's witty, and so on). The fundamental attribution error is the tendency to underestimate the impact of situations on other people, while overestimating the impact of situations when it comes to explaining our own behavior.

Multiple Choice Answers

1. The answer is *d*. Social psychology studies individuals as they interact with others; therefore, all the topics mentioned in the question, and many others, are studied by social psychologists.
2. The answer is *a*. Deindividuation has helped explain behavior as dramatic as lynching.
3. The answer is *d*. A fourth part of the bystander's decision tree, in addition to choices *a, b,* and *c* in the question, is deciding whether or not the bystander knows how to help.
4. The answer is *c*. Diffusion of responsibility tends to "divide up" responsibility among all bystanders, making it less likely that any *one* bystander will assume all the responsibility for acting.
5. The answer is *d*. The reason for social impairment on difficult tasks apparently has to do with levels of arousal that become too high for the task.
6. The answer is *c*. This phenomenon has been given the descriptive term *social loafing*.
7. The answer is *b*. This finding is consistent with the optimal levels of arousal, which indicate that easier tasks are easier to do when people are aroused.
8. The answer is *a*. Polarization refers to the fact that group discussions often lead its participants to take more extreme positions.
9. The answer is *d*. Group discussions can change opinions in subtle, but powerful ways.
10. The answer is *b*. Although Asch's study found that the majority of participants conformed to the group, most of the conformity was outward. When participants were allowed to make their judgments in private, there was little group conformity.
11. The answer is *c*. Asch's research reminds us about the tendency to yield to group pressure, even in the absence of a direct request to comply.
12. The answer is *a*. Both social roles and social norms provide guidelines. Norms, however, provide the spoken and unspoken rules for behaviors in particular situations.
13. The answer is *c*. In the studies, Milgram, in his lab coat and with a stern demeanor, acted as the authority figure.
14. The answer is *d*. An additional factor that lowered participants' obedience was when the "victim" was in the same room as the participant.
15. The answer is *b*. According to the text, attitudes are beliefs that predispose one to act and feel in certain ways.
16. The answer is *a*. Research has suggested that even speakers who are low in credibility can come to influence opinion after a period of time. This has been referred to as the sleeper effect.
17. The answer is *d*. Emotional appeals can be highly persuasive if all of the elements mentioned in the question are present.
18. The answer is *a*. Research suggests that less intelligent people are generally easier to persuade, except when the message is complex and difficult to understand.
19. The answer is *d*. The low-ball technique involves starting with a low priced offer; the price begins to work its way up, as the salesperson changes the deal ("Oh, you want an *engine* with that car?"). In the foot-in-the-door technique, you initially respond favorably to a small, reasonable request, which somehow turns into a larger and larger request.
20. The answer is *b*. When our attitudes and behavior are inconsistent, we are motivated to reduce the resulting discomfort. One way to accomplish this involves changing our attitudes.
21. The answer is *a*. According to cognitive dissonance theory, when attitudes and behavior are inconsistent, it creates discomfort; this discomfort is reduced when attitudes are modified to become consistent with behavior.
22. The answer is *b*. Attribution theory also explains why attitudes shift to become consistent with behavior, but the focus here is on our need to explain everything that happens or to attribute events to some cause.
23. The answer is *d*. Stereotypes are inaccurate generalizations that serve as the basis for prejudice.
24. The answer is *b*. According to some psychologists, "us versus them" prejudice helps to strengthen the prejudiced individual's self-esteem.
25. The answer is d. Another important factor is the extent to which group members view each other as being typical of their respective groups.

26. The answer is *a*. The impact of the primacy effect can be reduced with prolonged exposure, the passage of time, or knowing about primacy effects.
27. The answer is *a*. In person perception, the bad outweighs the good.
28. The answer is *b*. Situational attributions explain behavior as based on some external (environmental) cause, while dispositional attributions explain behavior as based on personal characteristics of the person. If Ron would have attributed his selling success to a superior product, he would be using a situational attribution.
29. The answer is *d*. The fundamental attribution error involves attributing others people's behavior to dispositional causes ("that's just how they are") while readily attributing our own behavior to situations.
30. The answer is *c*. This seemingly contradictory answer can be explained as follows: Although we are attracted to people who hold similar values and attitudes, we also are attracted to opposites when those opposite characteristics complement our own.
31. The answer is *c*. The emphasis on different factors in romantic relationships holds up across different generations in the United States and across other cultures as well.
32. The answer is *b*. Companionate love, while less intense than passionate love, is a blend of friendship, intimacy, commitment, and security.
33. The answer is *d*. According to equity theory, the actual perceived benefits people receive from each other do not have to be equal, but the *ratio* of these perceived benefits and contributions must be equal.
34. The answer is *d*. The suit, brought successfully against Price Waterhouse, was the first suit in which psychological testimony on gender stereotyping was introduced as evidence.

Answers to True-False Questions

1. T   6. F

2. F   7. T

3. F   8. T

4. T   9. F

5. T   10. F